GEOGRAPHY SKILLS ACTIVITIES KIT

Ready-to-Use Projects & Activities for Grades 4–8

James F. Silver

Associate Professor
Trenton (NJ) State College

Illustrated by Eileen Gerne Ciavarella

THE CENTER FOR APPLIED
RESEARCH IN EDUCATION
West Nyack, New York 10995

Library of Congress Cataloging-in-Publication Data

Silver, James F.
    Geography skills activities kit.
    ISBN 0-87628-354-7
    1. Geography—Study and teaching (Elementary)
I. Title.
G73.S44 1988   88-2821
910′.712   CIP

Printed in the United States of America

13 14 15 16 17 18 19

ISBN 0-87628-354-7

**THE CENTER FOR APPLIED RESEARCH
IN EDUCATION**
West Nyack, New York 10994

On the World Wide Web at http://www.phdirect.com

Prentice-Hall International (UK) Limited, *London*
Prentice-Hall of Australia Pty. Limited, *Sydney*
Prentice-Hall Canada Inc., *Toronto*
Prentice-Hall Hispanoamericana, S.A., *Mexico*
Prentice-Hall of India Private Limited, *New Delhi*
Prentice-Hall of Japan, Inc., *Tokyo*
Pearson Education Asia Pte. Ltd., *Singapore*
Editora Prentice-Hall do Brasil, Ltda., *Rio de Janeiro*

Dedicated to my wife, Edith, whose powers of analysis, unremitting loyalty, not to mention her command of the word processor, helped make this book a reality...

...And to Pamela, Beverly, Lorna Jean, Nancy Ann, and Frank, from whom I have learned much.

ABOUT THE AUTHOR

James F. Silver received his B.A. in social studies from Montclair (New Jersey) State College, his M.A. in history from Boston University, his M.A. in educational administration from Montclair State College, and his Ed.D. in curriculum and instruction from Pacific Western University in Los Angeles. Professor Silver also studied the psychology of reading at Temple University in Philadelphia, which led to his New Jersey state certification as a reading specialist.

Professor Silver's experience includes nine years as an elementary school teacher and principal in Morris County, New Jersey, and more than twenty-seven years in the education department at Trenton (New Jersey) State College, where he is now an associate professor. During this time, Professor Silver has written numerous teachers' manuals, geography and history skill development books, achievement tests for Silver Burdett & Co., and textbooks, including the two-volume *The United States Yesterday and Today* for Ginn and Company.

Professor Silver and his wife, a mathematics professor, live in Hopewell Township, New Jersey. They have five children and eight grandsons.

ABOUT THIS KIT

Geography Skills Activities Kit will help you teach students in grades 4–8 how to read and interpret geographic information presented in graphic form—maps, pictures, diagrams, tables, graphs—and narratives. The *Kit* also provides experiences that will enable students to develop nongraphic geography skills such as researching, experimenting, observing, recording, demonstrating, and constructing. Each activity is arranged in a handy two-page layout, with the teacher's page and the student's page facing each other.

To properly develop these geography skills, it is necessary to provide appropriate contextual situations. Although random exercises on a geography topic could help develop skills, the subject matter would be disjointed and unrelated. Thus, *Geography Skills Activities Kit* not only develops skills, but also develops connected and relevant geographic facts and understandings.

The topics covered in the *Kit* have universal geographic applicability, regardless of the curriculum arrangement or textbook used in any given classroom. Special effort has been made to include geographic content that, in general, follows curriculum guidelines, textbook offerings, and tests of basic skills used in grades 4–8.

The simplified format of *Geography Skills Activities Kit* gives a complete teaching-learning unit with each exercise. Here is how each two-page exercise is arranged.

The Teacher's Page

The left-hand page is the teacher's page. The title at the top of this page identifies the skill area and topics to be developed. Directly following the title is the background, which will help you gain insights into the lesson's topic. Statistics are sometimes presented that would otherwise take you considerable time and effort to uncover.

The book's eleven sections represent a summary of selected background information. Decisions on what to include in the background were made on the basis of affirmative answers to three questions:

1. Is the background information directly related to the topic?

2. Is it within the learners' capacities to understand and absorb the information if presented by the teacher?

3. Is the information interesting and meaningful to the children for whom the exercise was designed?

The "Student Involvement" section of the teacher's page helps you to teach the topic and skill elements of the lesson.

At the end of each teacher's page are the activity's answers and suggested responses.

The Student's Page

The right-hand page is the learner's page—the actual activity sheet. This can easily be reproduced as many times as needed for your students.

Each exercise sheet has two parts: (1) maps, tables, diagrams, graphs, pictures, and narratives, presented singly or in combination, and (2) questions or directions that are designed to elicit active written responses from the students. In some exercises, students must not only obtain information from the graphics or narratives, but must also add something to or make notations on the graphics. This approach helps students feel that they are doing more than just responding to questions. In a real sense, the graphics become the learner's graphics.

Some students may be able to complete some activities without prior instruction, but most students will need your guidance. The best way to maximize learning potential for all concerned is to introduce the lesson, provide some background information, and survey with the learners the exercise that will be developed. Then, after the students have completed the activity, there should be a follow-up during which answers are discussed, additional questions are asked, and supplementary information is given.

A special feature of *Geography Skills Activities Kit* is the section on enrichment activities at the back of the book. These activities provide your students with hands-on demonstrations and outside-the-classroom experiences. Each enrichment activity has been classroom-tested and requires no elaborate equipment or preparations.

Graphic interpretation skills, and especially map-reading skills, start with recognition of graphic symbols and proceed to higher-level skills that require analysis and application. The "Activities-Skills Index" suggests approximate grade levels for each exercise. Of course, the activities may be suitable at higher or lower levels, depending upon the students' achievement levels.

I wish you success in using *Geography Skills Activities Kit* and hope you and your students will enjoy the activities!

James F. Silver

ACKNOWLEDGMENTS

I would like to express my appreciation to the following organizations for permission to use their materials:

> The Pennsylvania Geological Survey for "Pennsylvania After the Ice Age"

> The State of Montana Department of Transportation for the official state road map

> Deserted Village of Allaire Map provided through the courtesy of Allaire Village, Inc. and Allaire State Park (New Jersey State's Parks Service)

> *Hunterdon County Democrat* for the map of the borough of Flemington, N.J.

The illustrations in Sections 8-2, 8-3, 8-8, 8-13, 8-14, 9-1, 9-2, and 10-1 are by Ann Gross of Pennington, N.J. They originally appeared in *Understanding Air, Soil, and Water* which was written by James F. Silver and published by InterAction Press, Pennington, N.J.

ACTIVITIES/SKILLS INDEX

About This Kit vii

Section 1   READING AND INTERPRETING MAPS.......................... 1

Activity Key	*Topic*	*Grade Level*
1-1	A Map Is a Kind of Picture	4–5
1-2	Map Symbols That Represent Natural Things	4–5
1-3	Map Symbols That Represent Man-Made Things	4–5
1-4	Symbols for Boundaries	4–5
1-5	Visualizing Symbols	4–5
1-6	Using a Compass to Find Directions	4–5
1-7	Using Directions to Locate Cities and States	4–5
1-8	Using Directions on Pictorial Maps	4–5
1-9	Locating Places Through Distance and Direction	4–5
1-10	Locating Places on a Street Map	4–5
1-11	A Walk Through a Small Town	4–5
1-12	Routes of Travel and Distances on Road Maps	4–5

Section 2   BASIC ENVIRONMENTS 27

Activity Key	*Topic/Skill*	*Grade Level*
2-1	How to Study a Geography Picture (*reading and interpreting a picture that depicts farming in the hot, dry climate of northern Mexico; applying a systematic approach to the reading and interpretation of pictures that have geographic content*)	4–5
2-2	A Mountain Occupation—Dairying (*reading and interpreting a picture that depicts dairying in the high altitudes of Switzerland*)	4–5
2-3	Desert Families Share the Work (*reading and interpreting a picture that depicts family activities in the hot, dry desert lands of northern Africa*)	4–5
2-4	A Map of a New Jersey Farm (*reading and interpreting a map that shows how a farm in the temperate eastern United States might be laid out*)	4–5

Activity Key	*Topic/Skill*	*Grade Level*
2-5	Working Together in Antarctica (*reading and interpreting a picture that depicts how humans adapt to transportation and settlement difficulties in the Antarctic environment*)	4–5
2-6	Keeping Back the Sea in the Netherlands (*reading and interpreting a picture that depicts a typical Netherlands coastal scene of a dike, with the sea and land clearly in evidence*)	4–5
2-7	Comparing Two Rivers (*reading and interpreting two pictures—one of a river in a hot, wet land, the other of a river in a hot, dry land—that offer sharp environmental and human usage contrasts*)	4–5

Section 3   THE FISHING INDUSTRY......................................43

3-1	The Fishing Harbor (*reading and interpreting a picture that depicts the varied activities that take place in a typical fishing harbor-village*)	4–5
3-2	Where Fish Are Caught (*reading and interpreting a a map that shows where the major fishing grounds of the world are located*)	4–5
3-3	Fish for the People of the World (*reading and interpreting a bar graph that compares the fish catches of the world's leading nations*)	4–5
3-4	Fishing Where the Fish Are (*reading and interpreting a cross-sectional diagram that shows fishing banks and continental shelves, and why fish are attracted to them*)	4–5
3-5	Catching Fish at Sea (*reading and interpreting a picture diagram that shows how fish are caught at sea by trawlers*)	4–5

Section 4   THE MINING INDUSTRY..55

4-1	Minerals Mined in the United States and the World (*reading and interpreting circle graphs that compare United States mineral production with the world's*)	4–5
4-2	Leading Mining States (*reading and interpreting a pattern map that shows the rank order of the important mineral-producing states*)	4–5
4-3	Understanding Strip Mining (*completing a scene that shows typical strip-mining activities*)	4–5
4-4	Understanding Underground Mining (*reading and interpreting cross-sectional diagrams of drift and shaft mines*)	4–5

Section 5   THE FARMING INDUSTRY 65

Activity Key   *Topic/Skill*   *Grade Level*

5-1   Corn—A Useful Grain (*reading and interpreting a   4–5
           sequence of pictures that illustrates the phases of corn
           agriculture from plowing to the consumer*)

5-2   The Growing Season (*reading and interpreting a   4–5
           pattern map that shows the length of the growing
           season as influenced by latitude in the Western
           Hemisphere*)

5-3   The Foods We Eat (*reading and interpreting a bar   4–5
           graph that compares the relative popularity of various
           food groups*)

**Section 6   MORE OF READING AND INTERPRETING MAPS AND
           DIAGRAMS** 73

6-1   Locating Places Through the Use of a Map Index   5–8
6-2   Reading a Road Map for City Size and Special   5–8
           Features
6-3   Identifying Water and Coastal Features   5–8
6-4   Identifying Land and Water Features   5–8
6-5   Earth Facts   5–8
6-6   The Spinning Earth Causes Day and Night   5–8
6-7   Locating Places with Lines of Latitude   5–8
6-8   Locating Places with Lines of Longitude   5–8
6-9   Locating Places with Latitude and Longitude   5–8
6-10   Using Latitude and Longitude to Compute Distances   5–8
6-11   Determining Direction with Latitude and Longitude   5–8
6-12   Telling Time with Longitude   5–8
6-13   Time Zones in the United States   5–8
6-14   Polar Maps and Direction   5–8
6-15   Flying Over the Polar Regions   5–8
6-16   The Four Seasons   5–8
6-17   Using a Scale of Miles to Find Air Distance   5–8
6-18   Rivers and River Systems   5–8
6-19   Understanding Altitude   5–8
6-20   Using Color to Show Altitude or Elevation   5–8
6-21   Determining Elevation on Flat Maps Through Color   5–8

Activity Key	*Topic/Skill*	*Grade Level*
6-22	Determining Elevation from Contour Lines	5–8
6-23	Finding Man-made Things on Topographical Maps	5–8
6-24	Locating Unnamed Places on Topographical Maps	5–8
6-25	Taking a Walk with a Topographical Map	5–8
6-26	Reading and Interpreting Pattern Maps I (*wheat production in the United States*)	5–8
6-27	Reading and Interpreting Pattern Maps II (*precipitation patterns in the United States*)	5–8
6-28	Reading and Interpreting Pattern Maps III (*distribution of national parks throughout the USA*)	5–8
6-29	Reading and Interpreting Pattern Maps IV (*relating a pattern map of transportation routes to a pattern map of natural resources*)	5–8
6-30	Reading and Interpreting Pattern Maps V (*relating a pattern map of agricultural products to a pattern map of elevation*)	5–8
6-31	Reading and Interpreting Pattern Maps VI (*relating a pattern map of earthquake occurrence to a pattern map showing the location of certain mountain ranges*)	5–8
6-32	Reading and Interpreting Pattern Maps VII (*reading a single pattern map that shows both cultural and physical symbols from which facts and inferences are derived*)	5–8
6-33	Reading and Interpreting Pattern Maps VIII (*transferring information derived from a table of temperatures to a blank map that evolves into a pattern map*)	5–8

Section 7   WORLD'S CONTINENTS, OCEANS, AND IMPORTANT WATER PASSAGES 135

7-1	Locating the Continents and Oceans	4–5
7-2	The Panama Canal (*reading and interpreting a map that shows the route of travel from Boston to San Francisco through the Panama Canal as compared to the all-water route around South America*)	5–8
7-3	The Suez Canal (*reading and interpreting a map that shows the route of travel from New York to Bombay, India, through the Suez Canal as compared to the route around Africa*)	5–8

Activity Key	*Topic/Skill*	*Grade Level*
7-4	The Strait of Gibraltar (*reading and interpreting a map that shows the route of travel from London, England, to Athens, Greece*)	5–8

Section 8   WATER AS A UNIVERSAL GEOGRAPHY SIGNIFICANT 145

8-1	Our Water Is Running Out (*reading and interpreting a line graph that shows the increase in water usage over a 55-year period*)	4–8
8-2	Raindrops Falling in a Watershed (*reading and interpreting a map-diagram that shows a typical watershed and its drainage system*)	4–8
8-3	Water Goes 'Round and 'Round (*reading and interpreting a diagram that shows the hydrologic cycle from evaporation to precipitation to drainage as a continuum*)	4–8
8-4	Thunder, Lightning, and Rain (*completing and interpreting a diagram that shows how rainfall is caused by convection currents*)	4–8
8-5	Rain in the Mountains (*reading and interpreting a diagram that shows how the presence of mountains causes orographic rainfall*)	4–8
8-6	The Battle of the Air Masses (*reading and interpreting a diagram that shows how cyclonic rainfall occurs when air masses meet*)	4–8
8-7	Water for Cities from Rivers and Lakes (*reading and interpreting picture-diagrams that show the sequences followed from water source to the household water tap*)	4–8
8-8	Water from Under the Ground (*reading and interpreting a cross-sectional picture-diagram of dug, artesian, and drilled wells*)	4–8
8-9	When Does the Rain Come Down? (*completing and interpreting a line graph that shows the monthly precipitation in three contrasting cities*)	4–8
8-10	Dams—Water Controllers (*reading and interpreting panoramic and cutaway views of Hoover Dam, a hydroelectric dam*)	4–8
8-11	High Dams of the United States and Canada (*completing and interpreting a bar graph that compares the heights of various dams*)	4–8

Activity Key	*Topic/Skill*	*Grade Level*

8-12   Electric Power from Water (*reading and interpreting*   4–8
            a cutaway view of the internal workings of a typical
            hydroelectric plant)

8-13   Polluted Water Kills Fish (*reading and interpreting*   4–8
            pictures that depict situations that cause water
            pollution)

8-14   Making Water Pure Again (*reading and interpreting*   4–8
            a series of picture-diagrams that show how water is
            purified)

Section 9   AIR AS A UNIVERSAL GEOGRAPHY SIGNIFICANT 171

9-1   Air Pollutants and the Atmosphere (*reading and*   4–8
            interpreting a diagram of the atmosphere)

9-2   How Does Air Become Polluted? (*reading and*   4–8
            interpreting pictures that show conditions that cause
            air pollution)

Section 10   NATURAL CONDITIONS AND PHENOMENA THAT
MODIFY THE EARTH 177

10-1   Forces That Act on Rocks (*reading and interpreting*   4–8
            pictures that show how rocks are reduced to small
            particles)

10-2   A Slice of Soil (*reading and interpreting a diagram*   4–8
            that shows a cross section of soil)

10-3   The Making of a Volcano (*reading and interpreting a*   4–8
            diagram that shows a cross section of an erupting
            volcano)

10-4   The Moving Earth (*reading and interpreting*   4–8
            diagrams that show a cross section of the earth and
            movements of the earth that cause earthquakes)

10-5   The Beginning of an Earthquake (*completing and*   4–8
            interpreting a diagram that shows how the waves of
            an earthquake spread to surrounding land)

10-6   Glaciers—Masses of Moving Ice (*completing and*   4–8
            interpreting a diagram that shows the birth and
            movement of a valley glacier)

10-7   All About Icebergs (*completing and interpreting a*   4–8
            diagram that shows how icebergs are formed from
            valley glaciers)

Activity Key	*Topic/Skill*	*Grade Level*
10-8	The Work of Glaciers (*completing diagrams that show how glaciers modify the surface of the earth*)	4–8
10-9	The Ice Age (*reading and interpreting a map of the Ice Age in North America; completing a table with information gained from the map*)	4–8

Section 11   STATISTICAL INFORMATION ON WORLD POPULATION AND PRODUCTION 197

11-1	The Sizes and Populations of the Continents (*reading and interpreting circle graphs that show the areas and populations of the continents*)	4–8
11-2	Wheat and Flour for the World's Bread (*reading and interpreting bar graphs that show the buyers of American wheat and the world's leading wheat producers*)	4–8
11-3	The World's Rice Bowls (*completing a bar graph on rice production from data extracted from a table*)	4–8

Appendix   GEOGRAPHY ENRICHMENT ACTIVITIES 205

Three-Dimensional Elevation Model • 205

Finding Compass Directions with a Bar Magnet • 206

Map Jigsaw Puzzles • 206

Demonstrating Contour Lines • 207

Three-Dimensional Pattern Maps • 208

Reading Road Maps • 208

Silhouette Map Flash Cards • 209

Clocks That Show "Times" Across the Country • 209

Making Rain • 210

Water Waste • 211

Model Conservation Farm • 211

Making Soil • 212

Sediment in Water • 213

Contours • 214

Reducing Rocks by Changes in Temperature • 215

Mountain Ranges and Peaks • 216

Erosion • 216

Evidence of Air Pollution • 216

Community Air Pollution • 217

Air Pollution and Plant Growth • 217

Wind, Dust, and Air Pollution • 217

Picture Collections • 218

Travel Posters • 218

Sand Table Models of Basic Environments • 219

Diorama Models • 219

Clay Models of Land Features and Land Usage • 220

Weather Charts • 220

Weather Graphs • 221

Postage Stamp Design • 221

Floating Icebergs • 221

Geography Bulletin Boards • 222

READING AND INTERPRETING MAPS

1-1 A Map Is a Kind of Picture
1-2 Map Symbols That Represent Natural Things
1-3 Map Symbols That Represent Man-Made Things
1-4 Symbols for Boundaries
1-5 Visualizing Symbols
1-6 Using a Compass to Find Directions
1-7 Using Directions to Locate Cities and States
1-8 Using Directions on Pictorial Maps
1-9 Locating Places through Distance and Direction
1-10 Locating Places on a Street Map
1-11 A Walk through a Small Town
1-12 Routes of Travel and Distances on Road Maps

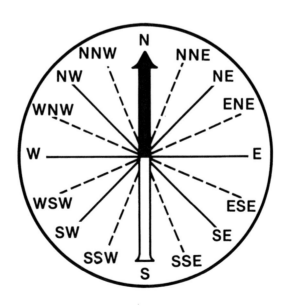

Reading and Interpreting Maps:
A Map Is a Kind of Picture

Background

1. The statement "maps are representations of portions of the earth's surface" is a truism. It is perhaps the most basic of all map understandings. All other map understandings and skills proceed from this assumption.

2. The efficient interpretation of maps rests on the recognition of map symbols. Just as they develop a sight vocabulary of words, learners should develop a sight vocabulary of map symbols. Those symbols that are not part of their sight vocabulary must be looked up in the legends or keys of the maps. A legend is the map equivalent of a glossary in a book.

Student Involvement

1. Most often when we look at a map, our eyes are above, looking down on the map. Likewise, when we are in an airplane we are looking down on the surface of the earth. If we were to take pictures of what we see, we would call the resultant photographs "aerial views." Map makers could take these aerial views and make maps from them. In so doing, they would utilize symbols to represent the objects shown in the photographs.

2. The learning activity on the facing page is based on the idea stated above. The learners have to put themselves in the position of being passengers in an airplane, looking down and taking a photograph of what they see. Then they have to render the photograph into a map.

3. The student exercise provides one experience in making maps from photographs. This experience should be repeated several times. An effective way to provide for this is to search through textbooks for photographs that present aerial views. Then, either as a class activity or as a learning center activity, instruct your learners to make maps based on the photographs. For encouragement and motivation, create a bulletin board that displays their maps and the photographs on which they are based.

Answers to the Exercise

1. House, trees, fence, telephone poles, wires, field, river, road, crossroad.

2. Accept any map effort that symbolically shows the picture items in reasonable relationship; e.g., a line for a road, squares for buildings, and so on.

Name _____   Date _____

A MAP IS A KIND OF PICTURE

1. The picture at the top of this column was taken from the air. Name at least eight things you see in the picture.

_____

_____

_____

_____

_____

_____

_____

_____

2. Maps can show all the things that pictures show, but they might show the things in different ways. In pictures, roads *look* like roads, but on maps roads might appear to be straight lines(—). In pictures, railroad tracks *look* like railroad tracks, but on maps they might be shown as lines with little cross-marks (—+—+—).

The map lines for roads and railroads are called *symbols*. Symbols represent or stand for the real thing. Almost everything shown in pictures can be shown on maps through the use of symbols.

In the box at the top of the second column, draw a map that uses symbols to show what is in the picture. Try to show on your map the roads, buildings, and other things in the same positions as in the picture.

Reading and Interpreting Maps:
Map Symbols That Represent Natural Things

Background

At this grade level, semipictorial symbols should frequently be employed. However, this is also the time when the transition to more abstract symbols should be made. Gradually, the use of abstract symbols should become dominant.

1. Item 1 of the activity can be supplemented by asking the question: What are some other symbols that are used to represent things? (Examples are highway signs showing animal images to indicate the presence of deer; highway numbers that stand for roads; signs showing silhouettes of bicycles to indicate bicycle paths; and logos that symbolize automobile makes.)

What are some symbols that are used to represent ideas or imaginary things? (Examples are balance scales to represent the idea of justice; hands clasped as in a handshake to indicate friendship; a V made with two fingers to indicate victory; and a cigarette with an X through it to warn against smoking.)

2. After the basic activity has been completed, your students can make additions to the map. Some suggestions:

—A range of mountains running lengthwise through the uppermost peninsula.

—A forest strip along the lower river.

—A lake within the island.

—Fish in the existing lake or any newly added lake.

—Tributary rivers entering the existing rivers. The rivers should begin in or near the mountain areas.

The suggestions above do not include directional terms such as north or south. Such terms are not needed for the successful completion of the activity. Information about the use of directions on maps begins with Activity 1-6.

Answers to the Exercise

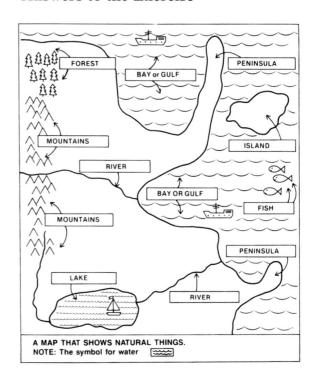

A MAP THAT SHOWS NATURAL THINGS.
NOTE: The symbol for water

Name _____   Date _____

MAP SYMBOLS THAT REPRESENT NATURAL THINGS

1. A *symbol* is a word, number, drawing, or object that stands for an idea or for a real thing. For example, the word *car* represents an automobile. The Statue of Liberty represents freedom. Your name stands for you.

Write a word that tells what each of the symbols represents:

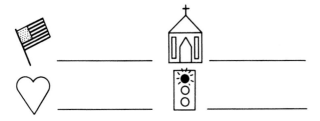

2. Often, maps show natural things such as mountains, lakes, and forests. Fish, cattle, and iron ore deposits are also examples of the kinds of natural things that can be shown with symbols on maps.

Sometimes, map makers try to make symbols look like the actual things. Study the symbols for natural things shown below. In the space underneath the symbols, write what you think each symbol stands for:

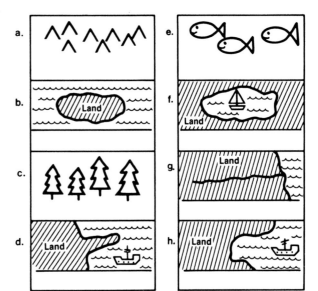

Here are the answers:
a. Mountains
b. Island
c. Forest
d. Peninsula (land that is nearly surrounded by water)
e. Fish
f. Lake
g. River
h. Bay or gulf (a part of an ocean or lake that extends inland)

3. All of the symbols for natural things that you identified above are shown in the map at left. There is a box near each symbol. Use the boxes to label each of the map symbols.

NOTE: To *label* a symbol on a map is to print or write the name of the thing that the symbol represents. Most map labels are printed because printing is usually neater and doesn't take as much space as script writing.

A MAP THAT SHOWS NATURAL THINGS.   NOTE: The symbol for water

Reading and Interpreting Maps:
Map Symbols That Represent Man-Made Things

Background

Visualization of the symbols used on maps and in map keys is of crucial importance to the correct reading and interpretation of maps. Therefore, the concept that is represented by the symbol should be carefully introduced and gradually expanded.

For example, children's concepts of "rivers" are limited to the real and vicarious experiences they have had with rivers. Perhaps the rivers the children experienced were shallow and not navigable. Although they may correctly identify the curvy line on a map as a river called "Mississippi," they may incorrectly visualize the Mississippi as being like the one they know—shallow, and not navigable.

One of the most effective ways to widen concepts is through the use of pictures, especially if they are accompanied by oral and written descriptions and questions. With reference to the river concept, many pictures should be shown of a variety of rivers—wide, deep, swift, sluggish, muddy, clear, with steep-sided banks, and so on.

Once this has been done, the next step is to help learners see the river in the context of the map. Otherwise, how will they know which aspect of the concept "rivers" to apply?

Just as deriving meaning from context is an advanced skill in reading words, so also is it an advanced skill in reading map symbols. But beginnings have to be made. With the guidance of the teacher, children can be helped to realize that a river in a mountain area will probably be swift, a river in a great plain will more than likely be slow-moving, a river emerging from a glacier will be cold, and so on.

Student Involvement

As in the previous activity, the map may be expanded. Some suggestions:
—Name and label the island and the lake.
—Locate, name, and label cities on the island and on the peninsulas.
—Locate two or three state parks at the source of the Indian River and the shores of the lake.

Answers to the Exercise

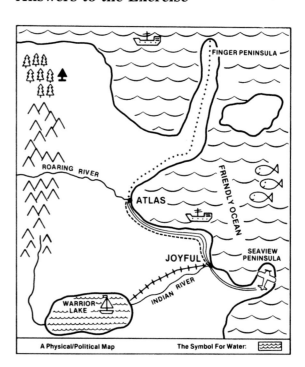

MAP SYMBOLS THAT REPRESENT MAN-MADE THINGS

SYMBOL	MEANING	REAL APPEARANCE
‖	ROAD	
+++++++	RAILROAD	
– – – –	ELECTRIC POWER LINE	
· · · · · · · ·	BIKE TRAIL	
✈	AIRPORT	
◢	STATE PARK	
•	CITY OR TOWN	

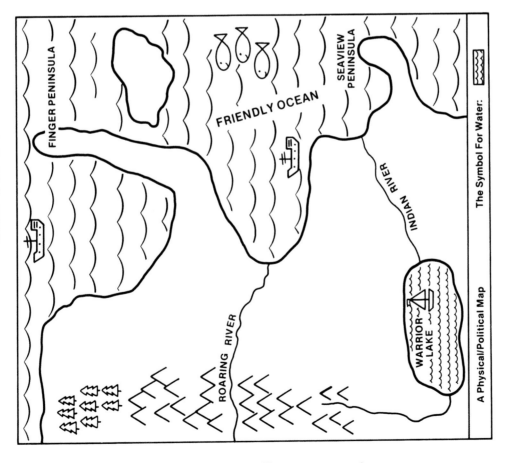

A Physical/Political Map

The Symbol For Water: 〜〜〜

The map in the left column is similar to the one you used in the previous activity. Add political symbols to the map by following the directions below. When the map is completed, you will have a physical-political map. In "map language," *physical* is another word for natural. Use the map key above for help in knowing how to draw the symbols.

1. Show a city at the place where Roaring River meets the ocean. Label the city *Atlas*.

2. Show another city where Indian River meets the ocean. Label the city *Joyful*.

3. Draw a road along the coast between Atlas and Joyful.

4. Draw a railroad along Indian River from Joyful to Warrior Lake.

5. Draw an electric power line along the road between Atlas and Joyful.

6. Draw a bike trail from Atlas to the end of Finger Peninsula.

7. Show an airport on Seaview Peninsula.

8. Draw a road along the coast from the airport to Joyful.

9. Show a state park near the forest.

In addition to natural things, man-made things such as roads and cities are also shown on maps. Maps that show man-made things are called *political* maps. Some of the kinds of symbols that are used on political maps are shown in the *Map Key:*

Reading and Interpreting Maps: Symbols for Boundaries

Background

This activity is concerned with recognizing and interpreting symbols that represent abstract things (i.e., imaginary lines). It follows the section on tangible symbols because, of the two, abstract symbols are the most difficult to teach and to learn.

Student Involvement

1. Item 2 presents the idea that boundaries are abstract (not real, not tangible) if they do not exist in some form, such as fences, walls, or painted lines. Some well-known boundaries that are marked by tangibles are the Berlin Wall, the Great Wall of China, and the Kremlin Walls. In former times, entire cities were enclosed by walls.

Also point out that it is impractical to mark some boundaries because of expense and upkeep. For example, none of the boundaries between Canada and the United States, some 3,000 miles, is walled or fenced.

Other imaginary lines on the earth's surface are the equator, the Arctic and Antarctic Circles, the Tropics of Capricorn and Cancer, and all of the parallels and meridians. Airplane and ocean routes can be considered to be imaginary, as shown on maps, because they don't exist as real things.

2. Note in Item d of the activity that city and town boundaries are in continuum; they show the shape of the cities.

3. Note in Item f of the activity that the size of the lettering decreases as one goes from the largest entities (countries) to the smallest entities (cities). Also, some maps show the relative sizes of the cities by different lettering sizes.

4. There have been some attempts among map publishers to standardize boundary symbols, but standardization should not be taken for granted. There are many deviations in the use of symbols from publisher to publisher. Your students should follow the rule: Always refer to the key to the map for correct interpretation of the symbols used on the map.

Answers to the Exercise

1. 3–6. [Check for correct labeling. Below is one version of how the map of Erehwon might look. Incidentally, Erehwon, spelled in reverse, reads "Nowhere."]

2. Four

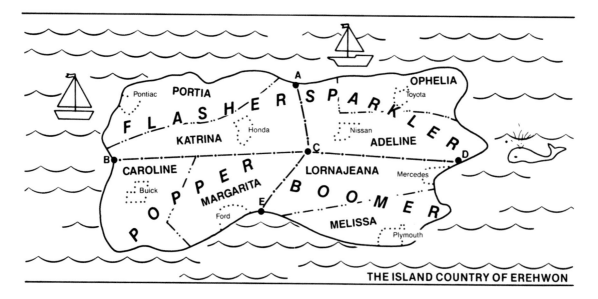

THE ISLAND COUNTRY OF EREHWON

Name _____   Date _____

SYMBOLS FOR BOUNDARIES

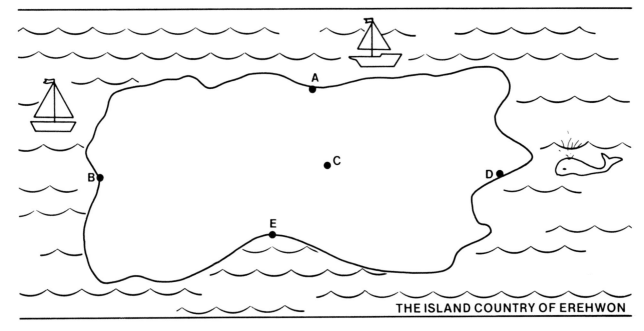

THE ISLAND COUNTRY OF EREHWON

Maps use symbols to represent real and imaginary things. Some of the imaginary things shown on maps are boundary lines of countries, states, counties, and cities. Boundary lines can be shown as going across both land and water.

Only a surveyor using instruments can tell you where boundary lines are located. Sometimes stakes are driven into the ground to indicate where boundary lines begin and end. If you wanted to, you could build a wall or fence by using the stakes as markers.

Show your understanding of boundary lines by completing the map of the make-believe country of Erehwon, shown above.

1. Draw − · − · − , the symbol for state boundaries, from:

    A to C   C to E   B to C   C to D

2. How many states have you made?

3. States are divided into counties. Here is one way to show county boundaries: − · · − · ·

Divide each state into two counties. The county lines can be straight or curved.

4. The boundaries of towns and cities can be shown in this way: CITY

Draw boundary lines for one city in each of the counties.

5. Make up a name for each state. Within the boundaries of each state, print its name in large letters.

6. Name and label each of your counties and cities. The county names should be printed in smaller letters than the state names. City names are printed smaller than county names.

Reading and Interpreting Maps:
Visualizing Symbols

Background

1. The foundation fact for all map reading is that symbols represent real and imaginary places. When reading word symbols, readers should visualize a table when they see the word *table*. The context surrounding the word will help the reader see the "correct" table. A sentence that reads "Set the dining-room table" conjures up a different image of a table than the sentence "The picnic table was covered with a gingham cloth." Thus, the word is first recognized, and then it is visualized according to the context.

2. In reading symbols on maps, the same psychological process takes place. Map readers recognize the symbol for *river*. Then they explore the context in which the symbol is placed. If they see that the river is high in the mountains, they should visualize a swift-running river coursing over rocks and boulders.

3. To provide practice in visualizing symbols, instructors should show pictures that represent the symbols. For example, if the symbol for mountain ranges is introduced, pictures showing various kinds of mountain ranges should be shown.

Student Involvement

1. Explain and illustrate the basic rationale of "symbols and context" as explained above.

2. Allow time for the students to match the pictures surrounding the map with the symbols on the map.

3. Discuss their choices.

4. Refer to a textbook map, preferably one that is currently being used. If this map shows, for example, that a vast area such as the Great Plains is all one color (indicating elevation), the scene might be described as "flat land stretching for miles with a gradual rise to the west."

In another situation, an island with contour lines might be described this way: "Surrounded by water. From the side it would look like a bowl turned upside-down."

Answers to the Exercise

Starting from upper left corner and reading clockwise: M, D, H, G, E, F, A, K, C.

Name _____ Date _____

VISUALIZING SYMBOLS

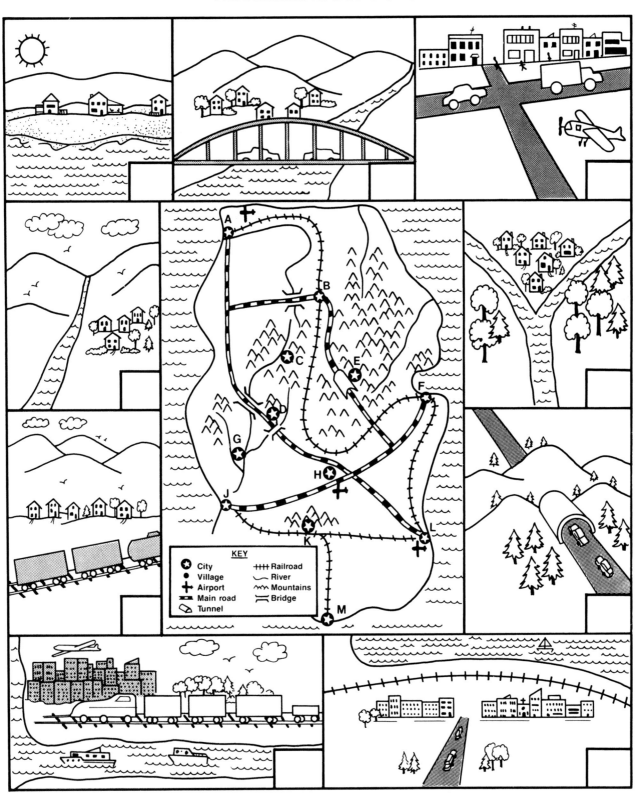

KEY

✪ City	┼┼┼ Railroad
● Village	‿ River
✚ Airport	⌃⌃⌃ Mountains
▬ Main road	⊟ Bridge
⌒ Tunnel	

Directions: Match the picture with the symbols. Note that there is a letter next to each map symbol. Find the picture that each symbol represents and write the corresponding letter in the blank square at the bottom right side of the picture. Remember that you are looking from south to north on the map.

Reading and Interpreting Diagrams: Using a Compass to Find Directions

1. A compass needle points to *magnetic* north. *True* north is in the direction of the North Pole. The degree difference between true north and magnetic north can be considerable, as much as 30 degrees in the continental United States.

The intersection of the "line" made by the arrow pointing to magnetic north and the "line" pointing to true north creates an angle. This angle is called the *declination.* Airplane pilots refer to the angle as *deviation.* The drawing below shows the magnetic declination for a location in Maine.

2. At the early grade levels, it probably would not be profitable to teach such technicalities. But to prevent misunderstandings, it would be well to call the children's attention to magnetic declination. When the class is using the compass, you can avoid contradiction of facts by saying, "The needle points in a northward direction," or a variation thereof.

Student Involvement

Some suggestions for teaching directions:

1. Show a compass. Have your students observe that no matter how the compass is turned, the magnetic arrow always points in the same direction: toward the north. Explain that this happens because there is a great area about a thousand miles south of the North Pole that attracts the compass needle. (The position of the magnetic field changes from year to year.)

2. Use a compass to establish in the classroom the eight directions practiced in this activity. Post a sign for "North" on the north wall, "South" on the south wall, "Northeast" in the northeast corner, and so on. Constantly refer to room locations by using compass directions. Say, for example, "Look at the bulletin board on the east wall," or "Class, let's make a learning center on the west wall."

3. Play direction games, for example, "Simon Says." Simon says, "Raise your east arm," or Simon says, "Face northwest," and so forth.

Answers to the Exercise

1*a*. South *b*. West *c*. East

2*a*. Southwest *b*. Northwest *c*. Southeast

3*a*. Northeast, east, southeast *b*. Northwest, west, southwest

4. [Check for accuracy.]

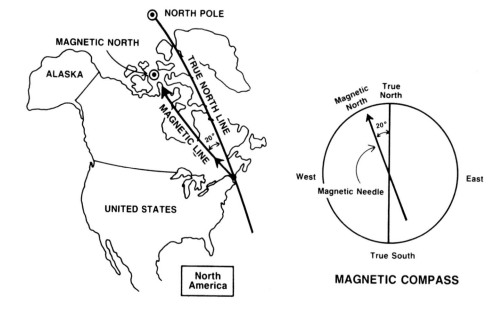

MAGNETIC COMPASS

Name _____   Date _____

USING A COMPASS TO FIND DIRECTIONS

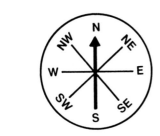

Left Hand   Right Hand

1. Finding direction is easy if you have a compass. This is because an arrow-shaped needle inside the compass always points *northward.* The other end of the needle points in the opposite direction: *southward.*

If you face *north,* as the girl in the drawing is doing, *east* is on your right and *west* is on your left.

a. Suppose that the girl in the drawing turned and faced in the opposite direction. What direction would she be facing?

_____

b. What direction would be on her right?

_____

c. What direction would be on her left?

_____

2. NE on the compass drawing is the abbreviation for northeast. As you can see, northeast is midway between north and east.

a. What direction is opposite northeast?

_____

b. What direction is midway between north and west? _____

c. What direction is opposite northwest?

_____

3a. Complete the following two sentences: The east side of the compass drawing shows three directions. They are:

_____

_____

_____

b. The west side of the compass drawing also shows three directions. They are:

_____

_____

_____

4. Try to label all the directions on the compass below without looking at the drawing above. Use abbreviations.

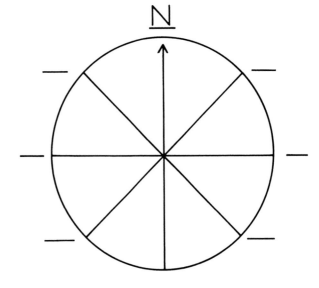

Reading and Interpreting Maps:
Using Directions to Locate Cities and States

Background

The "direction circle" is positioned on the map on the activity page to correspond with the geographic center of the contiguous United States. One definition of geographic center is "the center of gravity on the surface, or that point on which the surface of the area would balance" (*World Almanac and Book of Facts, 1986*).

Student Involvement

Before your students work on this activity, there are some elements that should be brought to their attention.

1. Point out that on maps the locations of cities are determined by special symbols. Symbols for cities may take different forms; for example, a colored dot (•), a circle and dot (⊙), or an outline of the shape of the city (⌂). Most maps will show in the key to the map the symbols used for cities.

A city's name should not be used as the location of the city because the name may stretch for hundreds of miles across the map (e.g., Indianapolis). Which letter stands for the location of the city? No one can tell; hence the use of a locational symbol.

2. Your students should realize that although *northeast,* for example, is technically a precise direction (45°N), it also indicates a general direction. On the exercise map, Maine is not precisely northeast of the direction circle's center, but the term northeast gives more information than north or east alone.

Later, after your students have become skilled in using cardinal and intermediate directions, they may learn the other points of the compass, as shown below.

3. "Table" may be an unfamiliar term to your students. If so, define it as an arrangement for listing information. A calender is a kind of table with which they are probably familiar.

It would be helpful to work out one of the listings with the students. An important part of the process: To find a "cell" in a table, it is necessary to use the horizontal and vertical axes. The cell is the point at which one axis intersects the other.

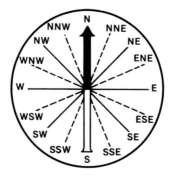

THE SIXTEEN POINTS
OF THE COMPASS

There are 11¼° between compass points, allowing for reasonable accuracy.

NNE means north-north-east; ENE is east-north-east, and so on.

Answers to the Exercise

The table should be completed as follows: Arizona, SW; Florida, SE; Maine, NE; Washington, NW; Atlanta, SE; Austin, S; Bismarck, N; Helena, NW; Madison, NE; New Orleans, SE; San Francisco, W; Washington, D.C., E

Name _____   Date _____

USING DIRECTIONS TO LOCATE CITIES AND STATES

Imagine that you are in the center of the direction circle shown on the map. You are deciding which direction you should take to go to the four states and eight cities shown on the map.

The table below lists the states and cities. Put a check (√) in the column that best tells the direction from your position to the place. Remember that the dot (•) shows the location of the city, not the printed name.

PLACE	DIRECTION FROM THE CENTER OF THE MAP CIRCLE							
(States)	N (North)	NE (Northeast)	E (East)	SE (Southeast)	S (South)	SW (Southwest)	W (West)	NW (Northwest)
Arizona								
Florida								
Maine								
Washington								
(Cities)								
Atlanta								
Austin								
Bismarck								
Helena								
Madison								
New Orleans								
San Francisco								
Washington, D.C.								

Reading and Interpreting Maps:
Using Directions on Pictorial Maps

Background

North on maps: North is not always at the top of a map page. East or west or some other direction may be shown at the top. If, for example, east were shown at the top of a page, then north would be to the left, as in the example below.

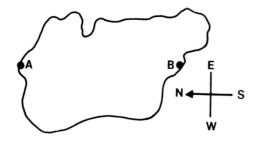

The map shows that A is the most northern point and B is on the south coast. If one were to travel from B to A, one would be traveling north. The rule to remember is: It is the compass direction and not the position of the map on the page that tells where north is.

It is important that your students realize that north is not always at the top of the map, because the tendency is to equate "top" with "up," and "up" with "north." The same kind of error is made in equating "south" with "down" as terms of direction. One goes south, not "down south," and one goes north, not "up north."

The correct use of words that express direction should be stressed. This is especially true for young learners, who are quite literal in their interpretations. Imagine the confusion that might arise in a student's mind if he or she heard that Magellan "sailed under South America."

"Up" as a map and globe direction is away from the center of the earth: "down" is toward the center of the earth. Learners who use those terms as compass directions are likely to find it difficult to believe that some rivers, such as the Allegheny (Pennsylvania) and the Nile (Egypt), flow north. Their reasoning is, "How can a river flow up?"

Student Involvement

With reference to the information given in the *background* section, call your students' attention to the fact that in the activity map north appears to be slightly askew, and the four sections seem off-balance. Assure your students that the map is correctly drawn. The compass arrow *is* pointing north, and the east–west line is at a right angle to the north–south line. See Activity 6-12 for more on this subject.

Answers to the Exercise

1. Paint Shop (NE), Slaughterhouse (NE), Foreman's Cottage (NW), Bakery (SW), Store (SE), Carpenter Shop (SE), Carriage Shop (SE), Sawmill (SW)

2a. Northeast   b. South   c. Southeast   d. West

Name _____   Date _____

USING DIRECTIONS ON A PICTORIAL MAP

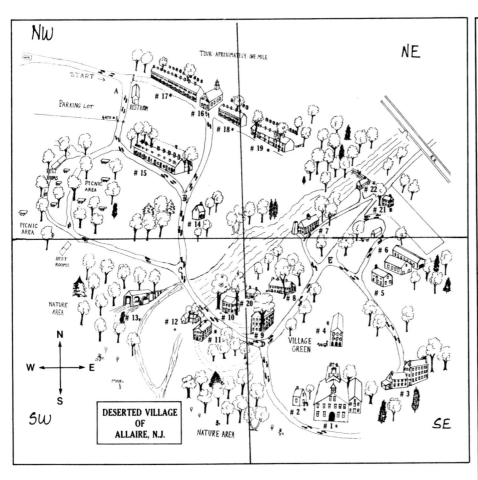

The Deserted Village of Allaire

Allaire, N.J. was once a very busy community. Its workers made things from iron. The iron came from nearby "iron bogs."

Great deposits of iron were discovered in other parts of the country. Soon, other communities could produce iron goods more cheaply than Allaire. There were no more jobs, so workers left the village. It became a deserted town.

Allaire is now being restored. The pictorial map shows Allaire as it once was.

Key to the Map

1–Furnace	12–Gristmill
2–Offices	13–Sawmill
3–Allaire's Home	14–Foreman's Cottage
4–Charcoal Depot	15–Workers' Homes
5–Farm Building	16–Church
6–Carriage Shop	17–Workers'
7–Paint Shop	18–Homes
8–Carpenter Shop	19–
9–Store	20–Manager's House
10–Bakery	21–Slaughter House
11–Blacksmith	22–Mill

1. Notice that the map is divided into four sections: northeast (NE), southeast (SE), southwest (SW), and northwest (NW). In which section is each of the following places?

In answering the question, be sure to use the key to the map. The numbers on the map are explained in the key. Also, use abbreviations for the sections.

___ Paint Shop   ___ Store

___ Slaughterhouse   ___ Carpenter Shop

___ Foreman's Cottage   ___ Carriage House

___ Bakery   ___ Sawmill

2. Suppose that you were to walk cross-country to the places listed below. Cross-country means that you are not going to follow the roads. You are going straight to each place over fields, roads, streams, and so on.

In what general direction would you be going if you went from:

a. The Store to the Slaughterhouse?

_____

b. The Church to the Blacksmith Shop?

_____

c. The Gristmill to the Offices?

_____

d. The Carpenter Shop to the Sawmill?

_____

Reading and Interpreting Maps:
Locating Places Through Distance and Direction

Background

If a map is not segmented into indexed quadrants, or if the map lacks lines of latitude and longitude, "distance and direction" are helpful place-locating tools. These tools may be used more often than is realized. When one asks, for example, "Where is Princeton?" and the answer is "About 15 miles northeast of here," direction and distance are being used as location references.

In the example given above, the respondent to the question knew where he was, and had also gained through experience a visualization of the approximate position of Princeton. The respondent actually went "cross-country" in his mind, much as a pilot of a small plane would fly to the place. Of course, the answer could have included a reference to roads, as, for example, "Go northeast on this road for 15 miles, and you'll find Princeton."

In teaching how to locate places on maps using distance and direction, there are four steps that your students can follow:

1. Establish the starting point—a town, a crossroad, a bridge, and so on.

2. Determine the direction *from* the starting point—for example, north, south, or southeast.

3. Lay a ruler or piece of paper from starting point to point of destination.

4. Determine the distance between the points through utilization of the scale of miles.

Student Involvement

1. Illustrate on the chalkboard how one would use distance and direction to locate places.

a. Draw this diagram:

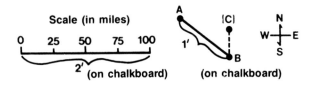

b. Ask: "How many miles and in what direction would one go to get from City A to City B?" Lay a string against the scale of miles. Read the answer (50 miles southeast).

c. Say: "City C is 25 miles directly north of City B. Watch while I locate City C." Lay the string along the scale. Pinch the string at 25 miles (6 inches). Make a point due north of B the length of the pinched string. Label the point *C*.

2. Direct your students to complete the exercise on the facing page.

Answers to the Exercise

1*a*. Alpha *b*. Ricksha *c*. Delta *d*. Parma *e*. Morris

2*a*. 80 miles west *b*. 80 miles northwest *c*. 80 miles east *d*. 100 miles southeast

3. Two

4. Four

5*a*. Morris *b*. Ricksha *c*. Essex *d*. Baxter

Name _____ Date _____

LOCATING PLACES THROUGH DISTANCE AND DIRECTION

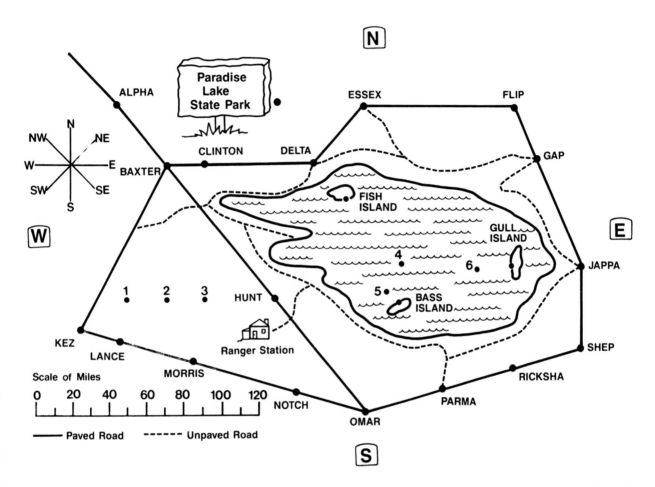

1. What town is:

   a. 40 miles northwest of Baxter? _____

   b. 80 miles east of Omar? _____

   c. 40 miles southwest of Essex? _____

   d. 100 miles southwest of Jappa? _____

   e. 120 miles southwest of Delta? _____

2. What is the *direction* and *distance* of:

   a. Essex from Flip? _____

   b. Clinton from Hunt? _____

   c. Parma from Notch? _____

   d. Gull Island from Fish Island? _____

3. An airplane crashed in the woods. Just before the crash, the pilot reported his position as 60 miles west of Hunt and 70 miles south of Baxter. Which of the numbered points in the western part of the map was the crash site:

   1, 2, or 3? _____

4. The best fishing spot in Paradise Lake is 20 miles north of Bass Island and 60 miles west of Gull Island. Which of the numbered spots in the lake is where the fish are:

   4, 5, or 6? _____

5. In what towns are these signposts located?

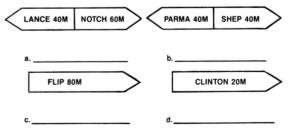

a. _____   b. _____

c. _____   d. _____

Reading and Interpreting Maps:
Locating Places on a Street Map

Background

1. Once a destination such as a town or city has been reached via the highways, the next consideration is to locate the particular address in which you are interested. Here is where orientation comes into play. To *orient* a map means to turn it in such a way that the symbols on the map "fit" the observable natural and cultural environment.

2. Of course, map orientation requires that you have a map of the town, city, or locale. If it is an important city, most likely it will be shown in large scale somewhere in the map folder. Also, detailed maps of cities can often be purchased at newsstands and bookstores.

3. The first step in orienting a street map is to orient yourself. This requires observation of the surroundings in order to identify street names, especially those of intersecting streets. When the observed streets are located on the map, you can say, "This is where I am on the map."

4. Next, orient the map; that is, place the map in such a position that symbols on the map are lined up with the actual objects that the symbols represent. For example, if the map shows a bridge near the intersection where you are standing, look for the actual bridge. Or, if a monument is shown on the map, try to spot it. Then place the map in your hand so that the symbols for the bridge or monument correspond to the location of the actual bridge and monument—to your right or left, or ahead of you or behind you, whatever the case may be.

5. If the symbols on the map and what you see match, then it should be relatively simple to go any place in the city that is shown on the map. After looking at the map, you might be able to say, for example, "I must walk six blocks straight ahead, turn left and walk four blocks."

Student Involvement

1. To explain and illustrate orientation, make a map of the classroom that shows important details—windows, doors, desks, and so forth. Then have your students physically orient themselves in various locations in the room with the help of the map.

2. Explain that the exercise on the facing page provides practice in reading a street map. The questions require adaptation to a variety of orientation situations.

Answers to the Exercise

1a. North b. North, east c. South d. North, west

2a. Drug store b. Police Station c. Town Hall

3. 250–300 feet

4. 1,100–1,200 feet

5. City Circle, Library

6. Three

7. He was going the wrong way on a one-way street.

8. "Walk through" the town with the students following on their maps. You should end up at the school.

LOCATING PLACES ON A STREET MAP

1. In which direction would you walk on the streets in going *from the school* to the:

   a. Police Station? West, then _____

   b. Library? West, then _____, then _____

   c. Motel? West, then _____

   d. Church? West, then _____, then _____

2. What building is immediately:

   a. west of the Shoe Store? _____

   b. north of the Theater? _____

   c. east of the Police Station? _____

3. How many feet is it from the X at Sweet Lane to the X on Broadway Boulevard? _____

4. How many feet is it around Children's Zoo on the Jogging Path? _____

5. If you are facing north at the intersection of Main Street and Flint Street, what place is to your left? _____ What building is to your right? _____

6. If you left the Theater to go to the Cafe, how many blocks south would you walk? _____

7. Mr. Hall was driving west on Lincoln Road. He turned left (south) onto Clinton Street. A police officer stopped him and gave him a ticket. Why? _____

8. Imagine that you took a walking tour of the town. Draw a dashed line on the map that shows your route.

   a. Start at the corner of Polar Lane and Third Avenue and walk west 200 feet.

   b. Walk north one block.

   c. Walk east to Broadway Boulevard.

   d. Walk south three blocks.

   e. Turn west and walk to the second building

   f. Go *through* the building, out the back door to the first street.

   g. Turn east, and walk as far as you can to the last building. What is it? _____

Reading and Interpreting Maps:
A Walk Through a Small Town

Background

The previous exercise was concerned with finding one's way around a portion of a town. The activity on the facing page is concerned with a whole town, Flemington, New Jersey.

Flemington is an old town dating back to 1756. The age of the town helps explain why the streets do not have a definite pattern. The lack of pattern makes reading and following routes more difficult.

Student Involvement

After your students complete the facing page, it would be productive for them to make their own street maps. The scope of the map should be limited. It would be well to map a single street. If the school is in a remote area, perhaps the school and grounds may be suitable for mapping. Following is a list of suggested steps:

1. Decide what is to be mapped. Let's assume that it is a city or town block.

2. Determine the length of the block in feet. If using a tape measure is impractical, determine the length by pacing. An adult's stride is about 3 feet. Obviously there will be inaccuracies in this type of measurement, but the results will be close enough for your purposes.

3. Decide on the scale of the map. A scale of 1 inch = 2 feet would be suitable. Thus, a street 200 feet in length would be represented by a 100-inch line drawn on chart paper.

4. Gather data for the map, for example:

Object	Frontage (width)
Drugstore on corner	20 feet
Church	40 feet
Cemetery next to church	60 feet
House	25 feet
House	25 feet
Bakery on the corner	30 feet

5. Make sketches of the various buildings for later use.

6. Divide the street line on the chart into segments. According to the scale, the drugstore is allotted 10 inches; the church, 20 inches; the cemetery, 30 inches; each house, 12½ inches; and the bakery, 15 inches.

7. Draw pictorial symbols of the buildings and cemetery and paste them on the map.

8. Add to the map miscellaneous items that were noted, such as trees, fire hydrants, parked cars, street signs, and so on.

9. The completed map may look like this:

THE SOUTH SIDE OF MAPLE STREET

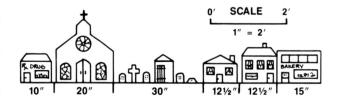

Answers to Exercise

1. Library (4), Baptist Church (6), Court House (2), Methodist Church (3), County Office Building (1), William Street (5)

2. Woman's Club, Post Office, County Office Building, Hall of Records, Court House

3a. Woman's Club b. Fleming Castle c. Flemington Raritan Public School d. Veterans of Foreign Wars

4. Church Street, Emery Avenue, Pennsylvania Avenue, Highland Avenue, East Main Street

Name _____   Date _____

A WALK THROUGH A SMALL TOWN

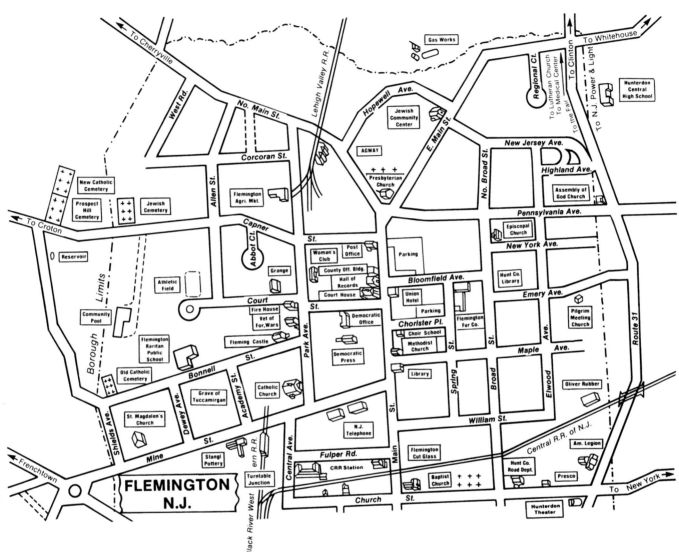

1. Number the places listed below in the order that you would meet them if you walked south from the Presbyterian Church at the junction of North Main Street and East Main Street.

___Library   ___Methodist Church
___Baptist Church   ___County Office Building
___Court House   ___William Street

2. What buildings are located on the block that is bounded by Capner Street, Court Street, Park Avenue, and Main Street?

_____

_____

_____

3. From which of the two places in each grouping below is the shorter walk to the Presbyterian Church? Underline the correct choice.

a. Library (Main Street) or Woman's Club (Park Avenue)?

b. Flemington Cut Glass (Main Street) or Flemington Castle (Bonnell Street)?

c. Hunterdon Theatre (Route 31) or Flemington Raritan Public School (Bonnell Street)?

d. Veterans of Foreign Wars (Park Avenue) or Pilgrim Meeting Church (Emery Avenue)?

4. What streets permit a car to enter Route 31?

_____

Reading and Interpreting Maps:
Routes of Travel and Distances on Road Maps

Background

1. Road maps are probably the most commonly used of all maps. It would be a rare driver of an automobile who hasn't consulted them for locations, distances, routes of travel, direction, and such secondary information as historic sites, city size, state and county boundaries, trails, state parks, marinas, and many other points of interest.

2. In a sense, all who use road maps are researchers. And as researchers they are interested, first of all, in arriving at the facts. Where is the place? What is its direction? How far is it? What kinds of roads will be encountered? How long will the trip take? Where are the rest stops on the limited access highway? And so on.

3. Thus, the instructor's first teaching task is to make sure that skill in "arriving at the facts" is developed. As in all such programs, skills are developed through repeated correct responses over a period of time until mastery is attained.

Student Involvement

1. To maintain and increase student skills in using road maps, many opportunities to read local road maps should be provided. Road maps useful for such experiences are often available free of charge from state departments of transportation. It would be highly desirable for each student to have one to study.

2. A complete state road map offers realistic opportunities for developing skills and knowledge. Even learning how to fold, and especially unfold, such maps is in itself a challenge! The next step after learning this sometimes baffling procedure is to survey the map for all of its special features, such as insets of metropolitan areas, state speed laws, lists of state parks, and so on.

3. Explain the legend that accompanies the large map so that students may realize the scope of information such maps provide.

4. Explain the partial legend that accompanies the map on the facing page. Give special attention to the meaning and use of "route of travel" and to the "distance between stars" method of computing distances.

5. Direct your students to complete the exercise on the facing page.

Answers to the Exercise

1a. 21 miles   b. 23 miles   c. 30 miles   d. 22 miles

2. Inwood, Hobart

3. Beaver, Churchill

4. Eight

5. Arrow City

6. Gretchen

Name _____ Date _____

ROUTES OF TRAVEL AND DISTANCES ON ROAD MAPS

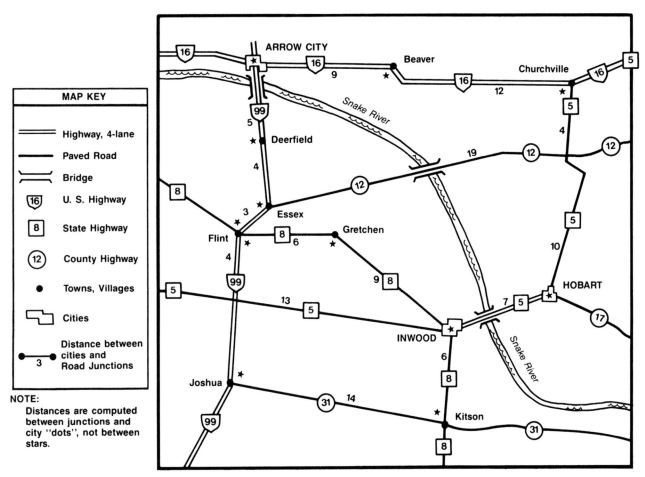

MAP KEY

Highway, 4-lane
Paved Road
Bridge
16 U. S. Highway
8   State Highway
12 County Highway
•   Towns, Villages
    Cities
3   Distance between cities and Road Junctions

NOTE:
Distances are computed between junctions and city "dots", not between stars.

1. How many miles is the drive from
   a. Arrow City to Churchville on U.S. 16?

   _____

   b. Essex to Churchville on County 12 and

   State 5? _____
   c. Essex to Churchville on U.S. 99 and

   U.S. 16? _____
   d. Flint to Hobart on State 8 and State 5?

   _____

2. What two cities are connected by a four-lane state highway?

   _____ _____

3. Name the cities in the order you would meet them if you drove from Arrow City to Hobart without crossing a bridge.

   _____

4. A long-distance run between Joshua and Kitson was held. Water stations were placed every two miles, including one at Joshua and one at Kitson. How many stations were set

up? _____

5. Imagine that you are in Joshua and someone gives you the following directions: Go east 14 miles, north 6 miles, west 13 miles, north 4 miles, northeast 3 miles, and north 9 miles, where are you?

   _____

6. Another direction/distance problem: From Hobart go north 14 miles, west 21 miles, south 9 miles, east 19 miles, south 10 miles, southwest 7 miles, and northwest 9 miles. Where are you?

   _____

BASIC ENVIRONMENTS

2-1   How to Study a Geography Picture
2-2   A Mountain Occupation—Dairying
2-3   Desert Families Share the Work
2-4   A Map of a New Jersey Farm
2-5   Working Together in Antarctica
2-6   Keeping Back the Sea in the Netherlands
2-7   Comparing Two Rivers

Basic Environments:
How to Study a Geography Picture

Background

Geography is concerned with the physical environment and human interaction with it. Using this simple but basic definition, it is possible to set up a list of questions that have universal applicability and that both instructors and students may use to study photographs and drawings for geographic data and relationships.

Student Involvement

1. Instruct your students on how to scan pictures for information. Encourage them to make notations on the lines next to each item on the activity's checklist.

2. As an initial experience, the students can react to the picture on the activity page. Suggested elements for discussion are written on the checklist shown on this page.

3. In the future, students may use photocopied checklists, or refer to a wall chart that contains the appropriate listings.

Answers to the Exercise

1a. Cactus and brush growing wild
b. None in evidence
c. High bare mountains; plains with low hills
d. Flowing stream, apparently from the mountains
e. Sunny in foreground, cloudy in background
f. Warm to cool, as shown by crops and clothing
2a. Very little except for plowing and hoeing
b. Nothing (no irrigation ditches or man-made ponds)
c. Goats, chickens
d. Planted crops of corn and vegetables
e. Flat-roofed houses of mud, adobe
f. No roads evident; no poles nor wires
g. Full clothing indicating warm to cool weather; broad hat for the sun

3. Garden-type farming; appearance of dryness; general lack of natural vegetation

Name _____ Date _____

HOW TO STUDY A GEOGRAPHY PICTURE

FARMING IN HOT, DRY NORTHERN MEXICO: Mexican families work together to supply enough food. Corn is the important crop. The goats supply milk, which is made into cheese. This family is very lucky to have a stream on their property.

1. What things does the picture show that were not made by people? Look at the
   a. plants: _____
   b. wildlife: _____
   c. land: _____
   d. water: _____
   e. weather: _____
   f. climate: _____

2. What things have people done to help them live in the area shown in the picture? Look at the
   a. land changes: _____
   b. water changes: _____
   c. animals: _____
   d. plants: _____
   e. houses and other buildings: _____
   f. aids to transportation and communication: _____
   g. clothing: _____

3. What are some other things that you notice in the picture? _____
   _____
   _____

Basic Environments:
A Mountain Occupation—Dairying

Background

Agriculture is concerned with three main activities: preparing soil, growing crops, and raising livestock. All of these activities take place in geographical settings. The next three activities will be concerned with helping your learners better understand the "geography" of agriculture while gaining proficiency in geographic information-finding skills.

Student Involvement

1. Read to the children the first sentence in the paragraph above. Then, to extend the meaning of "agriculture," analyze the parts of the definition, with your students making as many contributions as possible.

2. To organize the information coming from you and/or the children, set up three headings on the board (see below). Ask: "What things are a part of each of the three main agricultural (farming) activities?"

Preparing Soil

—fields
—plows (to turn the soil)
—animals or machines to pull plows and other farm machinery
—harrows (disks or spikes pulled over plowed fields to pulverize soil)

Growing and Storing Crops

—seeding
—fertilizing
—planting
—watering
—weeding
—harvesting (diggers, reapers, binders)
—packaging (bales, boxes, bags, crates, cans, barrels, baskets)
—conserving soil and water
—storing (barns, silos, grain elevators)

Raising Livestock

—animals (sheep, goats, cows, hogs, horses, poultry, caribou)
—pasture land
—shepherds
—corrals
—barns
—veterinarians
—milkers
—fleecers (wool, hair)
—renderers (butchers)
—dogs (helpers)

2. Proceed to the exercise on the facing page, which is concerned with raising livestock. What elements in the listing are directly or indirectly applicable to the picture?

Answers to the Exercise

1. To make the building and the fence
2. Eight
3. Forests
4. [Accept any reasonable reproduction.]
5. Alps
6. The milk will be made into cheese
7. The logs in the pile on the right are larger and can be cut into boards
8. Lower temperatures at high altitudes retard melting
9. Shelter, cheese production
10. Back-packing, possibly helicopters
11. Ventilation

Name _____ Date _____

A MOUNTAIN OCCUPATION—DAIRYING

DAIRY FARMING IN SWITZERLAND: In the summer, cows are taken to high mountain pastures called *alps*. The milk from the cows is made into cheese. In the fall the cows return to the valley below.

1. What are two ways that wood has been used? _____
   _____

2. How many cows are shown in the picture? Be sure you don't mistake cows for boulders!
   _____

3. What kind of vegetation covers the mountain slope in the far right of the picture?
   _____

4. Sketch the part of the house closest to the viewer. Supply as much detail as possible in your sketch.

5. According to the caption, what are high mountain pastures called?
   _____

6. What will be done with the milk that is produced? _____

7. Which of the piles of wood would be most likely to be cut into lumber?

   _____ Pile on left   _____ Pile on right

   Explain your answer_____
   _____

8. The picture shows a summer scene. But the mountains are snow-covered. Why is this so?
   _____
   _____

9. For what two purposes might the building be used? _____
   _____

10. There are no roads to this mountain pasture. How will the cheese be transported to the village below? _____
    _____

11. Notice that there is a chimney on the building. What might be the purpose of the other projection on the roof?
    _____

Basic Environments:
Desert Families Share the Work

Background

The contrasts between raising livestock in Switzerland and raising livestock in North Africa are very sharp. Some of the differences are readily apparent from the drawings used in this activity and the previous one, and some are implied. The following list includes most of the major differences of an environmental or social nature.

Rainfall

S: 30 inches or more per year, distributed over time and place

NA: Less than 10 inches per year, sporadic in terms of time and place; unreliable

Temperature

S: Cool summers, cold winters

NA: Year-round heat, with significant temperature changes from day to night

Vegetation

S: Lush grass in valleys, and more than adequate pasturage at higher altitudes

NA: Sparse, often thorny

Animals

S: Mainly cows, but some goats and sheep

NA: Goats, sheep, camels

Grazing areas

S: High pastures in summer, valleys in fall and spring, barns in winter

NA: Migratory; no storage of animal food for difficult times

Homes

S: Permanent; sturdy; barns attached

NA: Transient; no permanent farm buildings

Herding products

Essentially the same—milk, cheese, meat, leather. However, Swiss dairy products are sold domestically and internationally, while North African production is basically for subsistence.

Student Involvement

In this exercise, as in the previous one, the questions are divided evenly between fact and inference.

Question 1 is concerned with basic observation—What is in the picture? What is not? This treatment has its counterpart in reading sentences; that is, the first level of comprehension is to determine, with a minimum of interperation, what the author is saying.

Question 2 is concerned with combining information or data for the purpose of establishing relationships based on the facts. As in reading sentences, so also in reading pictures: Making inferences represents a higher order of comprehension.

Answers to the Exercise

1. The following items should *not* be checked: a water well, crops, tractors, two-wheeled carts, horses, trees, roads, a pond

  2a. Saddles
   b. Cloth
   c. Goats
   d. Heavy clothing
   e. No vegetables are visible
   f. Sparse pasture

Name _____ **Date** _____

DESERT FAMILIES SHARE THE WORK

MAKING A DESERT HOME IN NORTH AFRICA: Desert animal herders must be able to move quickly to places where there is grass and water. This whole camp can be put up or taken down in an hour or two.

1. Put a check before all the items in the list below that can be seen in the picture:

_____ Camels	_____ Two-wheeled carts
_____ Rugs	_____ Pottery
_____ Goats	_____ Horses
_____ Children	_____ Bells
_____ Sheep	_____ Trees
_____ Water well	_____ Roads
_____ Crops	_____ Pond
_____ Tractors	_____ Ropes and stakes
_____ Shepherd	_____ Sticks

2. What do you see in the picture that helps you to know that:

a. the people ride camels?

_____

b. the people know how to weave?

_____

c. the people eat cheese?

_____

d. it can be cool on the desert?

_____

e. vegetables are not an important part of the food eaten by the people? _____

_____

f. the people cannot stay in one area too long? _____

_____

Basic Environments:
A Map of a New Jersey Farm

Background

The farm shown on the map is typical of the Middle Atlantic and New England states. It is a farm that pastures cows in summer. In winter, the cows eat hay, as well as ensilage (cut corn plants) that is stored in the silo.

Wheat is grown on the farm as a cash crop. In other years, soybeans, barley, or some other crop that requires a minimum of attention may be grown.

What the farmer grows, beyond the corn and hay needed to feed the cows, is dependent upon what he or she perceives as being in demand in the marketplace. Also, crop rotation is effective as a method of soil conservation—the same crop in the same field each year will eventually lead to serious soil depletion of certain nutrients and minerals.

Student Involvement

Five major map-reading skills are given emphasis in the activity: interpreting the key to a map, using direction, computing distance, following a route of travel, and drawing inferences from map data.

Following are supplementary questions that will further develop these skills and that can be answered from the map.

1. *Direction:* "On which side of the lake is the dock?" (East.) "In what direction does the farm road run?" (North–south, or *vice versa.*) "What direction is the cow barn from the bridge on County Road 579?" (South.)

2. *Distance:* "How long in feet is the trail?" (1,300 feet.) "How many feet would be saved by walking along the stream from the bridge on the farm road to the bridge on County Road 579 (700 feet) as compared to walking on the roads to the same destination (980 feet)?" (A saving of 280 feet.)

3. *Following pathways:* "Traveling east on County Road 579, in what order would you see the following: trees, cornfields, farm road, Stony Brook bridge, wheat fields?" (In order: 3, 1, 2, 4, 5.)

4. *Thinking (inferencing):* "On the map, print an *X* where the stream *enters* Catfish Pond (west shore.) Which would be easier: to swim from the bridge on the farm road *to* Catfish Pond, or to swim from Catfish Pond to the bridge? Why?" (It's easier to swim from the pond to the bridge because you are swimming with the current.)

Answers to the Exercise

1. a
2. b
3. b
4. b
5. a
6. North
7. Trees
8. Cows
9. Wheat, milk, corn
10. Fence, Stony Brook, Catfish Pond

Name _____ Date _____

A MAP OF A NEW JERSEY FARM

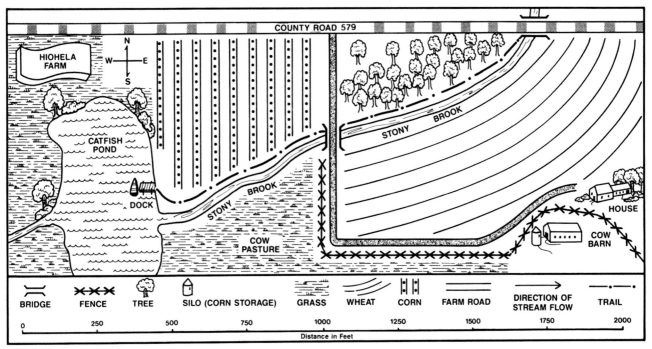

Using Direction

Circle the letter of the correct answer.

1. In what direction does County Road 579 run? *a.* East–West *b.* North–South

2. In what corner of the farm is the house? *a.* Northeast *b.* Southeast *c.* Southwest

3. In what direction is the stream flowing? *a.* To the southwest *b.* To the northeast

Distance

4. About how many feet is the drive from the house to County Road 579? *a.* 1,000 feet *b.* 1,500 feet *c.* 2,000 feet

5. About how many feet is it along Stony Brook from the Farm Road bridge to County Road 579? *a.* 750 feet *b.* 1,000 feet *c.* 1,500 feet

Following Pathways

Make believe you are walking on the trail *from* the dock *to* the bridge on County Road 579.

6. On which side of Stony Brook—north or south—are you walking?_____

7. What do you see to the north *after* you cross the farm road?_____

8. During the walk, which of these would you most likely see? Check the correct choice.

_____ Horses   _____ Pigs   _____Cows

Thinking

9. From what you see on the map, which *three* of the following are probably products of the Hiohela Farm? Check the correct choices.

_____Wheat   _____Wool   _____Eggs
_____Milk   _____Corn   _____Potatoes

10. What three things keep the cows from getting out of the pasture?

_____

_____

_____

Basic Environments:
Working Together in Antarctica

Background

1. Antarctic communities, certainly, are not typical communities. Nevertheless, all the needs of communities are present: food, clothing, shelter, transportation, sanitation, medical care, security, and recreation. As in all communities, but especially in Antarctica, cooperation of members is a crucial element.

2. Antarctica is not "owned" by any nation. Rather, eleven nations (Argentina, Australia, Chile, France, Japan, New Zealand, Norway, South Africa, the Soviet Union, United Kingdom, and the United States) have agreed to suspend territorial claims (to be resolved), and to reserve the continent for research.

Student Involvement

This activity is similar to several picture reading experiences already provided; that is, the learner first becomes aware of a picture as a whole, then concentrates on observing for details, then combines the details into new patterns and relationships.

A strong language component is provided in this activity; that is, the writing of paragraphs based on a unifying idea and supported with detail. That the writing is done in geographic contexts is helpful to the furtherance of subject matter understandings, as well as writing skills. Of course, the writer must use some imagination and think of elements not directly shown in the picture, but that are strongly implied. For example, in the picture no door is shown as being open in the airplane, yet there is a strong implication that a door, perhaps even in the bottom of the craft, or on the side of the plane not visible, had to be opened in order to eject cargo.

This activity has potential for "transfer" to other writing tasks because, essentially, all writing is based on the main topic/supporting detail/connecting links concept.

Answers to the Exercise

1. Airplane, parachute with cargo attached men on ground ready to receive the parachute, buildings (Quonset-hut type), radio receiving disc (on top of buildings), towers and wires, trucks, snow tractors, building under construction, open water, ship, unloading operations on ship, American flag, people involved in a variety of activities, vehicle tracks in snow.

2. Sample paragraph: In Antarctica, airplanes are used to deliver supplies. This is how it is done: The pilot guides his plane over an open field near the camp. A door in the airplane is opened. Supplies with a parachute attached are pushed out. The parachute opens and the supplies glide to the ground. Men on the ground recover the supplies and take them to camp.

Name _____ Date _____

WORKING TOGETHER IN ANTARCTICA

ANTARCTICA—A COMMUNITY IS SET UP: Everything—food, clothing, fuel, machinery—that is needed for humans to live must be brought to the world's coldest continent.

1. Imagine that you are a newspaper reporter. You are going to write a story about Antarctica. One of the first things you would do is make a list of what you see. You would use this information later when you write your story.

Study the picture carefully. Then make your list. For example, you could list *snow* or *ice*. Try to name at least ten things.

_____ _____

_____ _____

_____ _____

_____ _____

2. Write a paragraph for your story. Use some of the details from your list. Remember that a paragraph is made up of several sentences that tell about a main idea.

You might start your paragraph like this: *In Antarctica, airplanes are used to deliver supplies.* Then, from what you see in the picture, tell how this is done. Or you could write about the snow tractors, the mountains, or the look of the land.

_____

_____

_____

_____

_____

_____

_____

_____

_____

_____

_____

_____

Basic Environments:
Keeping Back the Sea in the Netherlands

Background

Following are some basic facts about the Netherlands:

—The country is about twice the size of New Jersey.

—The highest elevation is about 300 feet above sea level.

—About one-half of the country is below sea level.

—The population is about 15 million, with a population density of about 900 people per square mile.

—There are about 15,000 miles of dikes and 3,500 miles of canals. Major uses of canals: to drain water off the land and for freight transportation.

—About 70 percent of the land is agricultural.

—Amsterdam is the capital; Rotterdam is the largest city (1 million inhabitants) and the world's busiest seaport.

Student Involvement

1. Some pictures show physical or human-made features so clearly that they are called *definition* pictures. The dike in the picture in the exercise is a good example of a definition picture.

Have your students arrive at a word definition of a dike based on what they see. An example definition: Land raised to a level that will prevent water from going beyond it. Another possibility: A wall made of soil, stone, or concrete that controls or confines water.

2. It is important that your learners understand that the land at the right side of the picture (designated by the number 3)

is below sea level, and that without the dike the land would be water-covered. A simple diagram drawn on the board would prove helpful:

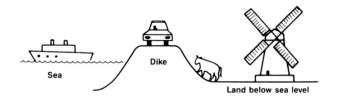

3. All of the questions in the exercise are of the inferential type. Therefore, any suggested answers that are seriously offered should be encouraged and accepted. After all suggestions have been made, the instructor should lead a discussion about them, giving as much credit and commendation as possible for logical thinking.

Answers to the Exercise

1. Three ways that dikes are useful: to hold back water, as a road for transportation, as grazing areas for cattle.

2. Rainfall and snow are heavy in the Netherlands. The steep roofs allow for fast shedding of precipitation.

3. The absence of trees in the picture indicates that lumber is not available. Note: The Netherlands does not have large forests that can be cut for construction purposes.

4. The fish they catch will add to the food supply.

5. They are fearful of storms that may blow water over the dike, or that may damage the dike.

Name _____ Date _____

KEEPING BACK THE SEA IN THE NETHERLANDS

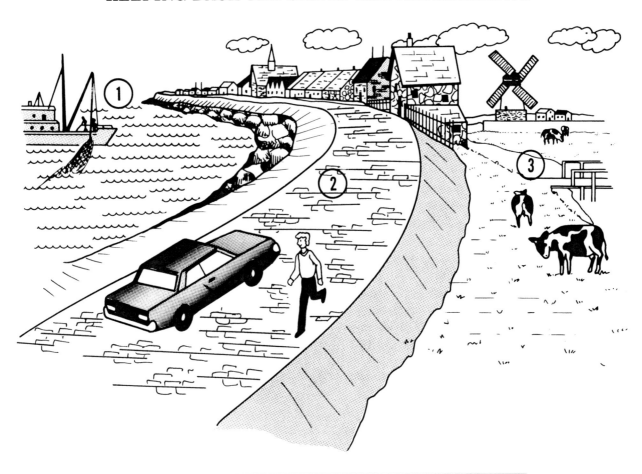

> THE NETHERLANDS: A seaside country whose people build walls to keep the sea from flooding the land.

1. In the picture, the water at ① on the left is the ocean. The ridge of land at ② is a *dike*. The houses and fields at ③ on the right are below the level of the ocean water.

From what you have read above and in the caption of the picture, and from what you see in the picture, try to list three ways that a dike is useful.

a. _____

b. _____

c. _____

2. Notice that each house has a steep roof. There is a good reason for this. What might be the reason? The answer has to do with rainfall. _____
_____

3. What is missing from the picture that helps explain why the houses are built of stone and brick? _____
_____
_____

4. In what way will the work of the people in the boat help feed other people? _____

5. The people who live on the land side of the dike keep close watch on the weather. Why would they be so careful? _____
_____
_____
_____
_____

Basic Environments:
Comparing Two Rivers

Background

The following information should prove helpful in developing this activity.

—The path of the Congo River resembles a three-quarter circle. It flows about 1,000 miles north from its sources and then makes a great arc toward the east.

—The Nile is longer than the Congo, but the Congo carries more water to the sea. In fact, the Congo carries a greater volume of water than any other river except the Amazon.

—The Congo flows through very warm, very wet lands—an area that is popularly called "the jungle." The Nile flows through arid or semiarid land, for the most part. Crops flourish for short distances on both sides of the river, but beyond that the desert dominates.

—Electricity is generated from power plants built on each river. Of the two rivers, however, the Congo probably has the greatest potential for future development of hydroelectricity. This is because the Congo has the greater volume of water and a more consistent flow.

Student Involvement

1. The main skill objectives of this activity are observing pictures for detail, making comparisons based on pictorial evidence, and making inferences based on factual evidence. The outcome should be an increase in knowledge of two basic environments—hot, wet lands along a great river, and hot, dry lands along a great river.

2. Refer to the inset map that shows the outline of the African continent. Show Africa's location on a larger map of the world.

Refer to the sources and general flow direction of the two rivers. Encourage your students to make generalizations about the rivers, such as:

—Both rivers are about the same overall length.

—The Nile flows into the Mediterranean Sea, the Congo flows into the Atlantic Ocean. (Use a larger map for additional place names.)

3. Direct the reading of the captions below the pictures. Give emphasis to the contrasts and similarities between the two river environments.

Answers to the Exercise

1a. T b. F c. F d. F e. F f. T g. T h. F i. T j. T

2a. Sandy, stony land with sparse vegetation.

b. Thick, loamy soil covered with many leafy bushes and trees.

TWO GREAT AFRICAN RIVERS—THE NILE AND THE CONGO

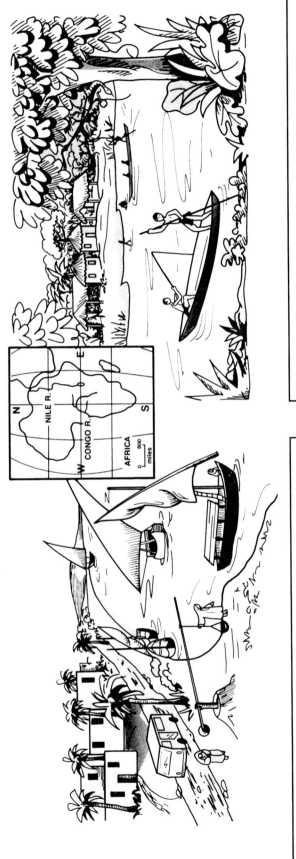

The Nile River flows through some of the world's driest land. The river water is used for crops. For short distances on each side of the river, the land blooms like a garden. Beyond that there is a great desert of sand, rocks, and scattered plants.

COMPARING TWO RIVERS

1. After studying the pictures, their captions, and the maps, decide whether the statements below are true or false. Put a T before the true statements and an F before the false statements.

_____ a. Both rivers are used for transportation.

_____ b. Both rivers show boats that are driven by the wind.

_____ c. Both rivers have thick forests on their banks.

_____ d. The homes on the banks of both rivers are made of the same kinds of materials.

_____ e. Both rivers flow through hot, wet lands.

_____ f. The waters of the Nile River are used to water crops.

The Congo River flows through some of the world's wettest land. There are miles of jungles on both sides of the river. The people who live along the river are dependent on it for much of their food.

_____ g. The Nile River flows in a northward direction.

_____ h. The Congo River flows toward the east.

_____ i. The people of the Nile have at least two other ways to travel along the river.

_____ j. The people of the Congo River use the river for fishing.

2a. What kind of land and vegetation would you expect to find a short distance away from the Nile River?

_____

_____

b. What kind of land and vegetation would you expect to find a few miles from the Congo River?

_____

_____

THE FISHING INDUSTRY

3-1   The Fishing Harbor
3-2   Where Fish Are Caught
3-3   Fish for the People of the World
3-4   Fishing Where the Fish Are
3-5   Catching Fish at Sea

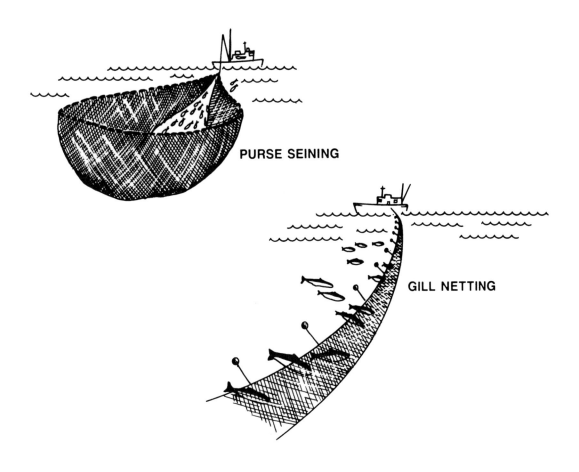

PURSE SEINING

GILL NETTING

The Fishing Industry:
The Fishing Harbor

Fishing and geography are inextricably related. The next five student activities provide opportunities to learn more about fishing as a universal occupation and to apply geography study skills in learning about it. The topics, in the sequence in which they are treated, are: pictures of a fishing community, a map of world fisheries, a graph of the world's important fish-catching nations, a diagram of the underwater terrain conditions conducive to catching fish, and a picture diagram of the trawler method of catching fish.

Student Involvement

1. The perspective in the top picture on the facing page is from the land *out* to the sea. In addition to the activity questions, other inferential questions that could be posed are:

—"Where did the rocks in the jetty come from?" (Probably from a quarry inland in the mountains.) "How did the rocks get to the harbor?" (By rail and-or truck; however, it is possible that they were transported by sea barge.)

—"Where would the greatest beach erosion occur—on the shores inside the harbor, or on the outside shores?" (Outside—because there the wave action is uninhibited.)

—"Why is it important that the cannery be located close to the docks?" (Fish require immediate processing; transportation costs are reduced.)

2. Pictures 1–3 depict harbor activities. Other activities include unloading fish from the hold, selling fish dockside, and maintaining and repairing the boats. Additional ways to preserve fish, other than the drying and canning methods shown, are pickling, salting, smoking, and freezing.

Answers to the Exercise

1a. The force of the waves is reduced when they break on the rock jetties; this results in quieter harbor waters.

b. The lighthouse, and the lights at the ends of the jetties.

c. The clouds are darkening and billowing, some rain is falling, and lightning is flashing.

2. Accept all titles that center around the main ideas of the pictures. For example:

Picture 1: "Nets are mended for the next trip," or "Few fish will escape after the nets are mended."

Picture 2: "The sun provides the energy to dry the fish," or "Drying fish on racks."

Picture 3: "Working in the cannery plant," or "Canning fish requires cooperation."

Name _____ Date _____

THE FISHING HARBOR

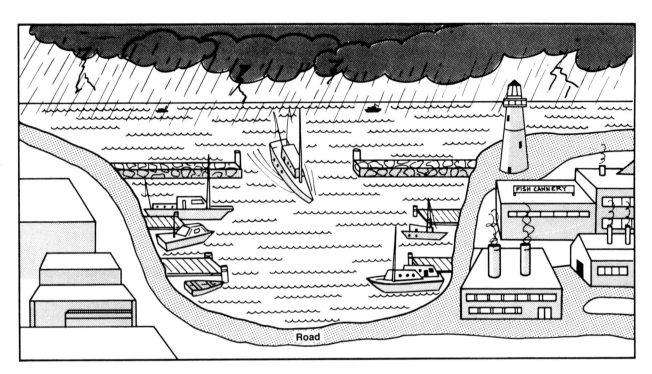

1. The picture at the top of the page shows the harbor of a fishing community. Study the picture for the answers to the questions.

  a. How is the harbor protected from the waves of the ocean? _____

_____

  b. What else protects the ships as they approach the harbor? _____

_____

  c. How can you tell that a storm may be breaking over the harbor? _____

_____

_____

2. The work of the fishermen does not end when they have returned to port. Some of their activities are shown in the numbered pictures above. On the lines below each picture, write a title that you think tells the main idea of the picture.

The Fishing Industry:
Where Fish Are Caught

Background

Just as the farmer is dependent upon soil, terrain, and the weather, so is the fisherman dependent upon elements of nature. The fisherman's "soil" is the water—that is where the fish grow. The farmer's hills, valleys, and plains all have their counterparts beneath the sea. The weather dictates whether the farmer's crops will thrive or wither, and whether or not he or she can work the fields. For the fisherman, the weather helps determine where the fish will school, and whether or not his or her fishing boat can even leave the harbor.

Student Involvement

1. Explain that all of the continents are shown on the map with the exception of Antarctica. The amount of fish caught in Antarctic waters is negligible. The cold water is not conducive to the growth of tiny sea plants and animals; thus, small fish are not attracted to the region. The scarcity of small fish results in the absence of the large fish that prey on them.

2. Lead to the observation that there are areas of the continents' coastlines where little commercial fishing is conducted. This does not mean that there is no fishing activity. Coastal inhabitants no doubt obtain fish for their own and local needs.

3. The flat map of the round world necessitates an arbitrary "cutoff" somewhere on the map page. With regard to the fishing map used in the exercise, the cut was made in the Pacific Ocean. Thus, Item 2 of the activity calls for labeling the Pacific Ocean twice.

Help your students realize the roundness of the earth by having them roll their map into a cylinder so that the two page edges touch. They should readily see that the "two" Pacific Oceans are really only one ocean.

The Arctic Ocean is so spread out on the map that it, also, is labeled twice. The reason for the spread is that a Mercator map projection such as this one grossly distorts sizes and distances in the polar regions. Thus, the Arctic Ocean, which is the smallest of the oceans, appears to cover an enormous area.

Answers to the Exercise

1–4. [Check for correct labeling of the continents and oceans, fishing areas, and map title.]

5. Along the coasts of the continents.

WHERE FISH ARE CAUGHT

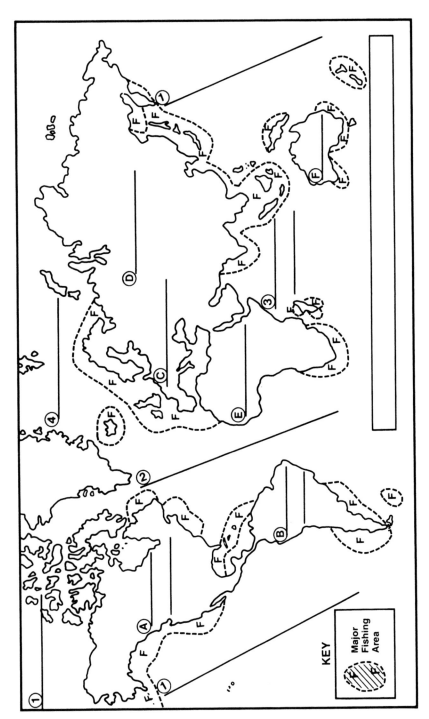

1. Follow instructions to show on the map where the world's fish are caught. On the map, label the continents as follows: (A) *North America*, (B) *South America*, (C) *Europe*, (D) *Asia*, (E) *Africa*, (F) *Australia*.

2. On the map, label the oceans as follows: 1 *Pacific Ocean*, 2 *Atlantic Ocean*, 3 *Indian Ocean*, 4 *Arctic Ocean*. Notice that there are two 1s and two 4s on the map.

3. Draw slanted lines in the fishing areas shown on the map.

Notice that the fishing areas are shown by the letter "f" enclosed by dashed (– – –) lines. See the map key.

4. Print the map title in the box: WHERE FISH ARE CAUGHT.

5. Where are most of the fish caught? Check the correct answer.

   _____ Along the coasts of the continents

   _____ In the middle of the oceans

The Fishing Industry: Fish for the People of the World

Background

The graph of the world's most prominent fishing nations offers some interesting observations. Japan leads the world. Why? Part of the answer lies in its dense population: 121 million people, about one-half of the United States' population, in a country about the size of California. When this fact is coupled with the fact that Japanese farms cannot come close to feeding the enormous population, the reasons why the Japanese turned to the sea are clear. Protein-laden fish supply food, and nonedible fish and fish parts provide the fertilizer needed to keep the intensively farmed soil productive.

Student Involvement

1. Young learners relate most easily to picture graphs because pictorial symbols are more readily understood than the abstract symbols utilized in bar and line graphs. Thus, the symbols employed in picture graphs should be instantly recognizable. In the graph on the opposite page, the fish (⋈) symbol would have much more meaning than, say, a rectangular (☐) symbol, even though both symbols could convey the same quantitative information.

In Item 4 of the exercise, your students are required to draw symbols that show Norway's fish catch. The repeated drawing of the fish symbol will be a constant reminder that it is *fish* that are being represented.

2. Most graphs, but especially picture graphs, are not designed to give exact figures. The basic message that graphs should convey is the *order* of the entries in relation to size or number and the *relative size or number* of an entry in comparison to another entry.

The relationship among the data presented should be given special attention; for example, "The United States and Chile caught about the same amount of fish," or "Russia caught three times as many fish as the United States."

3. Except in cases of very simple graphs, where, for example, one person equals one person-symbol, quantities are rounded for simplification. In the fish-catch exercise, amounts were rounded to the nearest 500,000 tons. For example, Chile's catch of 3,979,000 tons was rounded to 4 million.

Answers to the Exercise

1. Japan

2. 5 million tons more

3. 3½ million tons less

4a. 1 million b. Three c. [Three fish symbols should be drawn.]

Name _____   Date _____

FISH FOR THE PEOPLE OF THE WORLD

COUNTRY	THE WORLD'S GREATEST FISHING COUNTRIES*					
JAPAN	🐟 🐟	🐟 🐟	🐟 🐟	🐟 🐟	🐟 🐟	🐟 🐟 (1/2)
RUSSIA	🐟 🐟	🐟 🐟	🐟 🐟	🐟 🐟	🐟 🐟	
CHINA	🐟	🐟	🐟	🐟	🐟	
UNITED STATES	🐟	🐟	🐟	🐟		
CHILE	🐟	🐟	🐟	🐟		
NORWAY						

*For a recent year.   Key: Each 🐟 equals 1 million tons of fish

1. What country catches the most fish?

_____Russia _____Japan _____United States

2. How many more fish does Russia catch than China?

_____ 4 million tons more

_____ 5 million tons more

_____ 6 million tons more

3. If all the fish that the United States and Chile catch were added together, how many millions of tons less than what Japan catches would that be?

_____ 4 million tons less

_____ 5 million tons less

_____ 3½ million tons less

_____ 4½ million tons less

4. As you can see, there are no fish symbols for Norway. You can complete the graph by answering the questions and following the directions below.

a. How many tons does each fish symbol equal?

_____

b. Norway caught 3 million tons of fish. How many symbols would it take to show that many fish?_____

c. In the picture graph on the line next to Norway, draw enough fish symbols to show Norway's fish catch.

The Fishing Industry: Fishing Where the Fish Are

Background

In this activity, the topographical concept of "the ocean floor" is integrated with the physical concept of "the sun as a primary souce of energy" and the biological concept of "the food cycle."

Student Involvement

1. Help your students realize that the diagram in the exercise is a cross-sectional view. Comparison to a slice of layer cake may help them make the transition to the underwater scene.

2. It may take some convincing for your students to accept the idea that the ocean floor contains the same kind of topographical features as dry land. Part of their skepticism may arise from their experiences at the seashore. In most cases, beaches are level except for occasional dunes, and the levelness extends to the areas where people swim. Questioning can help them reach understanding:

—"Suppose that the water in the ocean were to rise and cover the land. What would happen to the plains, mountains, and valleys?" (They would be covered with water.)

—"Suppose that the water went away, dried up, what would you see?" (The land features would be visible again.)

—"Many thousands of years ago, the land beneath the ocean could be seen. The mountains and valleys were all visible. Then, after years and years of rain, the land was covered with water. All of the land features are still there, only we can't see them."

3. Quantities are often difficult for young learners to comprehend. They may not have had personal experiences that can be related to larger numbers. Thus, the depths shown on the left vertical edge of the diagram may need clarification: 100 feet may be translated as roughly three times the length of the average classroom, 200 feet as the length of ten or eleven full-sized automobiles lined up bumper to bumper, 300 feet as the length of the playing area of a football or soccer field.

Answers to the Exercise

1, 2. [Check for correct labeling and sketching.]

3. The water is not deep. The light and heat of the sun penetrate the water, which helps small sea plants and animals to grow. Fish are attracted to the area because food is plentiful.

4. Trench

5. 350 feet, 300 feet, 200 feet

6. Food would be scarce at B because it is too far underwater for plankton and zooplankton to flourish.

Name _____   Date _____

FISHING WHERE THE FISH ARE

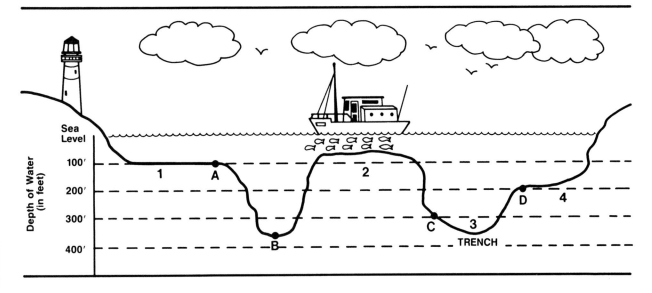

FISH AND LAND BELOW THE SEA

Fish can be caught almost anywhere in the oceans. But there may not be enough fish in one spot to pay for the expenses of the boat and its crew. So the captain of the boat sails to places in the ocean where many fish can almost certainly be found. The best places to fish are where the water is not deep. In the shallow water, the light and heat from the sun help small sea plants called *plankton* to grow. *Zooplankton,* which are very small animals, also grow well in the sunny water. Small fish feed on the plankton and zooplankton, bigger fish feed on the smaller fish, and so on all the way up to sharks.

---

1. The numeral 1 in the drawing shows a *continental shelf,* a shallow place where fish like to feed. Write *continental shelf* near the numeral 1 and draw several small fish swimming there.

2. Find another continental shelf at the numeral 4 in the drawing. Label this shelf and draw some fish over it.

3. The numeral 2 in the drawing shows a *fishing bank.* As you can see, there are many fish there. After reading the caption of the picture, explain why this is so.

_____

_____

_____

_____

4. What is the deep hole at the numeral 3 called? _____

5. The numbers on the left side of the drawing are used to measure the depth of the water. If you draw a line from point A on Continental Shelf 1 to the numbers, you can read that A is 100 feet under water.

How many feet under water is

Point B? ____ Point C? ____ Point D? ____

6. Why might there be fewer fish at Point B than at Point A?

_____

_____

_____

_____

The Fishing Industry:
Catching Fish at Sea

Background

Trawling as a method of catching fish is featured in this exercise. Two other methods that are widely used are explained below.

Purse seining: A huge net is let out from fishing boats. The net, which is often circular in shape, may encompass as much as an acre of ocean surface. Lead weights keep the sides of the net beneath the water; corks keep the net floating. The net stands in the water and is similar in appearance to a fence surrounding a house.

After the fish enter the net, a draw rope is pulled that closes the bottom of the net. Now the fish cannot escape through the bottom. The fish are then scooped aboard the fishing boats. Sometimes the fish are sucked through hoses into the holds of the boats.

Gill netting: A gill net stands in the water in much the same way as a purse seine. However, a gill net stands in a straight line, not unlike a snow fence standing in a field. Floats and weights are used, as in the purse seine.

Large fish, such as salmon and shad, swim into the net openings and become stuck. When the fish try to back out of the nets, their gills catch the netting; they cannot escape. Smaller fish swim through the netting. After sufficient fish have been impaled, fishermen in small boats collect their catch.

Student Involvement

1. Explain the methods of netting fish described above. It would be helpful to

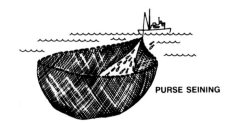

PURSE SEINING

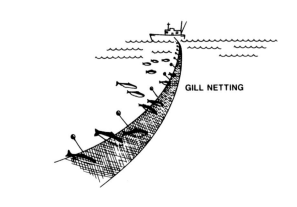

GILL NETTING

make board sketches of both purse seines and gill nets.

2. Direct the reading of the information at the beginning of the exercise. Also, discuss the picture, giving special attention to the mechanics of the net and the size and sophistication of the fishing boats.

Answers to the Exercise

1. [Check for correct sketching and labeling.]

2. The net catches all kinds of fish—big, small, edible, nonedible—some of which are "trashed," or thrown away.

3. Fish are highly perishable. The ice, which is "layered" over the fish, keeps them fresh.

Name _____   Date _____

CATCHING FISH AT SEA

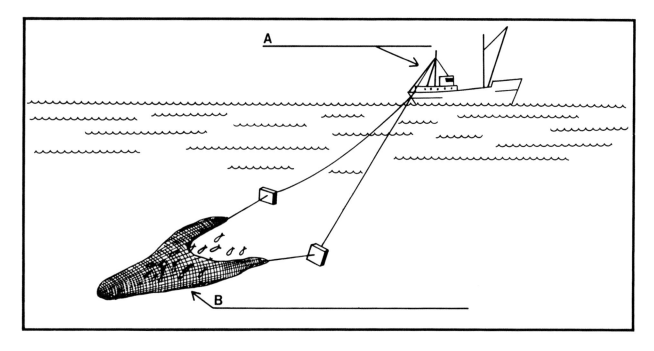

1. Perhaps the most efficient way to catch fish is to use nets. The picture above shows one way that it is done.

As the net is dragged behind the boat, it fills with fish. Some fish escape, but most of the fish stay inside the net. After the net is full, it is cranked to the side of the boat. Next, the net is lifted into the boat. The fish are dumped into the hold and covered with ice. The kind of net shown in the the drawing is called a *trawl*. You can see that it is shaped like a cone. Trawl nets are drawn along the ocean bottom. Notice the wooden floats near the mouth of the net. The floats keep the net from sinking too deep.

You can add to the drawing by doing the following:

a. Draw several small fish (⋈) swimming in the net and entering it.

b. Sharks and other big fish sometimes get caught in the net. Draw two or three sharks (⋈⊳) in and around the net.

c. The boat pulling the net is called a *trawler.* Write *trawler* on Line A in the drawing. Write *trawler net* on Line B.

2. Although a trawler can catch lots of fish, there are some things that are not good about catching fish that way. Try to think of one way that catching fish with trawlers can be harmful.

_____

_____

_____

_____

3. Sometimes trawlers stay out at sea for several days. What is the connection between that and having ice on the boat?

_____

_____

_____

_____

THE MINING INDUSTRY

4-1 Minerals Mined in the United States and the World

4-2 Leading Mining States

4-3 Understanding Strip Mining

4-4 Understanding Underground Mining

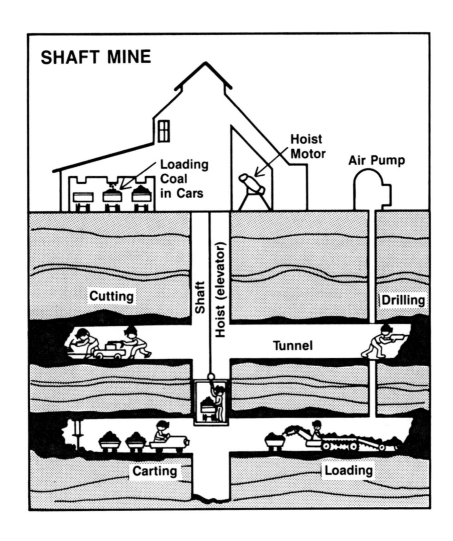

The Mining Industry:
Minerals Mined in the United States and the World

Background

The United States comprises about 6 percent of the world's surface and 5 percent of its population. Yet the nation produces a proportionately much higher percentage of the world's most important minerals, as shown in the graphs on the opposite page. Some other figures on the United States' share of the world's mineral production: natural gas, 30 percent; mica, 52 percent; sulphur, 18 percent; molybdenum (used in strengthening and hardening steel), 25 percent.

Nations that do not have as natural resources the minerals listed above and featured in the graphs suffer great handicaps in becoming industrialized. However, the disadvantages can be overcome, as in the case of Japan, if skilled, inexpensive labor is available and the methods of production are efficient. The savings derived from these two positive factors allow underresourced nations to absorb the expense of importing raw materials and to compete for world markets with manufactured products.

Student Involvement

1. Before your students begin the exercise, expand their understanding of the term *minerals*. Here is a definition that may prove helpful: A natural (not man-made) substance such as salt, sulphur, coal, or sand, usually obtained from the ground.

Additional insights:

—Minerals are not necessarily solid. Natural gas and petroleum are both minerals.

—Minerals are neither animal nor vegetable; they are inorganic.

—Minerals may be extracted from water; for example, manganese and gold.

—There are at least 1,500 different minerals. Stone is one of the most common; uranium is quite rare.

2. Item 2 of the exercise calls for a rank ordering of the minerals shown in the graphs. Coal and oil are exactly the same (18 percent) of the total. Thus, they receive the same rank order (3).

3. Your students should realize that the full circle represents 100 percent, the wedges a portion of 100 percent. Estimation is the chief measuring approach used in reading circle graphs. Circle graphs are not ordinarily designed to give exact data. Rather, they are best used to show general relationships among two or more elements.

Answers to the Exercise

1. [Check for correct lining of the graphs.]

2. Aluminum (2), coal (3), copper (4), iron ore (5), oil (3), phosphate (1)

3a. Iron ore b. Copper c. Phosphate d. Aluminum e. Coal f. Oil

Note: If *oil* is offered as the answer to 3e, accept as correct.

Name _____ **Date** _____

MINERALS MINED IN THE UNITED STATES AND THE WORLD

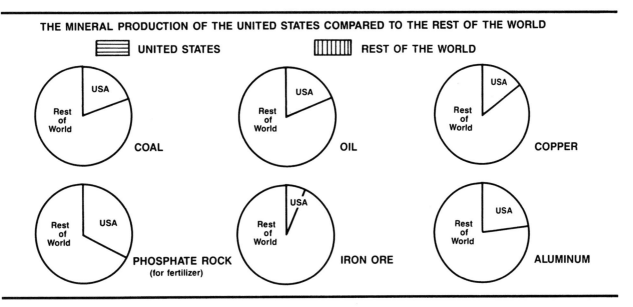

1. The mineral production shown in the graphs will "stand out" better if lines are drawn in the parts.

Draw lines in the two parts of each graph. The key to the graph will tell you how to make the lines.

2. All of the minerals that are shown in the graphs are listed below in alphabetical order. Which mineral do we have the most of in comparison with the rest of the world? Write the numeral 1 on the blank line in front of the mineral. Which was second? Number it with the numeral 2. Continue in this way for all of the minerals.

List of Minerals

_____ Aluminum   _____ Iron ore

_____ Coal   _____ Oil

_____ Copper   _____ Phosphate

3. Here is a thinking question: Some of the uses of the minerals shown in the circle graphs are listed below. On the line after each use, write the name of the mineral that is most important for that particular use.

a. To make automobiles and tractors:

_____

b. To make pipes for carrying water or wire for conducting electricity:

_____

c. To help crops to grow better:

_____

d. To make windows, siding for houses,

screen doors: _____

e. To heat homes, to provide energy for making electricity and material for making

plastics: _____

f. To make gasoline for cars, to help metal

parts move smoothly: _____

The Mining Industry:
Leading Mining States

Background

That life as we know it could not exist without miners and mining is an indisputable fact. The three basics of life—food, clothing, and shelter—are dependent upon miners and the results of their efforts. Some facts about the industry will increase your students' understanding and appreciation.

—It was during the Bronze Age that humans first learned to use metals. Copper and tin, both "soft" metals, were fused to make a harder metal, bronze; hence the term "Bronze Age."

—Europeans learned to use metals long before the Indians of North America. However, at the time of Columbus, some Indians had learned how to beat copper into ornaments.

—The most valuable nonmetal, nonfuel mineral mined in the United States in 1984 was crushed stone—almost $4 billion in value. The most valuable metal was iron ore—about $2 billion. The next most valuable metal was copper, at about $1½ billion.

Student Involvement

1. It is important that learners complete the activity correctly, but it is even more important that they recognize the skills they are developing. With such knowledge, and given opportunities to obtain and arrange information, there is reason to expect that they will become independent learners—one of education's goals.

This activity is designed to provide practice in obtaining information from a source (maps) and reorganizing it into another form (a table). Two means of arranging information are used in the table: alphabetization (of the states) and listing items in rank order.

There is a choice implicit in the way that the table is arranged. The states could be listed in order of production, rather than alphabetically. Ask: "What would be one of the disadvantages of such an arrangement?" (It is more difficult to find a particular state, to determine if it is listed. However, at times it is more advantageous not to list items alphabetically.) The *Minerals Yearbook,* from which the data for the table was obtained, lists the states alphabetically, but some of the hundreds of tables in the book do not utilize alphabetical listings.

Answers to the Exercise

1. Rank order: CA, TX, MN, FL, AZ, MI, GA, MO, PA, NM

2a. Cement   b. Copper, iron ore

3. California

4. Texas, Florida

5. Florida

6. Pennsylvania

Name _____ Date _____

LEADING MINING STATES

1. Which are the ten leading mining states in the United States? The map will tell you. The state with the numeral 1 is first, numeral 2 shows the second leading state, and so on.

In the table of figures, write each state's rank, or position, in the blank spaces.

2a. What mineral is most valuable in four of the states? _____

b. What two minerals are listed twice as most valuable? _____

3. What leading mineral state borders on the Pacific Ocean? _____

4. What two leading mineral states border on the Gulf of Mexico? _____

_____

5. What leading mineral state borders on both the Gulf of Mexico and the Atlantic Ocean? _____

6. What is the only leading mineral state that is located in the northeastern United States? _____

Leading Mining States*

States (Alpha-betical Order)	Rank	Most Valuable Mineral
Arizona		Copper
California		Cement
Florida		Phosphate rock
Georgia		Clay
Michigan		Iron ore
Minnesota		Iron ore
Missouri		Cement
Pennsylvania		Cement
New Mexico		Copper
Texas		Cement

*Does not include fuel minerals: gas, oil, coal.

The Mining Industry:
Understanding Strip Mining

Background

Strip mining is undoubtedly a much easier way to mine than shaft and tunnel mining. However, there are some disadvantages, especially to the environment.

—A great amount of dust, containing air pollutants, is created by the earth-moving machines.

—The waste materials—slag, topsoil, subsoil, below-par minerals—must be disposed of. Huge piles of debris accumulate. These materials, left uncovered, erode. Streams and rivers become clogged with sediment, sand bars build, shell fisheries at the mouths of the rivers are destroyed, and so on.

—The stripped land is often left bare, exposing it to the erosion effects of wind and water.

Many communities have passed laws to regulate strip mines. These laws require mine operators to take measures to alleviate conditions that injure the environment. Nevertheless, strip mines are still major sources of environmental contamination.

Student Involvement

1. Direct your students' attention to the drawing. Stress the fact that the unmined coal is lying just below the surface, and that bulldozers have stripped away the topsoil and subsoil to get at the coal.

2. Your students should realize that the picture is incomplete, and that it will be their job to draw in some details. Some students may prefer to cut out the accompanying drawings and paste them in the proper places in the picture. Also, coloring the picture will enhance its appearance.

The picture can serve as a model for a large mural showing strip-mining operations. One way to arrange for this is for the instructor to sketch a background (horizon, the washer, the mine office, etc.) on chart paper. The students draw large vehicles at their desks. After the drawings are completed, they are pasted on the mural.

3. Some thought questions to ask concerning the drawing:

—"What steps in coal processing are shown in the top middle section of the drawing?" (Bulldoze coal, load coal on conveyor belt, wash coal, load coal from hopper into trucks.)

—"Why is coal washed?" (To remove coal dust that can pollute the air, to make it less "dirty" for consumers, especially when used to heat homes.)

—"What else could be shown in the drawing?" ("Crushers" that break large chunks into smaller parts, "sorters" that separate coal into various sizes, railroad cars to transport the coal.)

Name _____

Date _____

UNDERSTANDING STRIP MINING

Coal

Coal

Coal

Coal

Conveyor Belt →

Coal Washer

Tank

Mine Office

FL

DT

TT

B

B

There are several ways to take minerals from the ground. One of the most important ways is called *strip mining*. This kind of mining takes place on the surface of the land. Machines such as *bulldozers* push the earth into piles. Other machines, such as *crushers* and *washers*, process the materials. Trucks and railroad cars carry the material away. Much of the coal we use is obtained by strip mining.

Definitions and drawings of vehicles used in strip mining to move materials are explained in the word list below.

Bulldozer (B)—Pushes materials into piles.

Dump truck (DT)—Driver's cab and load box are part of the same unit.

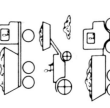

Front loader (FL)—Picks up materials and dumps them.

Tractor-trailer (TT)—Driver's cab is separate from the trailer.

1. The drawing above of a strip mine is incomplete. Complete the picture by drawing one of the machines used in the mine.

Where you see a letter and a dashed box in the drawing, draw the machine shown in the word list that matches the letter. For example, one box has the letter B in it. In the word list, the letter B is in parentheses after the word *Bulldozer.* Try to draw the machines about the same size as they are shown in the word list.

2. The line across the top of the drawing is the *horizon*, where the earth seems to meet the sky. Draw trees ( ), a water tank ( ), and telephone poles ( ) on the horizon. Put some clouds ( ) in the sky.

The Mining Industry:
Understanding Underground Mining

Background

Following is some general information about mine safety that may prove helpful in presenting and discussing the mining industry.

Hazards

—Inhalation of dust, especially coal dust, into the lungs.
—Explosions resulting from the igniting of underground gases or fine dust particles.
—Caving in of ceilings and walls, caused by excessive weight, water seepage, and weakening by explosions designed to loosen ore.
—Flooding from streams whose waters percolate into the mines.

Precautions

—Use of protective clothing: hard hats, steel-tipped shoes, shatterproof goggles, safety lights operated by batteries.
—Ventilating fans to pump fresh air in and stale air out, to keep air moving so that pockets of gas are prevented.
—Reinforcement of mine roofs with timbers and steel beams.
—Drainage system or water pumps to remove excess water.
—Individual breathing respirators to prevent lung contamination from dust and gases.

Student Involvement

1. Help your students orient themselves to the diagrams. They should realize that the drawings are cross-sections, and that they are looking inside the buildings as though the walls, soil, and so on were stripped away.

2. The drift mine activity requires that your students correlate the text ("In a drift mine...") with the steps implicit in the diagram. They should realize that the end result of the mining activity is extraction. Note: If the text is not followed closely, it is possible that some students will proceed from left to right, as they do in reading, in interpreting the diagram. They may think that the materials are going from the truck to the mine. However, the text and logic would show this to be an incorrect assumption.

Answers to the Exercise

1. The story can be completed in various ways. Here is one possible ending: Then, a moving belt carries the materials to funnels. Below the funnels are empty trucks. The trucks are filled with the materials.

2a. Tunnels b. Hoist, miners, materials c. Air d. Cutting, carting, drilling, loading e. Dump truck
[Note: Accept reasonable variations from the suggested answers; e.g., "men" or "workers" for "miners."]

Name _____   Date _____

UNDERSTANDING UNDERGROUND MINING

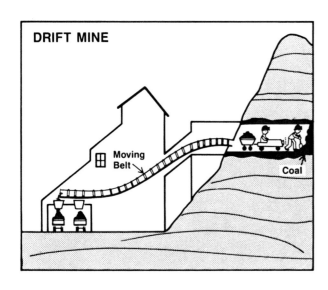

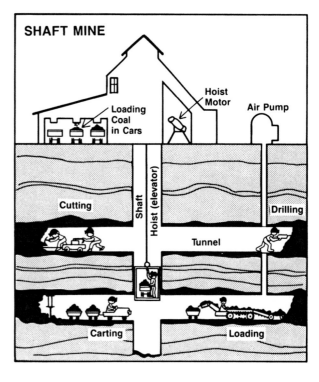

Sometimes minerals and metals, such as coal and copper, can't be obtained by strip mining. They are too deep in the earth. So mining must take place underground.

The two most important kinds of underground mines are *drift* mines and *shaft* mines. The diagrams at the top of the page will help you understand how they are worked.

1. Drift Mines

From what you see in the diagram, complete in your own words the story that follows.

In a drift mine, a tunnel is dug into the side of a mountain. The minerals are dug out. Next, they are moved to the entrance in little wagons. Then...(You complete the story.) _____

_____

_____

_____

2. Shaft Mines

The sentences below have some words missing. Complete the sentences about shaft mines with information from the diagram.

a. A shaft or hole is made into the earth. From the shaft, _____ are dug to the left and right.

b. An elevator, which is also called a

_____,

carries _____

and _____ to the surface.

c. The machinery in the pump house pumps _____ to the miners.

d. The four mining activities carried out by the miners are _____,

_____, _____,

and _____.

e. After the materials are brought to the surface, they are loaded into a

_____

THE FARMING INDUSTRY

5-1   Corn—A Useful Grain
5-2   The Growing Season
5-3   The Foods We Eat

The Farming Industry:
Corn—A Useful Grain

Background

—Corn has been defined as a tall, coarse grass that bears *spikes,* or ears of grain.

—Some of the things for which corn is used, other than food for animals and humans, are paints, soaps, fibers for cloth, rayon, explosives, glues, pharmaceuticals, paper, packing materials, plastics, cigarette paper, alcohol as a fuel for motor vehicles, and a variety of building materials.

Student Involvement

1. Written paragraphs have main ideas and supporting details, and so do pictures. This activity is designed to provide opportunities for your learners to determine the main ideas of pictures.

A second objective of the activity is to provide experiences in recognizing sequences in a process—in this case, corn production.

2. It is easier to select a main idea from several choices than it is to compose a main idea. To provide opportunities in composing main ideas, and to further emphasize the geographic content of the activity, the following is suggested: With your help, your learners can recompose the main ideas in Items 1 and 2. This can be done using a language approach. For example, the titles for Pictures A–E are sentences. They can be restated as sentence fragments. However, be sure that all of the fragments have parallel construction. These are the suggested titles for the picture sequence, as depicted: plowing land; planting seeds; spreading fertilizer; removing weeds; cutting corn.

Pictures F–J, which are sentence fragments, can be reworded into sentences. These are the suggested titles for the picture sequence, as depicted: fresh corn is sold in roadside stands; corn is stored in silos; breakfast cereals are made from corn; corn is canned in factories; hogs are fattened on corn.

3. How the main idea of a picture is perceived and expressed is dependent upon the point of view of the observer. Suppose, for example, that a farm machine salesperson used the pictures to help sell machines. How might the pictures be titled? Suggestions: our plows dig deep furrows; FarmTech drillers seed four rows at a planting; FarmTech spreaders spread evenly; no weeds escape our cultivators; FarmTech corn cutters cut and husk in one operation. (FarmTech is a fictional name.)

Answers to the Exercise

1. (A) Land is plowed; (B) Seeds are planted; (C) Fertilizer is spread; (D) Weeds are removed; (E) Corn is cut.

2. (F) Sold in roadside markets; (G) Stored in silos; (H) Eaten as cereals; (I) Packed in cans; (J) Fed to hogs.

3. Popcorn, corn oil, corn syrup, corn flour.

Name _____   Date _____

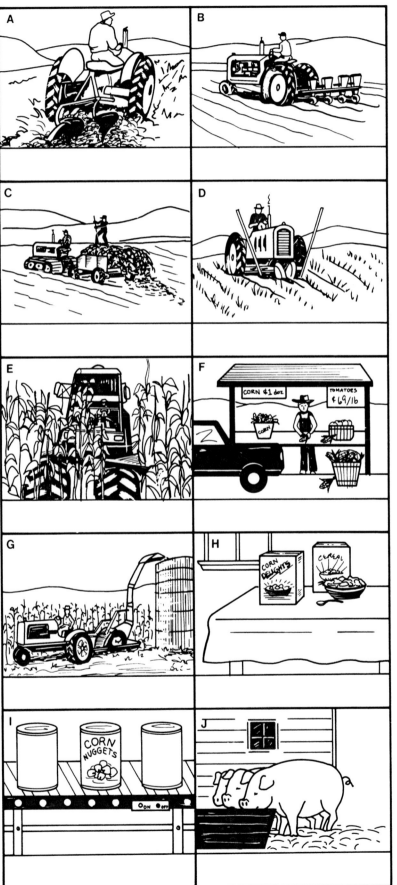

CORN—A USEFUL GRAIN

1. Many steps must be followed to grow corn. Pictures A–E show the steps in the order in which they occur. Match the picture titles printed below with the pictures. Print the titles in the blank spaces in the pictures.

Seeds are planted.
Weeds are removed.
Corn is cut.
Fertilizer is spread.
Land is plowed.

2. Pictures F–J show what is done with the corn after it is harvested. Print on the blank lines in the pictures the titles printed below.

Stored in silos
Eaten as cereals
Sold in roadside markets
Packed in cans
Fed to hogs

3. Think of some other ways to use corn that are not shown in the pictures.

_____

_____

_____

_____

_____

The Farming Industry:
The Growing Season

Background

Pattern maps sometimes show prodigious amounts of information. This is both a weakness and a strength. There is a danger that young learners will make sweeping conclusions, as well as important exclusions. For example, it appears on the map that about 75 percent of South America has a growing season of 240 days or more. This *is* true, but within the area there are pockets of land (mountains) that have very few "growing" days. On a small-scale map, such areas would be impossible to show.

Student Involvement

1. The map in the exercise is a pattern map. Its primary purpose is to show the growing season for two continents. Call attention to the key, which is crucial to effective utilization of the map.

2. This book often asks students to add something to maps and other graphics. This is done because it compels the learners to respond mentally and physically to the instructional aids. Also, in the case of adding place names to a map, the act of labeling helps develop a mental image of places—their configurations and other specifics. If the same place names are repeated on several maps, there is reason to think that the place names will stay in the minds of the learners.

3. In Item 3 of the exercise, it is important to call attention to South America's proximity to the equator. This fact is the dominant reason for the growing season of more than 240 days.

4. The fact that climate becomes colder as distance north and south of the equator increases is crucial to geographic understanding. Care should be taken, however, to help children realize that the growth of plants is determined by several variables. Altitude increases result in lower temperatures. Thus, Place A, at the foot of a mountain on the equator, might have a 365-day growing season, but Place B, at the top of the mountain, may have no growing season.

Also, it is possible for a place to have temperatures suitable for all-year cultivation but lack the rain needed to make crops grow, as in deserts.

5. Item 5 concentrates on the question: Are there enough *days* to grow certain crops? Other variables, such as hours of sunshine, rainfall, and soil fertility, are not considered.

Answers to the Exercise

1. [Check for proper labeling.]
2. 240 days
3. Shorter, shorter
4*a*. No, no, yes *b*. No, yes, yes *c*. Yes, no

THE GROWING SEASON

The number of days when it is warm enough for seeds and plants to grow is called "the length of the growing season." In some places the growing season is the entire year. In other places the growing season may be less than 60 days. Very cold places have no growing season at all.

The map shows the length of the growing seasons for North America and South America.

1. Print on the map the names of the following places.

A—North America   C—Pacific Ocean

B—South America   D—Atlantic Ocean

2. What is the length of the growing season in most of South America? _____

3. Complete this sentence by drawing a circle around the correct words in the parentheses.

As we go north of the equator, the growing season becomes (shorter, longer), and as we go south of the equator, the growing season becomes (shorter, longer).

4. Answer yes or no to each of the following questions after studying the map, especially the key.

a. Corn needs about 140 days to grow from the time it is planted until it is picked. Is the growing season long enough in Place 1 to grow corn? _____ Place 3? _____ Place 4? _____

b. Cotton needs about 175 days of growth before it can be picked. Is the growing season in Place 2 long enough? _____ Place 4? _____ Place 6? _____

c. Suppose that you live in New York, and you want to make a garden. You would like to plant tomatoes, which need about 75 to 85 days to become ripe. Is the growing season long enough? _____

Could you grow tomatoes in a garden in Iceland? _____

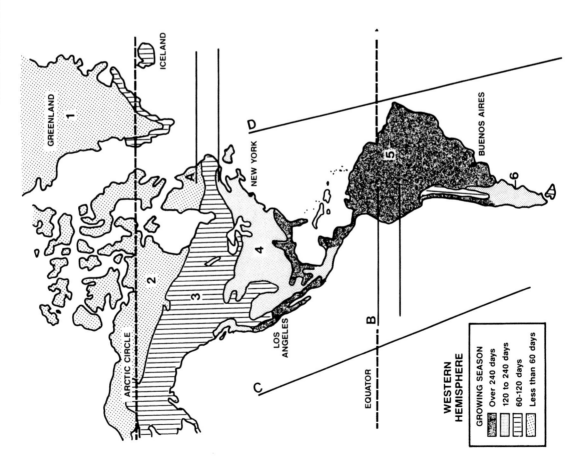

WESTERN HEMISPHERE

GROWING SEASON
- Over 240 days
- 120 to 240 days
- 60-120 days
- Less than 60 days

The Farming Industry:
The Foods We Eat

Background

Food production is *the* essential human occupation. All else depends upon a sufficient and constant flow of nutritious food from the land and the sea. As helpful as the sea is in furnishing food, the amount of food we obtain from it is but a small portion of what is needed to feed the world. For example, the average American eats about 14 pounds of fish annually, as compared to 144 pounds of meat. With regard to food, the bumper sticker seen on the back of an automobile may have said it all: No farmers, no food.

Student Involvement

1. Point out various elements of the graph, such as the title, the horizontal axis with its range of 0 to 300 pounds in 20-pound divisions, and the vertical axis with its eight food groups.

2. Your students should realize that the food groups are large categories that have components: "Dairy Products" includes milk, cream, butter, and cheese; "Grains" includes wheat and corn; "Meats, Poultry, and Poultry Products" includes beef, mutton, lamb, pork, chicken, turkey, and eggs; "Vegetables" includes standards such as carrots and tomatoes; "Fruits" includes juices as well as raw fruit; "Potatoes" includes sweet potatoes; "Fats" includes oils, margarine, and lard.

3. Perhaps your students have not encountered the statistical concept of "average." If not, it should be brought to their attention. Help them to understand the concept, if not the computation. In the case of food consumption per person, the focus of this activity, the average is determined by dividing the amount of food(s) consumed in each category by the entire population of the country. Your students should understand that the average is a "middle" figure. A three-year-old, for example, doesn't eat as much meat, poultry, and poultry products as an adult. Some people must have eaten far more than the average amount of foods in the category.

Answers to the Exercise

1. Dairy Products

2. Potatoes

3. Matchings: Dairy Products (268); Vegetables (159); Grains (246); Sugar (71); Meats, Poultry, and Poultry Products (201); Fruits (140)

4. Butter–Dairy Products; Wheat –Grains; Carrots–Vegetables; Apples–Fruit; Cider–Fruit

Name _____ Date _____

THE FOODS WE EAT

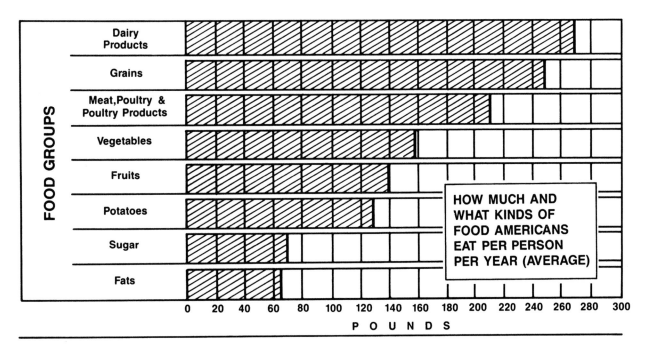

American farmers have a big job in growing enough food for all the people. People in the United States eat about ten times their weight in food each year. This means that if you weigh 100 pounds, you eat about 1,000 pounds of meat, potatoes, eggs, and other things each year. This activity will help you understand how much of each food group the average American eats.

1. Which food group is the most popular?

_____

2. Which food group shows a bar twice the length of the "Fats" food group bar?

_____

3. By drawing a line from one to the other, match the food group with the number of pounds eaten.

Food Group	Number of Pounds Eaten Yearly
Dairy Products	140 pounds
Vegetables	268 pounds
Grains	208 pounds
Sugar	159 pounds
Meats, Poultry, and Poultry Products	246 pounds
Fruits	71 pounds

4. Each of the food groups shown in the graph are made up of different kinds of food. For example, "Fats" includes margarine, lard, and other fats.

Write the name of the food group of which each of the following is a part:

a. Butter _____

b. Wheat _____

c. Carrots _____

d. Apples _____

e. Cider _____

MORE READING AND INTERPRETING MAPS AND DIAGRAMS

6-1   Locating Places through the Use of a Map Index
6-2   Reading a Road Map for City Size and Special Features
6-3   Identifying Water and Coastal Features
6-4   Identifying Land and Water Features
6-5   Locating Places with Lines of Latitude
6-6   Locating Places with Lines of Longitude
6-7   Locating Places with Latitude and Longitude
6-8   Using Latitude and Longitude to Compute Distances
6-9   Determining Direction with Latitude and Longitude
6-10   Telling Time with Longitude
6-11   Time Zones in the United States
6-12   Polar Maps and Direction
6-13   Flying Over the Polar Regions
6-14   The Four Seasons
6-15   Using a Scale of Miles to Find Air Distance
6-16   Rivers and River Systems
6-17   Understanding Altitude
6-18   Using Color to Show Altitude or Elevation
6-19   Determining Elevation on Flat Maps through Color
6-20   Determining Elevation from Contour Lines
6-21   Finding Man-Made Things on Topographical Maps
6-22   Locating Unnamed Places on Topographical Maps
6-23   Taking a Walk with a Topographical Map
6-24   Reading and Interpreting Pattern Maps I
6-25   Reading and Interpreting Pattern Maps II
6-26   Reading and Interpreting Pattern Maps III
6-27   Reading and Interpreting Pattern Maps IV
6-28   Reading and Interpreting Pattern Maps V
6-29   Reading and Interpreting Pattern Maps VI
6-30   Reading and Interpreting Pattern Maps VII
6-31   Reading and Interpreting Pattern Maps VIII

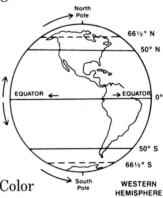

More Reading and Interpreting Maps:
Locating Places Through the Use of a Map Index

Background

1. The Rand McNally *Cosmopolitan World Atlas* lists thousands of place names in its index. There are twenty-four Washingtons, twenty-one Jacksons, and twenty-seven Springfields in the United States. The same atlas contains some 350 maps.

2. It is obvious that a system for finding places on maps had to be devised. Major map makers developed a way of using grids to localize the search for a particular place; that is, the searcher is directed to a particular map square in which the place is located.

3. In some cases, lines of latitude and longitude form the boundaries of a map square. In other cases, arbitrary north–south and east–west lines form the boundaries. In either case, letters and numerals printed along the top and sides of the map make square identification easy.

Example:

Thus, Hilltop is located in square B3 and Foxtown is located in square D6.

4. Maps of metropolitan areas may have fifty or more place names in a designated square. In such cases, map searchers have to scan the square systematically from top to bottom until the place is found.

Student Involvement

1. Distribute the facing page. Present as much of the foregoing information as seems appropriate for your group.

2. Provide practice opportunities in which the learners are guided in finding places on the map.

3. Read to the learners the directions at the bottom of the facing page. The multiple-choice element will help them narrow down the search for places.

4. Here are some additional indexed square problems:
—"Through what three squares does Highway 22 run?" (B1, C1, C2).
—"What square has only two named towns?" (B1).
—"Which one of these four squares—C1, C2, C3, B3—does not have any part of Highway 94?" (C3).

Answers to the Exercise

1. Big Sheep Mountain, B2; Blue Mountain, B3; Circle, B2; Cohagen, B1; Louie & Scottie Creek, C1; Mildred, C3; Sidney, A3

2. Jordan, Cohagen

3. 94, 12, 446, 22

4. Two

Name _____   Date _____

LOCATING PLACES THROUGH THE USE OF A MAP INDEX

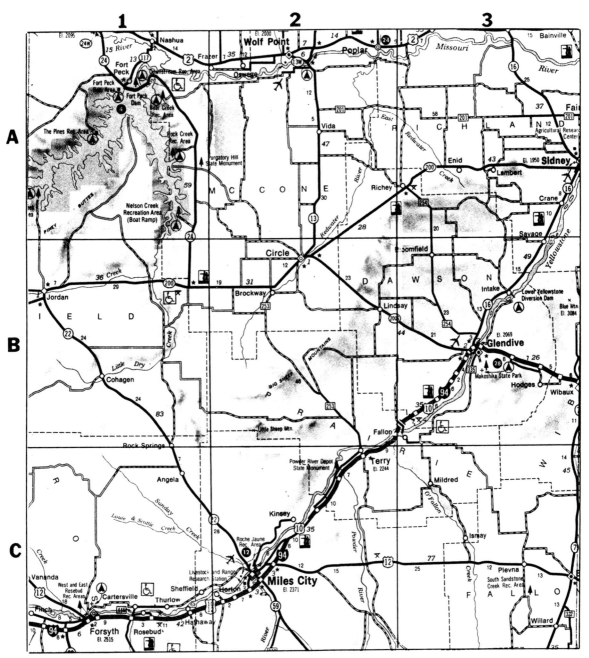

1. Some of the places shown on the map are listed below in alphabetical order. Draw a circle around the map index combination that tells the square on the map in which the place is located.

Big Sheep Mountains	A1	B2	B3
Blue Mountain	B1	B2	B3
Circle	B1	B2	A1
Cohagen	A3	C2	B1
Louie & Scottie Creek	C1	B2	A3
Mildred	B3	C1	C3
Sidney	B2	A1	A3

2. Name all the towns in B1. _____

_____

3. Name all the numbered highways in C1. (Hint: It may be necessary to look in another square to find the numbers of the highways.) _____

4. How many airports (✈) are in A3 and B3 combined? _____

© 1988 by The Center for Applied Research in Education

More Reading and Interpreting Maps:
Reading a Road Map for City Size and Special Features

Background

There are three ways that populations of cities and towns are shown on road maps: (1) through a special table, perhaps the map index, where communities and their populations are listed; (2) through the use of differentiated symbols, each symbol representing a population range; and (3) through the use of differentiated print, the size and heaviness of which indicates the range of population.

Unfortunately, the symbols used on road maps to indicate the populations of communities may vary from map to map. This presents no great problem if the map reader has acquired the habit of referring to the key to the map.

Student Involvement

1. Quantitative figures used in designating community populations are sometimes meaningless to students. This is because they cannot relate the numbers to their experiences. If a student has never experienced 1 million people, smog, great stores, traffic jams, high buildings, and so on, it is hard for them to "see" the city when they identify the symbol. Conversely, students who live in large cities may have difficulty visualizing a crossroads hamlet.

2. If the situation described above exists in your classroom, the next best remedy—after taking the students to various size communities—is to use pictures. Show them pictures of small towns, medium-sized towns, and so on. Then relate the pictures to their representative symbols on the map.

Another helpful instructional aid to use in this regard is to make simple board sketches similar to these:

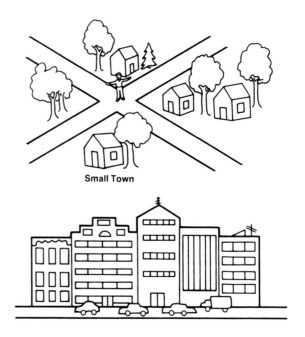

Small Town

Large City

3. Explain the key to the map on the facing page. Give special attention to the two ways that community size is shown and to the special feature symbols. Note that the populations are shown through the use of both symbols and special size print—the larger and heavier the print, the larger the city.

4. Point out that in Item 1 of the exercise, information gained from the map is being organized into a table—a useful work-study skill.

Note: The map shows a portion of eastern Montana as taken from an official Montana highway map.

Answers to the Exercise

1. Glendive, Miles City: 10,000–30,000; Baker, Sidney: 2,500–10,000; Circle, Poplar: 1,000–2,500; Bloomfield: Under 1,000

2. Miles City

3. Checked: Glendive, Sidney, Wolf Point

4a. 3,084 feet b. 2,244 feet c. 1,950 feet

5. Campsites: Froid, Glendive

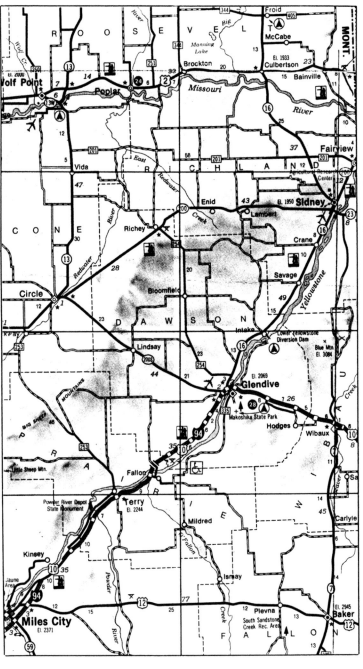

Name _____

Date _____

READING A ROAD MAP FOR CITY SIZE AND SPECIAL FEATURES

The map shows a portion of eastern Montana. Also, the map index location of each city is shown in parentheses.

1. Put a check in the chart under the population heading that best fits each listed city.

City	Population			
	Under 1,000	1,000– 2,500	2,500– 10,000	10,000– 30,000
Glendive (B3)				
Circle (A2)				
Miles City (A4)				
Baker (B4)				
Bloomfield (B2)				
Sidney (B2)				
Poplar (A1)				

2. Which of the two following cities is closest to the Rest Area on U.S. 12?
Miles City (A4) _____ Baker (B4) _____

3. Put a check before each of the cities that is served by a commercial airport.
a._____ Glendive (B3) d._____ Wolf Point (A1)
b._____ Sydney (B2) e._____ Circle (A2)
c._____ Baker (B4)

4. Which of the following places has a campsite nearby?
a._____ Baker (B4) c._____ Richey (A2)
b._____ Froid (B1) d._____ Glendive (B3)

SPECIAL FEATURES

✈ Airports Commercial

▲ St. Parks

⚑ Campsites

✕ Rest Areas

CITY POPULATIONS

○ Under 1,000 Conner
◉ 1,000-2,500 Townsend
◉ 2,500-10,000 Livingston

⬡ 10,000-30,000 **Havre**
⬡ 30,000 and over **Billings**

0   11   22   33   44
One inch represents approximately 22 miles

More Reading and Interpreting Maps: Identifying Water and Coastal Features

Background

Map legends supply information needed to interpret special symbols on maps. However, legends rarely depict frequently used "standard" symbols, such as those for gulfs and peninsulas.

Student Involvement

1. Make a transparency of the "Glossary of Water and Coastal Terms" listed below.

2. Distribute copies of the glossary and the facing page to your students.

3. Present each term and on a wall map point out an example of the feature.

4. Call attention to the map of northern Europe on the facing page. Point out that some of the water and coastal features of the region are named and numbered in the box.

5. Direct your students to neatly write the names of the features next to their corresponding numbers of the map.

Answers to the Exercise

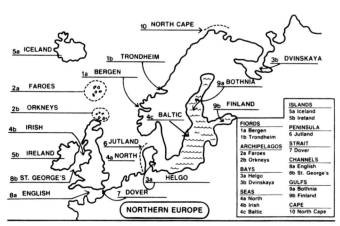

GLOSSARY OF WATER AND COASTAL TERMS

archipelago: a group or "string" of islands

bay: similar to a gulf, but usually smaller; usually narrower at the entrance than at the middle (see *gulf*)

fiord: a long, narrow arm of the ocean protruding deep into the land; usually with high hills or mountains on its sides

gulf: a large portion of an ocean or sea that protrudes into the land

islands: a piece of land completely surrounded by water

isthmus: a narrow strip of land that connects two larger pieces of land

peninsula: land that noticeably juts into a body of water; land with water on three sides (Note: a *cape* is similar to a peninsula. Capes are often found at the end of peninsulas; important capes usually have a name: Cape Cod, Cape Horn, etc.)

sea: a large body of water; usually part of an ocean; sometimes surrounded by land as, for example, the Caspian Sea

strait: a narrow strip of water that connects two large bodies of water (Note: *sounds* and *channels* are similar to straits.)

Name _____ Date _____

IDENTIFYING WATER AND COASTAL FEATURES

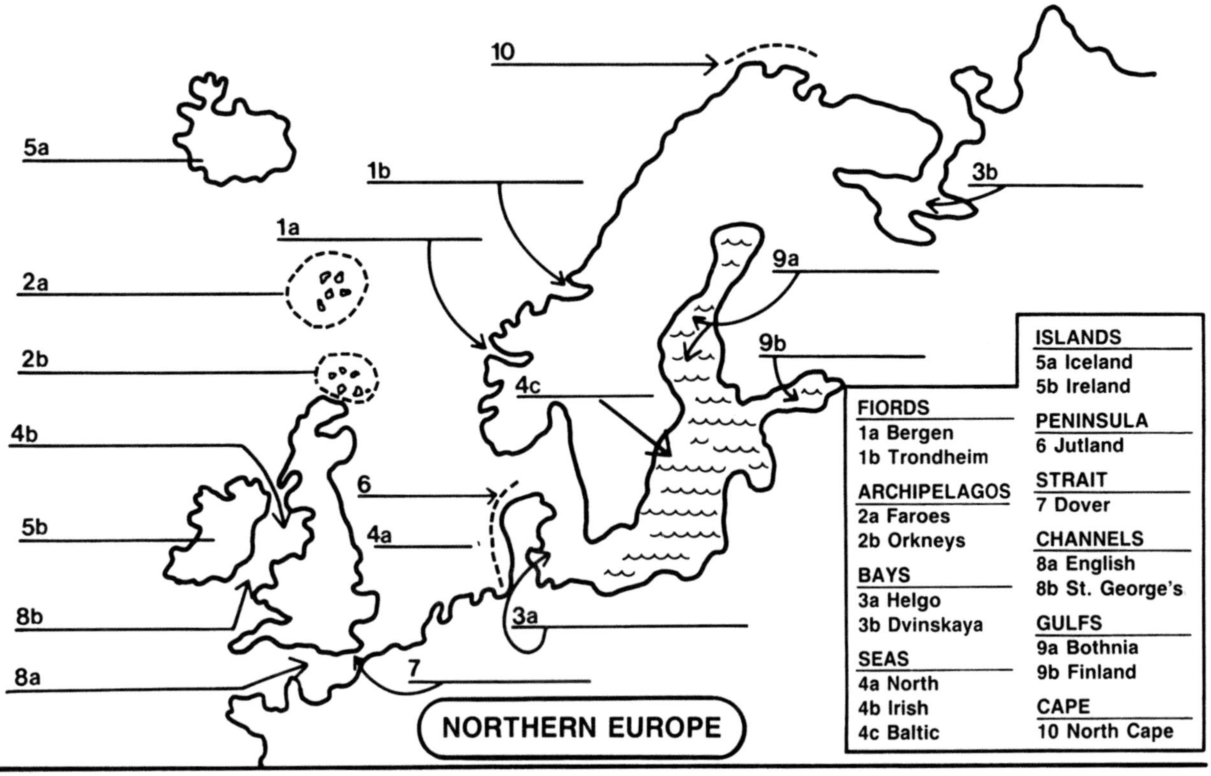

NORTHERN EUROPE

FIORDS
1a Bergen
1b Trondheim

ARCHIPELAGOS
2a Faroes
2b Orkneys

BAYS
3a Helgo
3b Dvinskaya

SEAS
4a North
4b Irish
4c Baltic

ISLANDS
5a Iceland
5b Ireland

PENINSULA
6 Jutland

STRAIT
7 Dover

CHANNELS
8a English
8b St. George's

GULFS
9a Bothnia
9b Finland

CAPE
10 North Cape

Directions: Draw your own coastline. Try to show all of the land and water symbols explained in the glossary. Give your features names, such as Paradise Archipelago, Cape Snow, and so on.

More Reading and Interpreting Maps: Identifying Land and Water Features

Background

The visualization of terms and symbols is an important map-reading skill. But it is difficult to visualize that which has never been seen. Geography, especially, is often remote from the learner's experiences.

Student Involvement

1. Distribute copies of the glossary printed below and the pictorial map.

2. Explain and illustrate each term.

3. Have your students complete the exercise on the facing page.

Answers to the Exercise:

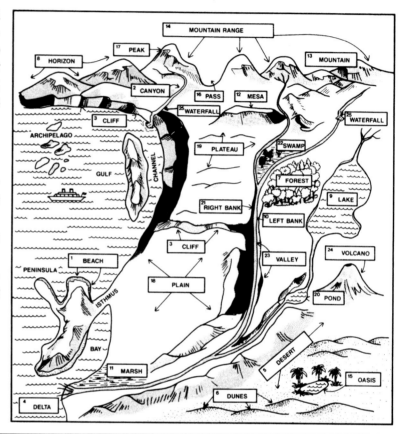

GLOSSARY OF LAND AND WATER TERMS

1. **beach:** a place where the water meets the land; the land between low and high tides

2. **canyon:** a deep cut in the earth's surface through which a river flows

3. **cliff:** land that rises almost straight up from the water or earth's surface

4. **delta:** land formed from the soil carried by a river and deposited at its mouth

5. **desert:** a large area of land with little rainfall and sparse vegetation

6. **dunes:** hills or ridges of sand found in deserts and on beaches

7. **forest:** a large area of land covered by a great number of trees and undergrowth

8. **horizon:** a line in the distance where the earth or ocean appears to meet the sky

9. **lake:** a body of water surrounded by land

10. **left bank:** the river bank on one's left when facing downstream

11. **marsh:** soft, wet land with grasslike vegetation; often near coasts

12. **mesa:** a flat-topped hill with steep sides, usually in an arid area

13. **mountain:** a part of the earth's surface that projects very high above the land around it

14. **mountain range:** a series of mountains and hills that might extend for hundreds of miles

15. **oasis:** a place in a desert where there is water from a well or spring

16. **pass:** a low place through mountains that allows for passage of people, cars, and so forth

17. **peak:** the pointed top of a mountain; sometimes a mountain that stands by itself

18. **plain:** a large, level area of land, usually at lower altitude than a plateau

19. **plateau:** a large elevated area of land; generally flat, but may have hills and valleys

20. **pond:** a small body of water surrounded by land, usually smaller than a lake

21. **right bank:** the river bank on one's right when facing downstream

22. **swamp:** wet, spongy land, some parts of which may be covered by water; usually has trees

23. **valley:** a level area of land, sometimes many miles in length, with high land on its sides

24. **volcano:** a cone-shaped hill or mountain with a hollow center (crater)

25. **waterfall:** a place where the water in a stream or river drops suddenly over a steep place

Name _____ Date _____

IDENTIFYING LAND AND WATER FEATURES

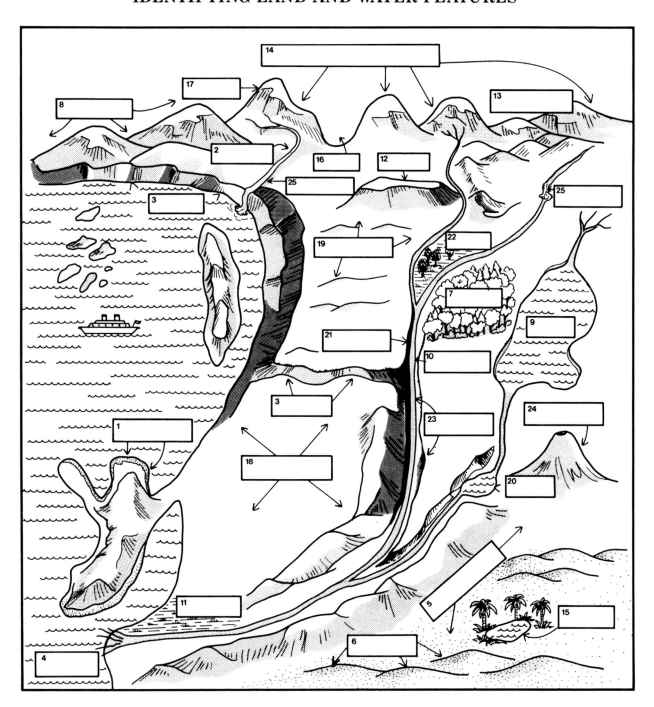

1. Each glossary term is numbered, and each box in the pictorial map is numbered. Write in the boxes the correct term for each feature shown.

2. Review question: On the map, write the following terms where you think they belong: Bay, Gulf, Isthmus, Channel, Archipelago, Peninsula.

More Reading and Interpreting Maps:
Earth Facts

Background/Student Involvement

There are several words and concepts in this activity that may need elaboration.

1. The equator is an imaginary line that marks the beginning of latitudinal measurement. Point out that all things that are measured must have a starting point, or a standard against which things are compared. The birth of Christ is the point from which the Western world measures time: events occurred either before Christ (B.C.), or after Christ (A.D., from *anno domini,* the Latin term for "in the year of our lord"). Likewise, places on earth are either north or south of the equator, or on the equator.

Longitude need not be introduced at this time. However, just as latitude measures north and south distances, longitude measures east and west distances. (See Activity 6-6.) East-west distances proceed from the zero degree of longitude, also called the prime meridian. One is either east or west of the prime meridian or actually on it.

2. Stress that in using latitude, it is necessary to designate either north (N) or south (S). If neither north nor south are designated, there is no way to determine which hemisphere a place is in. It may be either the Northern Hemisphere or the Southern Hemisphere.

3. That temperature decreases as one goes north or south from the equator is a significant concept. A common misconception is that as one proceeds south, it becomes warmer and warmer even *beyond and south of the equator.* Suggestion: On a large map or globe, glue several paper human figures. Distribute the figures widely on the surface. Ask your students: "Which is most likely to be in a cold climate, Person A or Person B?" and so on.

4. It should be realized that latitudinal position is only one of the factors that influence temperature. Some other factors:
Altitude: Temperature decreases as altitude increases. Thus, on the equator it is possible to have perpetual snow in the high mountains.
Water proximity: Large bodies of water help cool or heat the land.
Winds: The prevailing wind direction of an area can bring cool air masses from the north and warm air masses from the south. (The reverse is true in the Southern Hemisphere): Cool air masses come from the south, warm air masses from the north.)

The factors of temperature do not act independently. All of the factors combine to produce the air temperature of any given place.

Answers to the Exercise

1–4. [Check for correct labeling.]
5a. 50° N   *b.* 50° S
6. [Check for correct labeling.]
7. Higher

Name _____   Date _____

EARTH FACTS

1. The earth is about 25,000 miles around at the equator. If you could walk four miles in an hour day and night without stopping, it would take you more than eight months to walk 25,000 miles.

Write *25,000 miles* between the arrows on the equator line in the diagram.

2. As you go north from the equator, climates get colder. The same thing is true if you go south from the equator.

You can show on the diagram that it gets colder as you go from the equator to either the North Pole or the South Pole. Write *Colder* in the big spaces between the arrows on the outside of the earth diagram. Notice that there are *two* places to write—one is north of the equator, and the other is south of the equator.

3. Find the dash line near the North Pole. The places north of the line are in the *Arctic* region of the world. It is very cold in the Arctic during the winter.

Write *Arctic* in the space between the dashed line and the North Pole.

4. Find the dashed line near the South Pole. The places south of the line are in the *Ant-*

arctic region of the world. The Antarctic is also a very cold region.

Write *Antarctic* in the space between the dashed line and the South Pole.

5. The equator has another name. It is also called a *line of latitude*. The equator is neither north nor south. It is the beginning line of latitude. All places on earth are either north or south of the equator. Of course, a place could be right on the equator. Because it is the beginning, the equator is at zero degrees (0°) of latitude.

a. What is the number of the line of latitude

north of the equator? _____

b. What is the number of the line of latitude

south of the equator? _____

6. The regions near the equator are warm. Show this on the diagram by writing *Warm* on the equator.

7. Which shows the colder regions—the higher or the lower numbers of latitude?

_____

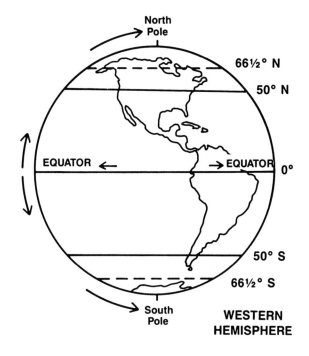

More Reading and Interpreting Diagrams:
The Spinning Earth Causes Day and Night

Background/Student Involvement

1. There are three basic concepts that should be taught in connection with the causes of day and night: rotation, axis, and the west-to-east spin of the earth.

a. *Rotation:* Young learners often confuse *rotation* with *revolution.* It would be wise to not teach revolution, which is a key element in understanding the causes of the seasons, until rotation is thoroughly understood and assimilated.

It would be helpful to have the children themselves physically rotate. Simply ask them to stand and then to turn around and around in one spot. Tell them that they are rotating, and write the word on the board.

Then ask them if they have ever seen ice skaters rotate themselves on the points of their skates, as is done in Olympic and other competitions. Give as many examples of rotation as possible: merry-go-rounds, a drill bit biting into wood, a pinwheel, a ball spinning on the tip of a basketball player's finger, the second hand of a clock sweeping around the clock face, and so forth.

b. *Axis:* The invisibility of an axis is what makes the concept difficult for learners to grasp. But the axle of a wagon, bicycle, or automobile wheel is quite tangible. Show with an actual axle (a toy car will do) that the wheel rotates around the axle. Point out that *axle* and *axis* are from the same root word.

c. *The west-to-east spin of the earth:* Obtain a globe that is set on a stand in such a way that it may be rotated. Glue on the globe a symbol that represents a person. Spin the globe in a counterclockwise direction (that is, from left to right, which corresponds to the earth's west-to-east rotation). Next, shine a flashlight on the globe as it spins. Your students will readily see that the person symbol goes from light to darkness to light to darkness. Point out that the east receives the rays of the sun before the west; that is, the eastern United States enters the sunlight before the western United States.

2. Before assigning the exercise, it would be helpful to orient the children to the diagram, and to direct their reading of the explanation in the first column.

Answers to the Exercise

1, 2. [Check for correct labeling of the diagram and the copying of the title.]

3. Example: The sun shines on the earth. The earth rotates on its axis. The half of the earth that faces the sun is having daytime. The other half is having night.

Name _____   Date _____

THE SPINNING EARTH CAUSES DAY AND NIGHT

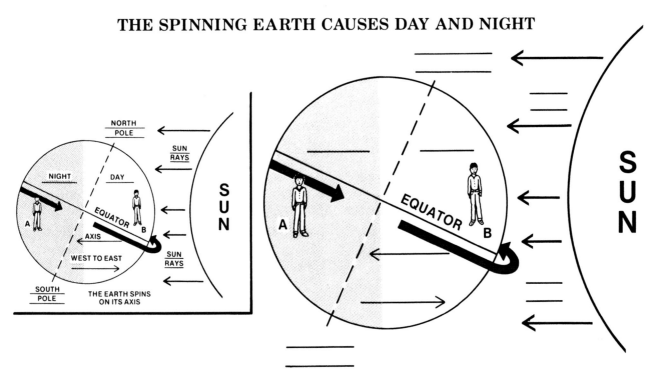

As the earth travels through space, it spins. Another word for spin is *rotate*. So to rotate means to turn around and around.

You've probably seen lots of things rotate. Tops rotate, and so do eggbeaters. Each of these things is spinning on its *axis*. An axis is an imaginary line around which a thing spins. The drawing shows what the axis of a top looks like. The small diagram above shows the earth's axis.

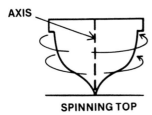

SPINNING TOP

When half of the earth is in sunlight, the other half is in darkness. The large diagram shows two people standing in different places on the earth. Person B is in the sunlight, while on the other side of the earth, Person A is in the dark. It takes 24 hours, which is one *day,* for the earth to make a complete rotation. This means that Person A and Person B will be in sunlight during part of the 24-hour day and in darkness during the other part.

You should also notice that the diagram shows that the earth turns from west to east.

Title _____

Explanation _____

_____

_____

_____

_____

_____

_____

_____

_____

At the top of this column is a large copy of the small diagram, except that some words are missing. Follow these directions to complete the diagram.

1. Copy the title from the small diagram. Write the title on the blank line in the box.

2. Label your diagram with the same words that are in the small diagram.

3. In the box below the title, tell in your own words why the earth has night and day.

More Reading and Interpreting Maps:
Locating Places with Lines of Latitude

Background

Lines of latitude, also called parallels, serve three basic purposes on maps and globes:

1. They are necessary, along with lines of longitude, to determine the position of places.

2. They provide data relative to climate.

3. They can be used to determine distances.

The activities that follow will be concerned with the first and second listed above.

Student Involvement

1. Make a transparency of the facing page.

2. Distribute copies of the facing page.

3. Explain that the students should complete the diagram of the globe on their own copies as you complete the diagram on the transparency.

4. Lines of latitude are imaginary lines that extend west and east across the globe or map. (Have students write *West—East* on two lines of latitude, one north of the equator and one south of the equator.)

5. The equator lies midway between the north and the south poles. (Have students label the equator, the North Pole, and the South Pole.)

6. The equator divides the earth into two equal parts, the *Northern Hemisphere* and the *Southern Hemisphere*. (Have the students label the hemispheres on the lines provided to the right of the global diagram.) All circles, including lines of latitude which are circles, may be divided into 360 equal parts or units. Each part is called a *degree*. The symbol for degree is °, as in 50°.

7. Lines of latitude are generally numbered in increments of ten degrees, starting at the equator. Occasionally other divisions are used.

The Tropics of Cancer (23½° N) and Capricorn (23½° S), the Arctic Circle (66½° N), and the Antarctic Circle (66½° S) are shown by numbered dash lines on the student map. (Have the students number all the lines of latitude; 90° N and 90° S should also be numbered.)

8. For drill and practice, have the students complete the exercise at the bottom of the page.

Answers to the Exercise

1. H: *SH*   E: *NH*   G: *Neither*
   B: *NH*   A: *NH*   I: *SH*
   D: *NH*   F: *NH*   J: *SH*

2. A: 50° N F: 5° N C: 35° N J: 30° S
B: 40° N   H: 20° S   I: 40° S   G: 0°

   3a. 20   b. 40   c. 60   d. 85

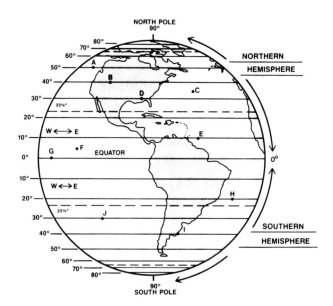

Name _____   Date _____

LOCATING PLACES WITH LINES OF LATITUDE

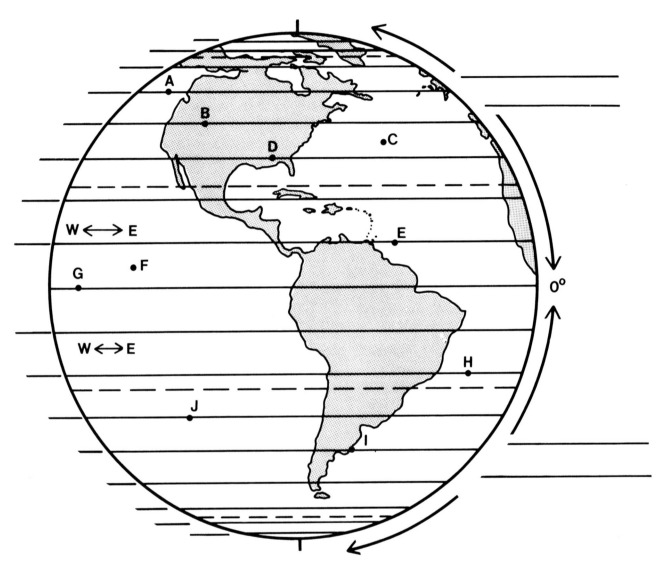

1. In which hemisphere is each of the following located? Write NH for Northern Hemisphere, SH for Southern Hemisphere.

Point H_____ Point E_____ Point G_____

Point B_____ Point A_____ Point I _____

Point D_____ Point F_____ Point J _____

2. What is the latitude of the following points on the map? Be sure to write N for north or S for south after the latitude numerals. Example: 20° N, 45° S.

A_____   F_____   C_____   J_____

B_____   H_____   I_____   G_____

3. How many degrees of latitude are there between each of the following?

  a. 30° N and 50° N? _____

  b. 20° S and 60° S? _____

  c. 30° S and 30° N? _____

  d. 45° S and 40° N? _____

More Reading and Interpreting Maps:
Locating Places with Lines of Longitude

Background

Lines of longitude, also called meridians, serve three basic purposes on maps and globes:

1. In conjunction with lines of latitude, they help determine the location of places.

2. They are helpful in measuring time and determing time zones.

3. They can be used to measure distances.

This activity is concerned with the use of longitude in locating places. Other aspects of longitude are treated on later activity pages.

Student Involvement

1. Make a transparency of the facing page.

2. Distribute copies of the facing page.

3. Direct your students to complete their diagram as you complete the transparency. Present those parts of the following information that are appropriate for your class.

4. Lines of longitude are imaginary lines that extend from the North Pole to the South Pole. Lines of longitude, unlike lines of latitude, are not parallel. (Have the students label the North Pole and the South Pole.)

5. All measurements of longitude start with the prime meridian, which is 0 degrees. Longitude is measured in increments of fifteen degrees starting with the prime meridian. The enumeration continues for 180 degrees to the east and 180 degrees to the west of the prime meridian. (On the map, have the students enumerate in 15-degree intervals. Point out that because only part of a globe can be shown at one time, the numbering stops at 75 degrees west and 75 degrees east.)

6. The prime meridian and its counterpart on the other side of the world (the 180-degree line) divide the world into two equal parts—the Eastern Hemisphere and the Western Hemisphere. (Point out the boxes inside the diagram. Have the students print the names of the hemispheres in the boxes.)

7. For drill and practice, have the students complete the exercise on the facing page.

Answers to the Exercise

1. A: 60°W   D: 30°W   I: 75°E   C: 75°E
B: 45°E   H: 37½°W   G: 45°E   E: 22½°E

2a. 30°   b. 30°   c. 90°

3. D: WH   C: EH   I: EH   G: EH
F: WH   A: WH

4. A: NW&WH D: NH&WH G: SH&EH
B: NH&EH   F: SH&WH

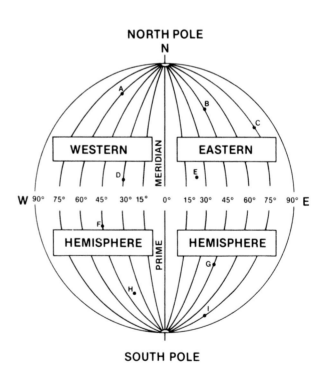

Name _____   Date _____

LOCATING PLACES WITH LINES OF LONGITUDE

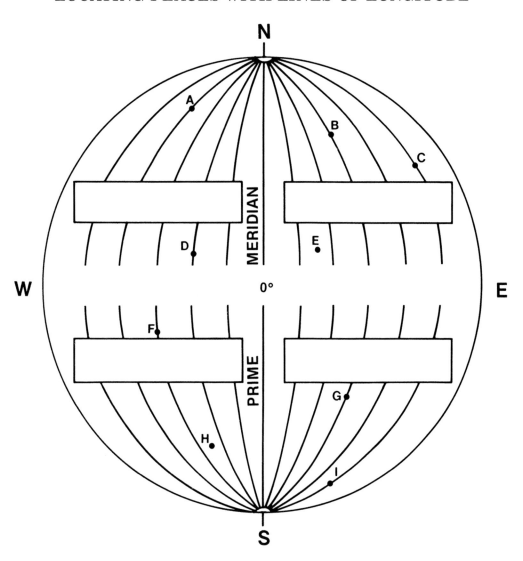

1. What is the longitude of the following points on the map? Be sure to write E for east or W for west after the longitude numerals. Examples: 15° E, 45° W.

A _____   D _____   I _____   C _____

B _____   H _____   G _____   E _____

2. How many degrees of longitude are there between each of the following?

a. 30° E and 60° E? _____

b. 45° W and 75° W? _____

c. 60° W and 30° E? _____

3. In which hemisphere is each of the following located? Write EH for Eastern Hemisphere or WH for Western Hemisphere.

Point D_____ Point C_____ Point I _____

Point G_____ Point F_____ Point A_____

4. Notice the equator and recall what you learned on the previous exercise. In which

two hemispheres is A? _____   D? _____

G? _____   B? _____   F? _____

More Reading and Interpreting Maps:
Locating Places with Latitude and Longitude

Background

Mercator maps are most useful for determining location. The straight north–south, and east–west lines on the Mercator allow for easy reading of the coordinates. That the Mercator distorts distances and the sizes and shapes of the land masses has no detrimental effect on the accurate reading of latitude and longitude. Globes and globe maps are rarely used for latitudinal and longitudinal locations because it is difficult to read between their curved lines.

Student Involvement

1. Reproduce and distribute the Mercator map of the world shown on the facing page.

2. Make a transparency of the map for projection.

3. Direct your students to complete their map as you complete the transparency. Present those parts of the following information that are appropriate for your class.

4. It would be almost impossible to find a place on a line unless it is known *where* on the line the place is located. To help solve this problem on maps, the lines of latitude are crossed by intersecting lines—that is, lines of longitude.

5. Lines of latitude are numbered from the equator, lines of longitude from the prime meridian. Ask your students to make these entries on their maps:

a. Label the *prime meridian* and the *equator*.

b. Number all the grid lines, including the Tropics of Cancer and Capricorn and the Arctic and Antarctic Circles.

c. Write *East* in the horizontal box in the Eastern Hemisphere, *West* in the horizontal box in the Western Hemisphere, *South* in the vertical box in the Southern Hemisphere, and *North* in the vertical box in the Northern Hemisphere.

6. Demonstrate how to determine the location of Point A on the map (60° N, 60° W).

7. For drill and practice, have the students complete the exercise on the facing page.

Answers to the Exercise

1. A: 60° N - 60° W,   B: 50° N - 45° W, D: 30° N - 150° E,   E: 5° S - 135° W, F: 30° S - 75° W,   J: 50° S - 45° W

2. A&B: 10°, B&J: 100°, C&G: 70°, D&H: 70°

3. G&F: 120°, G&H: 105°, E&F: 60°, B&C: 90°

4. 70° N - 45° W

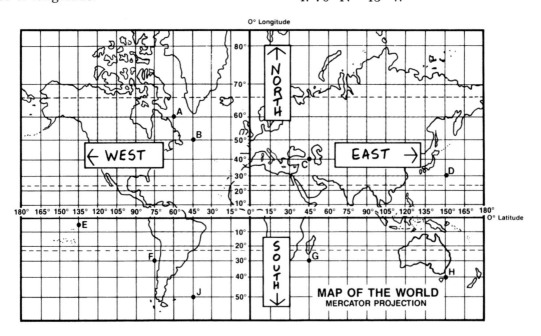

Name _____ Date _____

LOCATING PLACES WITH LATITUDE AND LONGITUDE

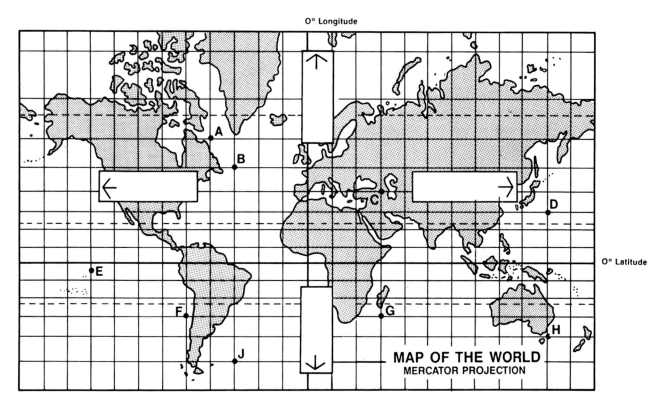

1. Write the latitude and the longitude of the following places shown on the map.

A _____   B _____   D _____

E _____   F _____   J _____

2. How many degrees of latitude are there between:

A and B? _____   B and J? _____

C and G? _____   D and H? _____

3. How many degrees of longitude are there between:

G and F? _____   G and H? _____

E and F? _____   B and C? _____

4. Challenge: Start at Point A on the map.

a. Go south 30°. Write a *w* at that point.
b. Go east 45°. Write an *x* at that point.
c. Go north 40°. Write a *y* at that point.
d. Go west 30°. Write a *z* at that point.
What is your latitude and longitude at *z*?

_____

5. Suppose a ship is sinking at sea. The radar operator sends a message: "We need help. Sinking fast. Location is 30°S - 45°W." Draw a small ship at that location.

More Reading and Interpreting Maps:
Using Latitude and Longitude to Compute Distances

Background

Latitude and longitude offer a way to quickly estimate direct east–west or north–south distances. For example, there are about 12 degrees of latitude between New Orleans and Chicago. This translates into 840 miles. You can calculate this answer quickly because a degree of latitude is equal to about 70 miles; thus, 12 × 70 = 840.

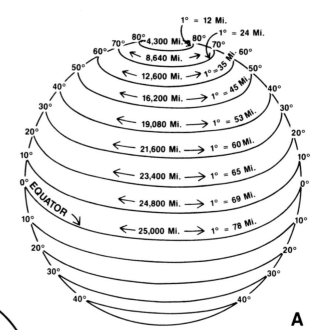

A

Student Involvement

Have your students follow the steps outlined below to learn how distances on the map can be computed using latitude and longitude.

1. The distance around the world on the equator is approximately 25,000 miles.

2. Since the equator is a circle, it contains 360 degrees, as do all circles.

3. Each degree of longitude on the equator is about 70 miles. How is this figure obtained? The circumference of the equator in miles is divided by the total number of degrees; thus 25,000 ÷ 360 = 70. (The answer is rounded off.)

4. Since each degree of longitude on the 10°S line is approximately 69 miles, an airplane flying from Point A (10° E) to Point B (40° E) flies 30 degrees, or 2,070 miles.

5. The parallels of latitude become shorter in circumference as they approach the poles. Diagram A shows the approximate lengths.

Thus, as Diagram B shows, an airplane that flies along the 30° S line of latitude from point C to point D flies 30 degrees. A degree on the 30° S line is 60 miles. Therefore, the airplane will fly 1,800 miles (30 × 60).

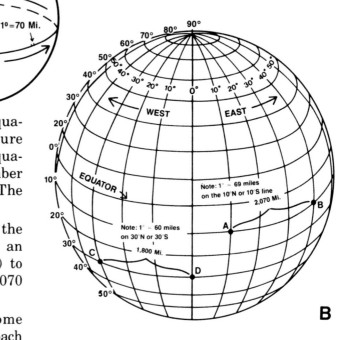

B

Answers to the Exercise

1a. 1,350   b. 1,800   c. 1,800
d. 2,070   e. 2,100   f. 4,140
2a. H to J   b. A to B
3a. 700   b. 2,800   c. 4,200   d. 3,500
4. 9,690

Name _____   Date _____

USING LATITUDE AND LONGITUDE TO COMPUTE DISTANCES

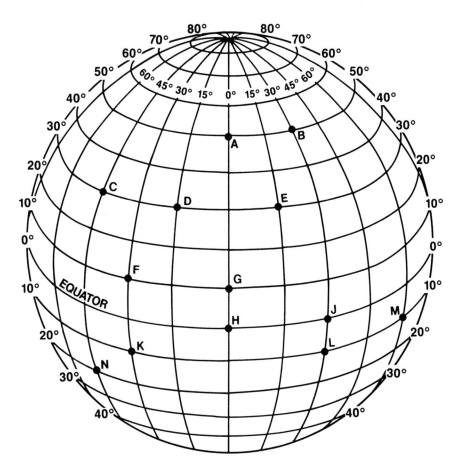

Number of Miles in One Degree of Longitude on Certain Lines of Latitude	
Latitude	*Miles*
Equator	70
10° N or S	69
20° N or S	65
30° N or S	60
40° N or S	53
50° N or S	45
60° N or S	35
70° N or S	24
80° N or S	12

Use the information in the chart above for help in doing the exercise below.

1. How many miles is it from:

   a. A to B? _____   d. F to G? _____

   b. C to D? _____   e. H to J? _____

   c. D to E? _____   f. K to L? _____

2. Which would be the shortest trip:

   a. C to E, or H to J? _____

   b. A to B, or L to M? _____

3. All lines of longitude are the same length—about 12,500 miles. Each degree of latitude is equivalent to about 70 miles. Using this fact, how many miles is it from:

   a. H to G? _____   c. L to B? _____

   b. G to A? _____   d. C to N? _____

4. Challenge: Using only lines of latitude and longitude, can you calculate how many miles an airplane would fly to get from A to B to L to K?

_____

More Reading and Interpreting Maps: Determining Direction with Latitude and Longitude

Background

1. Often, the apparent location of a place on a map can be deceiving. A place may appear to be farther north, south, east, or west of another place than it really is. Here is an example:

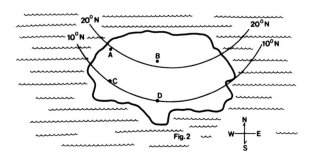

Fig. 1

In Fig. 1 above, Point A appears to be farther north than B. And from the data on the map, one would be justified in coming to that conclusion.

2. However, when we impose lines of latitude on the map (Fig. 2), we see that B is farther north than A. We know this because B is north of the 20° N line of latitude and A is south of the 20° N line.

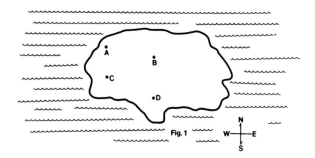

Fig. 2

Similarly, C and D are both the same distance north of the equator, although C appears to be farther north.

3. Misperception of direction can also occur if longitude lines are not shown. It appears in Figs. 1 and 2 that A and C are equally west of the prime meridian. But when lines of longitude are drawn, as in

Fig. 3, it is clear that A is approximately 61° W, while C is approximately 59° W. Likewise, B is farther west than D.

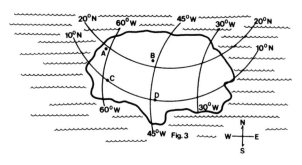

Fig. 3

Student Involvement

1. Explain the foregoing to the extent that is appropriate for your class. Sketches and diagrams will add significantly to their understanding.

2. Illustrate the use of the grid as an indicator of true direction by showing a typical map of the United States on which its northern boundary, 49° N, is shown as curved. On a globe, that line would be perfectly straight.

3. Point out that on maps of small areas, direction is not significantly inaccurate if there are no lines of latitude and longitude, but on maps of large areas the grid is necessary for accuracy.

4. Have your students complete the exercise on the facing page.

Answers to the Exercise

1a. Ankara   b. Cairo   c. Durban

2. London, Accra

3. Aden

4. Naples, New York

5a. A   b. D   c. C

6a. A   b. F   c. C

7a. B   b. B

Name _____   Date _____

DETERMINING DIRECTION WITH LATITUDE AND LONGITUDE

1. Leningrad is on the 30° E line of longitude. What three cities are almost directly south? a. _____

b. _____ c. _____

2. Oran is on the 0° line of longitude. What city is almost directly north?

_____

What city is almost directly south?

_____

3. What city is almost directly south of Baghdad on the 45° E line of longitude?

_____

4. Ankara is close to the 40° N line of latitude. What two cities are almost directly

west? _____

_____

Note: Use the map at the bottom of this column to answer the following questions.

5. Which point is farthest north?
a. A or B _____ b. C or D _____
c. C or E _____

6. Which point is farthest west?
a. A or C _____ b. F or D _____
c. C or F _____

7. Which point is farthest east?
a. D or B _____ b. B or G _____

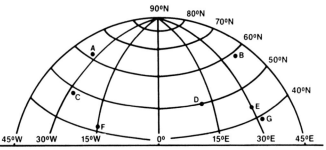

More Reading and Interpreting Maps: Telling Time with Longitude

Background/Student Involvement

Earth-sun relationships are often difficult for young learners to understand. There is nothing more "real" than the earth and the sun, but the variables of space, distance, rotation, and revolution, all interacting simultaneously, are quite complex and abstract.

Before assigning the activity on the facing page, there are some facts that should be brought to the attention of your students:

1. The earth rotates in a west-to-east direction toward the sun. This fact makes it appear that the sun is "rising" in the east and "setting" in the west. Actually, the earth is constantly turning a new face, as it were, to the sun. Thus, people at a given place on the earth experience dawn, then noon, then dusk, then night. The cycle begins again with a new dawn.

2. The fact that the earth turns toward the sun is basic to an understanding of how time is reckoned on earth. The earth has a circumference of 360 degrees. Since the earth makes one complete turn in 24 hours, it follows that it turns 15 degrees every hour (360 ÷ 24 = 15). This is why most maps show longitude lines every 15 degrees. Each 15 degrees stands for the passage of one hour of time.

3. The abbreviation A.M. is from the Latin phrase *ante meridiem*. This phrase means "before noon." Thus, 9:00 A.M. is the ninth hour of the day before noon.

P.M. is the abbreviation for the Latin *post meridiem,* or "after noon." Therefore, 10:00 P.M. means ten hours past noon, or ten hours past the middle of the day.

4. The idea that places on the earth observe different times can be disconcerting. For example, a speech may be given at 3:00 P.M. in London, but people in New York may be listening to it at 10:00 A.M. New York time, while people in San Francisco are listening to the speech at 7:00 A.M.

Answers to the Exercise

1. 11 A.M.; 10 A.M.

2. 30° W—10 A.M.; 60° W—6 A.M.; 120° W—4 A.M.; 150° W—2 A.M.

3. 7 A.M.; 4 A.M.

4. 9 P.M.; 7 P.M.

5. 12 hours

Name _____   Date _____

TELLING TIME WITH LONGITUDE

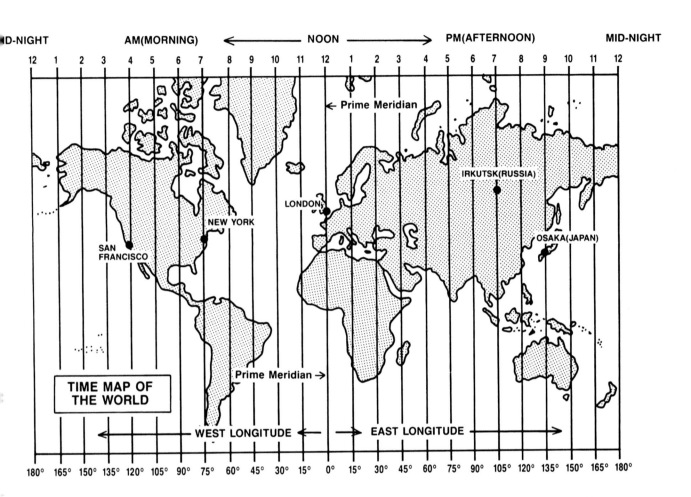

1. Find the prime meridian (zero degree longitude) on the map. If you follow the line to the top of the map, you can see that it is 12:00 noon on the prime meridian. This means that it is 12:00 noon in all the places on earth through which the prime meridian passes.

What hour of the day is printed on the 15° W line of longitude? _____30° W? _____

2. As you have discovered, for every 15 degrees the earth turns toward the sun there is a one-hour change in time. Using this understanding and the information on the map, complete this table.

Longitude	Time	Longitude	Time
0°	12:00 Noon	120° W	
30° W		150° W	
60° W		180° W	12:00 Midnight

3. Find New York on the map. Follow its line of longitude to the top of the map. What time is it in New York when it is 12:00 noon in London? _____San Francisco? _____

4. Suppose that it is 12:00 noon in London and that you are going *east* of the prime meridian toward Europe and Asia. It is past noon (P.M.) in those places, and the people are doing afternoon and evening activities. You can see on the map that on the 15° E line of longitude it is 1:00 P.M., at 30° E it is 2:00 P.M., and so on.

When it is 12:00 noon in London, what time is it in Osaka, Japan?_____

in Irkutsk, Russia? _____

5. How many hours' difference in time is there between New York and Irkutsk?

_____

More Reading and Interpreting Maps:
Time Zones in the United States

Background

The following information on the reasons for standard time zones should prove useful in introducing the accompanying learner activity. The drawing below can be readily copied onto the chalk board.

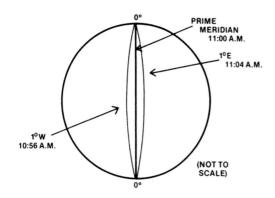

The idea that "Time never stands still" is a truism. The earth is constantly rotating toward the sun. Each degree of longitude varies four minutes from the one preceding or following it. So when it is 11:00 A.M. on the prime meridian, or zero degree longitude, it is 11:04 A.M. on 1° E and 10:56 A.M. on 1° W.

If "sun time" were used, people who lived only a few miles apart would have different times. Obviously, this would lead to great confusion. For example, each town along a railroad track would have its own local time.

Standard time was devised to alleviate the problem. The United States was divided into four time zones (six if Alaska and Hawaii are included). The 75° W, 90° W, 105° W, and 120° W lines of longitude were used as approximate boundaries of the zones. Every place in a zone uses the same time. Persons who go from one zone to another add or subtract one hour from their watches, depending on whether they are going east or west.

The zone lines are irregular in order to avoid dividing cities, railroad terminals, and so on. Even so, as can be seen on the map, some states are divided into two time zones.

Student Involvement

Item 5 of the activity will probably require special explanation.

First, determine from the map what the time was in California when the airplane left New York. Since the plane left New York at 1:00 P.M., the time in California was 10:00 A.M..

Second, add the number of hours the plane was en route (six) to the California time. Thus, it was 4:00 P.M. when the plane arrived at its destination.

In formula form: destination time at time of departure + hours of flight = arrival time (10:00 A.M. + 6 hrs. = 4:00 P.M.)

Answers to the Exercise

1. Eastern, Central, Mountain, Pacific

2. 3 P.M., 2 P.M., 1 P.M.

3. 4 P.M., 5 P.M., 3 P.M.

4. The following states should be checked: Oregon, Nebraska, Tennessee, Kentucky

5. 4 P.M.

Name _____ Date _____

TIME ZONES IN THE UNITED STATES

4 p.m.

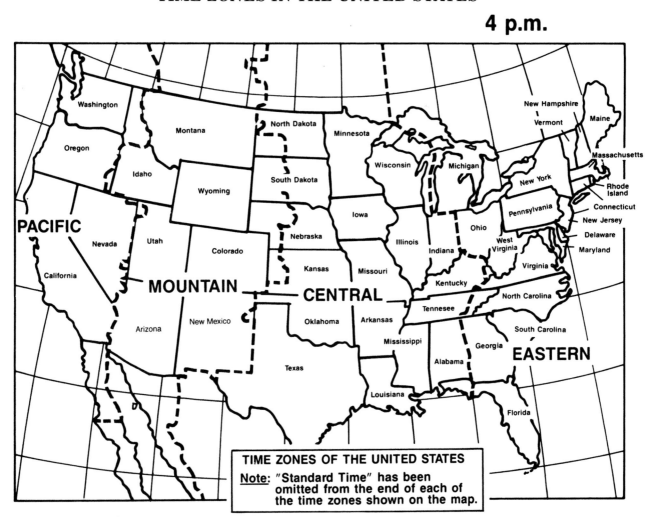

TIME ZONES OF THE UNITED STATES
Note: "Standard Time" has been
omitted from the end of each of
the time zones shown on the map.

1. The United States, not including Alaska and Hawaii, is divided into four time zones. *Zone* is another word for area or region, except that a zone has definite boundaries.

What are the names of the zones, according to the map?

_____ _____

_____ _____

2. There is a one-hour difference in time from zone to zone. You can see on the map that the sample time in the Eastern Standard Time Zone, called Eastern for short, is 4:00 P.M. What is the time in the Central Standard

Time Zone (Central)? _____

the Mountain Standard Time Zone (Mountain)? _____

the Pacific Standard Time Zone (Pacific)?

_____

3. Suppose that it were 6:00 P.M. in the Eastern zone. What time would it be in the Mountain zone? _____

in the Central zone? _____

in the Pacific zone? _____

4. Check on the list below those states that have two time zones within their borders:

__ Oregon   __ Texas
__ Nebraska   __ Tennessee
__ California   __ North Carolina
__ New York   __ Kentucky

5. Suppose that you were to fly from New York to California. You leave New York at 1:00 P.M. The flight takes six hours. What time would it be in California when you arrived?

_____

More Reading and Interpreting Maps: Polar Maps and Direction

Background

Since the advent of the airplane, polar maps have become increasingly important. Formerly, when oceangoing ships carried most of the world's freight and passengers, Mercator maps or variations of them were most frequently used by the public. Now that airplanes routinely fly over or near the poles, especially the North Pole, polar maps are needed to show proper distances and true routes of travel.

One of the elements that makes polar maps difficult for some to read is that established ideas of direction are challenged. Normally, a Mercator map shows east to the right, west to the left, south behind, and north straight ahead! But on a polar map, east and west are read on a great circle, and north and south are read on straight lines coming from all points of the compass and converging on the poles.

A few experiences with polar maps, however, can overcome established ideas on how to read direction. One begins to see the beautiful logic of the parallel and meridian grid system as applied to the polar regions of the world and elsewhere.

Student Involvement

The polar map should be explained before you assign the exercise. Here are some suggestions that will make the map more understandable:

1. Show a globe with the North Pole tipped toward and facing the students. Relate the polar regions as shown on the globe to the flat map they are using. Point out the North Pole, the parallels and meridians, and the prime meridian on both the globe and the map.

2. Explain that on the exercise map, parallels and meridians are shown only in the water regions.

3. Point out the west–east direction arrows at the bottom of the map.

4. Point out that only a few of the parallels are numbered, but the enumeration sequence is a clue to the number of all the parallels.

5. Read the introduction to the exercise. Explain and illustrate where necessary.

Answers to the Exercise

1.
A: North	F: North
B: North	G: North
C: South	H: South
D: North	I: South
E: North	J: North

2.
1: West	5: West
2: East	6: East
3: East	7: West
4: East	8: East

3. A, E, I, D

4. 1, I, A, G

POLAR MAPS AND DIRECTION

Polar maps present views of the world that are quite different from the maps used most often in books, magazines, and newspapers. Here are some things to remember when you work with direction on polar maps:

—North or south is usually located at or near the center of the map.

—All *straight* lines on polar maps are lines of longitude (meridians).

—If you are traveling along a line of longitude, you are going either straight north or straight south.

—Lines of latitude (parallels) are shown as circles on polar maps. Lines of latitude go directly east and west. Even if the line appears to be going "up" or "down," it is still going east and west.

1. On the north polar map in the next column, some of the small airplanes are traveling along the lines of longitude. They are marked with capital letters. In which direction is each one going? Answer either *north* or *south*.

Airplane	Direction of Travel	Airplane	Direction of Travel
A		F	
B		G	
C		H	
D		I	
E		J	

2. Other small airplanes are traveling on the lines of latitude. They are marked with numerals. In which direction is each one going, east or west?

① _____   ⑤ _____
② _____   ⑥ _____
③ _____   ⑦ _____
④ _____   ⑧ _____

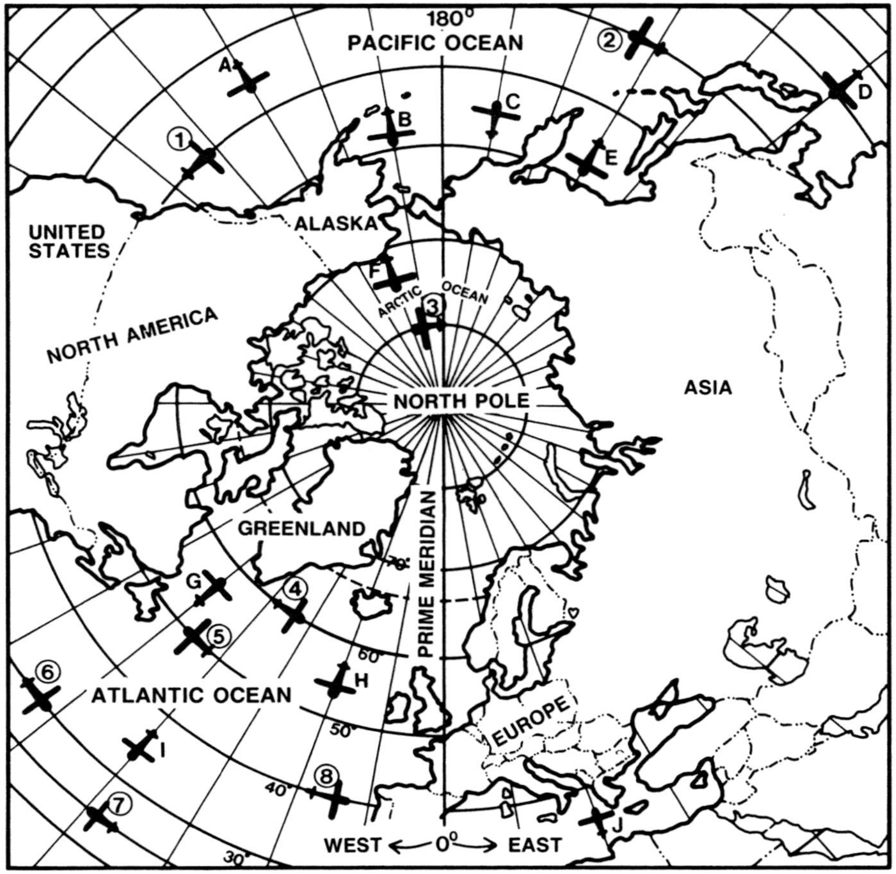

3. Which airplane is farthest south?

A or B _____   H or I _____
F or E _____   D or H _____

4. Which airplane is farthest west?

1 or G _____   A or 6 _____
I or J _____   G or I _____

More Reading and Interpreting Maps:
Flying Over the Polar Regions

Background

Seventy-five years ago, if you were traveling to Tokyo, Japan, from Washington, D.C., it is most likely that you would have traveled by train to the west coast and then embarked on a long sea voyage over the Pacific Ocean to the shores of Japan. In today's world, the vast majority of travelers between the two cities fly a Great Circle route—that is, a route that takes them over Alaska and across the North Pacific Ocean.

Unfortunately, many of the maps used in classrooms today help instill erroneous ideas about travel routes. The Mercator map, for example, with its east–west orientation, is one of the worst offenders in the matter of travel routes. Ask typical young learners to trace on a Mercator map the route from Washington to Tokyo and they will draw a straight line between the two points. They will do this because it is the most apparent way to go.

Student Involvement

1. Demonstrate on a globe the Great Circle route to Tokyo from Washington, as follows:

a. Stretch a string taut between the points that mark the two cities. Affix the string to the globe with small pieces of tape. The route shown by the string is the Great Circle route. Point out the places one would fly over if the route were followed.

b. A north polar map such as the one in the student exercise will also accurately show Great Circle routes. Simply draw a line from the point of departure to the point of arrival.

c. Point out on the exercise map that a plane traveling along either the Great Circle route or the alternate route will not make a direct flight between the two cities because it must stop for refueling. On a globe, a Great Circle route is the shortest distance between two points. Also, Great Circle routes that bring United States airplanes over the Soviet Union are not strictly followed because of airspace restrictions imposed by the Soviet Union.

2. Contrast the Great Circle route to Calcutta with the land–sea route to that city from Washington, D.C.

Answers to the Exercise

1. 3,350 miles; 3,500 miles; 6,850 miles
2. 8,900 miles; 2,050 miles
3. Arctic

Name _____   Date _____

FLYING OVER THE POLAR REGIONS

The polar map above shows the route an airplane could take when flying from Washington, D.C., to Tokyo, Japan. The route is called a *Great Circle* route. When planes are flying between continents, Great Circle routes can save them hundreds of miles of flight and hours of time.

1. According to the polar map, what is the flight distance from Washington, D.C., to

Anchorage, Alaska? _____

from Anchorage to Tokyo, Japan? _____
    What is the total distance between Washington and Tokyo? _____

ington and Tokyo? _____

2. It is possible to fly west from Washington, D.C., over the Pacific Ocean to Tokyo. The route is shown on the map.
    The first part of the flight, from Washington to Honolulu, Hawaii, is about 5,000 miles. The second part of the flight, from Honolulu to Tokyo, is about 3,900 miles. What is the total distance of the flight?_____
    How many miles are saved by flying the

Great Circle route? _____

3. Draw on the polar map the route an airplane would take to go from Washington, D.C., directly to Calcutta, India. Over what

ocean would it fly?_____

More Reading and Interpreting Diagrams:
The Four Seasons

Background

Because many students experience difficulty grasping earth–sun relationships, the step-by-step procedure outlined below should prove helpful to their understanding.

1. *Directions to students:* Title Diagram 1 "Summer in the Northern Hemisphere." Title Diagram 2 "Summer in the Southern Hemisphere."

Explain: "When it is summer in the Northern Hemisphere, it is winter in the Southern Hemisphere. After you complete this exercise, you will better understand why this is so."

2. *Read and Demonstrate (RD):* "It takes 365¼ days (one year) for the earth to revolve around the sun. Diagrams 1 and 2 show a half revolution, which is about 183 days, or 6 months."

Directions to Students (DS): Write "183 days—6 months" on Line A, which shows the direction of the earth's revolution.

3. *RD:* "The tilt of the earth (23½ degrees) remains the same as the earth revolves around the sun."

DS: Write "Constant tilt" on the dashed lines labeled C in the two diagrams. Each dashed line represents the earth's axis.

4. *RD:* "In our summer, the Northern Hemisphere tilts toward the sun."

DS: Write "Northern Hemisphere tilts toward the sun" on the line below the title of Diagram 1.

5. *RD:* "In our winter, the Northern Hemisphere tilts away from the sun."

DS: Write "Northern Hemisphere tilts away from the sun" below the title of Diagram 2.

6. *RD:* "When the Northern Hemisphere has summer, the sun's rays strike the earth directly. The concentration of the rays in a small area makes it hot."

DS: Write "Direct rays" on the lines labeled D in Diagram 1.

7. *RD:* "When the Northern Hemisphere has summer, the sun's rays strike indirectly on the Southern Hemisphere, as shown in Diagram 1. Because the rays glance off the earth's surface, their effect is not as great. This makes for cold and winter in the Southern Hemisphere."

DS: Write "Indirect rays" on lines labeled E.

8. *RD:* "In Diagram 2, the earth has revolved halfway around the sun. The Northern Hemisphere is tilted away from the sun, and the Southern Hemisphere is now getting direct rays."

DS: Write "Direct rays" on lines labeled F. Ask: "In Diagram 2, which hemisphere is receiving indirect rays?" (Northern Hemisphere.) Write "Indirect rays" on lines labeled G.

9. *RD:* "The diagram at the bottom of the page shows the earth's position in all four seasons. Notice the constant tilt of the earth's axis, the direct sun rays of summer, and the indirect rays of winter."

Name ______________________ Date ______________________

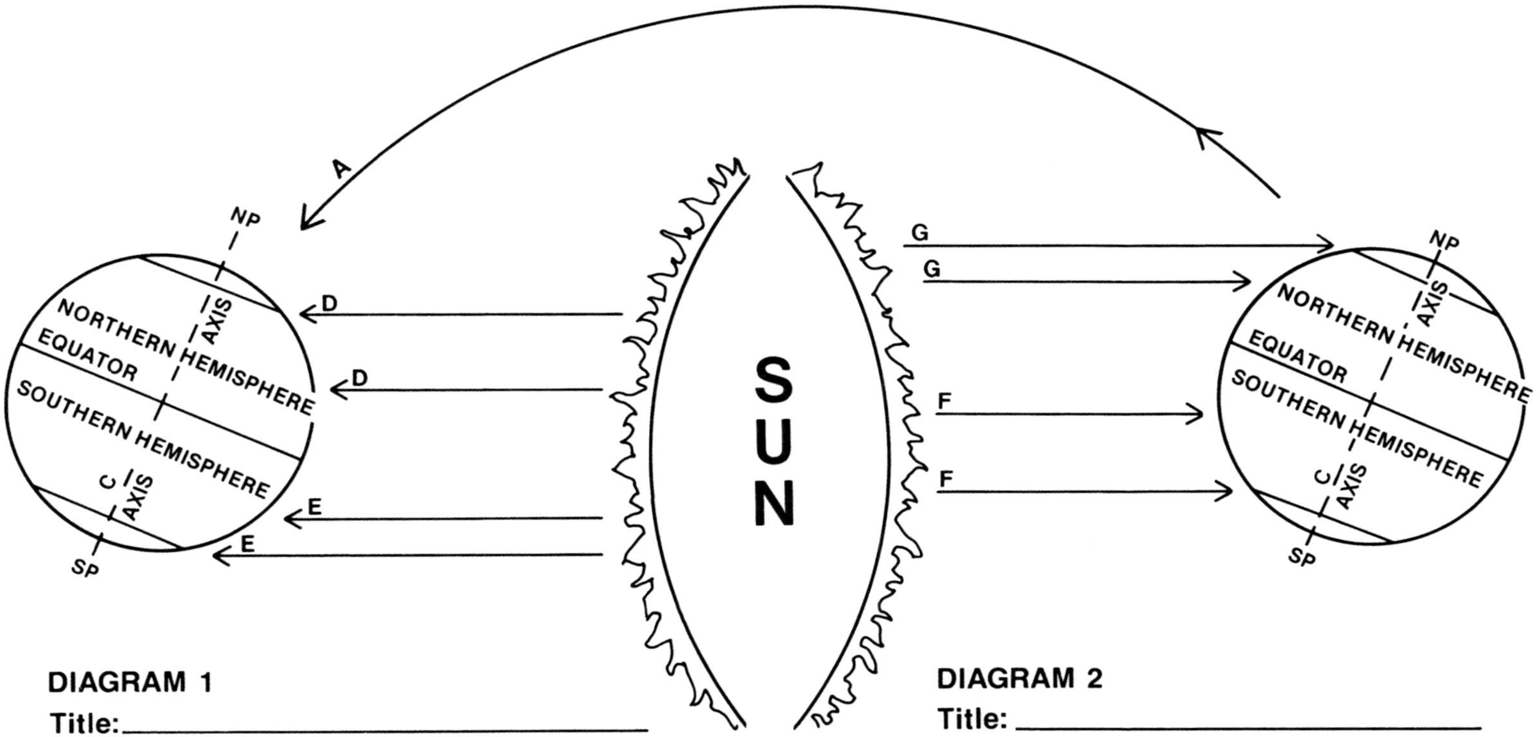

A
NP
AXIS
NORTHERN HEMISPHERE
EQUATOR
SOUTHERN HEMISPHERE
C
AXIS
SP
D
D
E
E
SUN
G
G
F
F
NP
AXIS
NORTHERN HEMISPHERE
EQUATOR
SOUTHERN HEMISPHERE
C
AXIS
SP

DIAGRAM 1
Title: ______________________

DIAGRAM 2
Title: ______________________

THE FOUR SEASONS

The diagram on the right shows the position of the earth in relation to the sun in the four seasons of the year. When the Northern Hemisphere is tilted toward the sun, the Arctic has six months of light and the Antarctic has six months of darkness. The reverse is true when the Northern Hemisphere is tilted away from the sun.

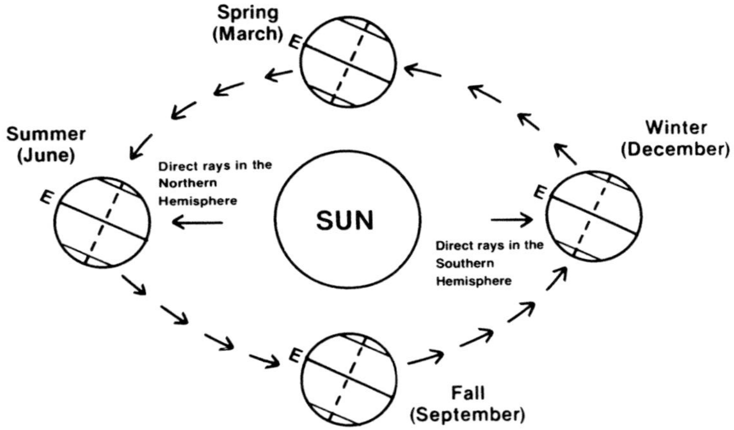

Spring
(March)
Summer
(June)
Winter
(December)
Fall
(September)
SUN
Direct rays in the Northern Hemisphere
Direct rays in the Southern Hemisphere
E
E
E
E

More Reading and Interpreting Maps: Using a Scale of Miles to Find Air Distance

Background

1. The air distance and the overland distance to the same destination are quite different. The air distance is invariably shorter. Air distances convey a more accurate understanding of distance relationships. To be completely realistic, both air distances and road distances should be thought of in terms of time: "How long does it take to get there?"

2. Many travelers find distances to destinations by using an "air distance table." However, there are occasions when the relevant air distance table cannot be found.

3. This activity is designed not only to help learners find air distances by using a scale, but also to provide them with an opportunity to organize map data into a table.

4. The learner exercise on the facing page requires twenty-five active responses relative to distances in the United States. The result should be not only increased skill in using the distance gauge, but also enhanced understanding of distance relationships in the United States.

Student Involvement

1. Distribute the facing page and a blank piece of paper to each student.

2. Put a corner of the paper on the dot that locates the city.

3. Make a mark on the edge of the paper where it touches the dot for the other city.

4. Lay the paper along the scale of miles at the top of the map and read the distance where the mark meets the scale.

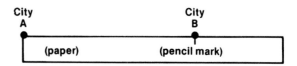

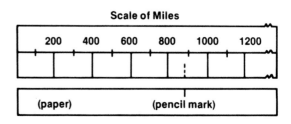

City A is 890 miles distant by air from B. Note: Explain that it is sometimes necessary to estimate distances if the mark falls between numbers on the scale.

5. To enter the distance from Chicago to Salt Lake City (1,240 miles), first find Chicago on the vertical axis. Then find Salt Lake City on the horizontal axis. The cell where the two axes intersect is the space where the student should write the distance.

Answers to the Exercise

Boston: 1,350, 2,450, 1,000, 2,060, 410
Chicago: 825, 1,700, 240, 1,240, 610
Los Angeles: 1,650, 960, 1,550, 550, 2,350
Miami: 650, 2,700, 1,050, 2,040, 880
Pierre: 1,175, 1,050, 675, 600, 1,300

Name _____   **Date** _____

USING A SCALE OF MILES TO FIND AIR DISTANCE

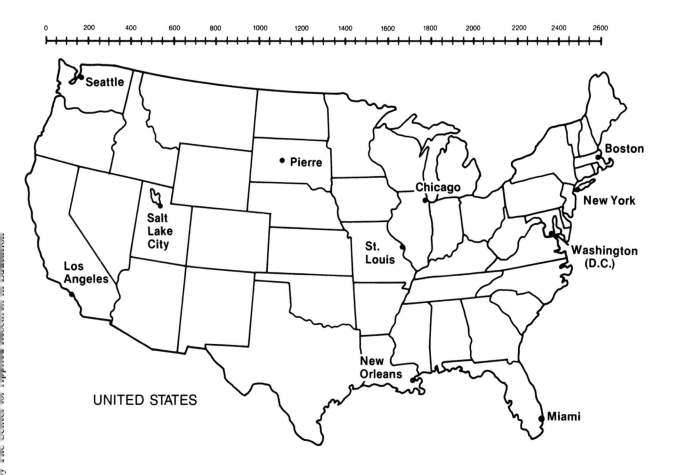

Cities	New Orleans, LA	Seattle, WA	St. Louis, MO	Salt Lake City, UT	Washington, D.C.
Boston, MA					
Chicago, IL					
Los Angeles, CA					
Miami, FL					
Pierre, SD					

More Reading and Interpreting Maps: Rivers and River Systems

Background

1. Possibly no geographic feature has played a more important part in shaping human destiny than rivers. Rivers have acted as either barriers or aids in war, transportation, and settlement. One has only to think of the part played by the Rhine River as the last obstacle to the invasion of Germany in World War II, or the use of the St. Lawrence River as a natural highway into the interior of North America, to realize the multiple roles that rivers have played.

2. Rivers can reveal much about elevation and land slope. Many students do not understand that rivers flow downhill from interior elevations. This leads to another common misunderstanding—the notion that rivers cannot flow north. This belief comes about because north is equated with *up*. Those who hold this idea think that the Nile River, for example, flows from the Mediterranean Sea to the interior mountains.

3. Rivers determine the boundaries of nations and the locations of cities. As sources of water for human use—drinking, washing, manufacturing, irrigation, hydroelectric power—rivers have no equal.

Student Involvement

1. Present and illustrate as much of the foregoing as seems appropriate.

2. Present and discuss the technical terms listed below. Notice that the terms are numbered. Students may write brief definitions of the terms on their exercise page.

3. Students write the correct technical terms in the blank boxes on the map. For example, *Tributary* is written wherever (2) appears on the map; *Mouth* wherever (3) appears, and so on.

4. Have the students respond to the questions at the bottom of the page. Discuss the answers.

5. Frequently reinforce the acquired understandings and skills in subsequent lessons.

Terms Associated with Rivers

(1) *River systems:* all the secondary rivers and streams that contribute to a main river.

(2) *Tributary:* a stream that flows into a larger stream.

(3) *Mouth:* the place where a river empties into another river, a lake, or the ocean.

(4) *Source:* the place where a river begins.

(5) *Upstream:* against the current.

(6) *Downstream:* with the current.

(7) *Confluence:* the place where two rivers meet to form one river.

(8) *Delta:* soil deposited at the mouth of a river.

Answers to the Exercise

1. South; west
2a. A   b. D   c. C   d. A
3. Seven
4. [Check for arrow pointing north.]

Name

Date

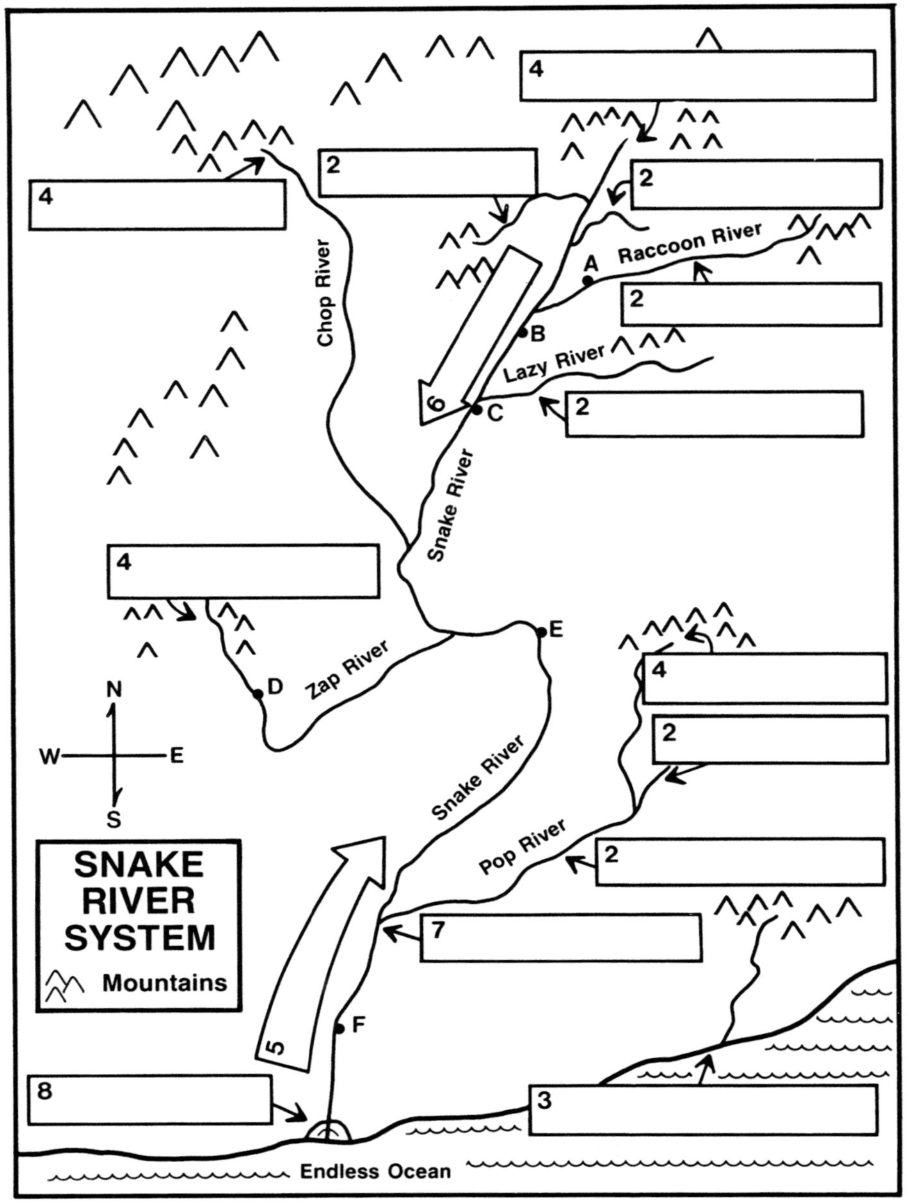

RIVERS AND RIVER SYSTEMS

River Vocabulary

1. River system: _____

2. Tributary: _____

3. Mouth: _____

4. Source: _____

5. Upstream: _____

6. Downstream: _____

7. Confluence: _____

8. Delta: _____

1. In what general direction does the Snake River flow? _____

2. Which has the higher elevation: _____ Raccoon River?
   a. A or B? _____   c. C or F? _____
   b. D or E? _____   d. A, B, or F? _____

3. How many tributaries are there to the Snake River? _____

4. Draw an arrow that points *upstream* next to the Chop River.

SNAKE RIVER SYSTEM

^^ Mountains

Raccoon River

Lazy River

Snake River

Chop River

Zap River

Pop River

Snake River

Endless Ocean

A
B
C
D
E
F

N W E S

More Reading and Interpreting Diagrams:
Understanding Altitude

Background

Elevation, or altitude, is the distance in feet or miles that a place is above or below sea level. Here are some interesting facts about altitude.

1. All altitudes are measured from sea level. But the level of the sea changes as tides come and go. In some places there can be as much as a 30-foot difference between low tide and high tide. *Sea level* as used in expressions of altitude means the average between low and high tide.

2. Some places on the earth are below sea level. Ocean water doesn't flood these places because they are surrounded by high land that dams out the sea. The Dead Sea, for example, is 1,290 feet below sea level.

3. As one goes higher in the atmosphere, there is less air. Thus, it is extremely difficult to breathe at high altitudes such as the summit of Mount Everest, which is 29,028 feet high.

4. Temperature decreases as altitude increases. As a rule of thumb, the temperature drops 3 degrees for every 1,000-foot increase in altitude. At 20,000 feet, the temperature may be zero, but in the valley below it may be 60 degrees.

5. Altitude exerts a great influence on crops and natural vegetation. Even on the equator, trees will not grow above an altitude of 10,000 feet. Potatoes and hardy grains such as barley, oats, and rye will grow at the 10,000-foot level in highlands along the equator, for example, the high plains of Bolivia.

Student Involvement

1. The diagram on the facing page shows that altitude is the distance from sea level up to an imaginary line drawn parallel to the sea from a point on the land.

2. Explain that the diagram shows a modified cross section of land and ocean. It is as though a cake were sliced through and the layers and filling were exposed.

3. After communicating as many of the facts outlined above as seem appropriate for your group, have your students complete the exercise on the facing page.

Answers to the Exercise

1a. 14,000' b. 1,000' c. About 300' below sea level d. About 1,500' e. About 7,200' f. 12,000' g. 6,000' h. About 7,200'

2. About 1,000'

3. 2,000'

4a. 10,000' b. 9,000'

5. About 1,000'

6. About 5,000'

7. [Look for scattered clouds in the 2,000'–6000' areas. Note: Cumulus clouds range from near the surface to about 6,500'.]

8. [Look for a row of trees along the 10,000-foot line. "Spruce" trees have been designated because they are non-deciduous.]

Name —————————

Date —————————

UNDERSTANDING ALTITUDE

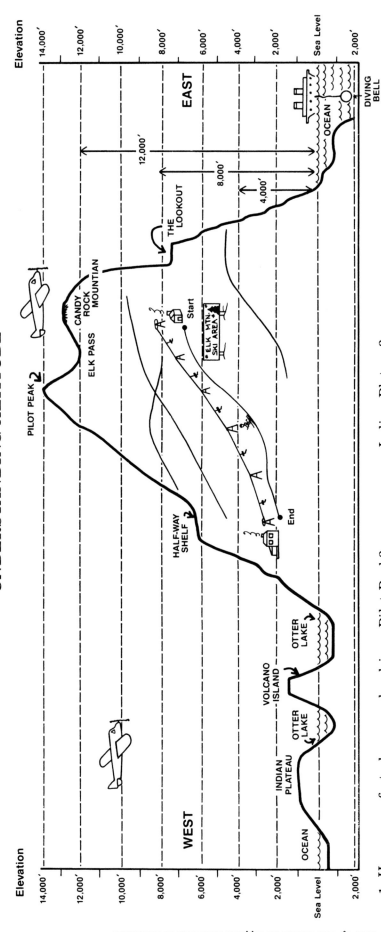

1. How many feet above sea level is a. Pilot Peak? ————
b. Indian Plateau? ———— c. the surface of Otter Lake? ————
d. the top of Volcano Island? ———— e. the top of
Candy Rock Mountain? ———— f. Elk Pass? ———— g. Half-
Way Shelf? ———— h. the Lookout? ————

2. How many feet of space below sea level is the bottom of
Otter Lake? ————

3. Notice the ship on the east side of the diagram. How far
below sea level would a diving bell descend from the ship before
reaching the ocean floor? ————

4a. What is the *sea level* altitude of the airplane flying over
Indian Plateau? ————
b. What is its *overland* altitude? ————

5. How many feet are there between Candy Rock Mountain
and the airplane above it? ————

6. Notice the Elk Mountain Ski Area. What is the "drop" in
feet of the ski run? ————

7. Draw some cumulus clouds (🌥) in the space
between 2,000 feet and 6,000 feet.

8. Trees do not usually grow above 10,000 feet. The place
where the trees stop growing is called the *Tree Line.* Show a line
of spruce trees (🌲) on the 10,000-foot line of the mountain.

More Reading and Interpreting Diagrams: Using Color to Show Altitude or Elevation

Background

1. One way to show elevation on maps is through the use of color. As the diagram shows, shades of green indicate the lower elevations. "Greens" are topped by "yellows," "browns," and "reds." Each of the major colors may be subdivided into various shades; for example, light green for elevations from 0 feet to 500 feet and darker green for elevations from 500 feet to 1000 feet.

2. The colors used to designate elevations are standardized. Sometimes, however, nonstandard colors are used. In such cases, reference to the map legend is necessary for proper interpretation.

3. A significant limitation of color representation of elevation is that some hills and depressions may not be shown within a colored area. For example, a large area encompassing several thousand square miles could be shown completely red (10,000 feet or more) but could still contain deep valleys with floors less than 10,000 feet above sea level. Also, there may be mountain peaks in the region as high as 25,000 feet.

Student Involvement

1. Explain and illustrate each of the points made in the foregoing section. Then, for greater depth of understanding among your students, the following demonstration is suggested:

a. Mold clay over a bowl that has considerable incline on its sides

(This: ⛿ not this: ⛾).

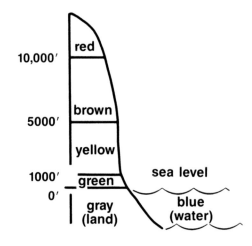

b. Color the sides of the bowl with successive layers of gray, green, yellow, and red, as in the diagram at the top of the first column.

c. Place the bowl right side up and explain that the bowl represents a mountain.

d. Use a broad-point pen to write the various elevations on the layers.

e. Make a drawing of the bowl on the board, but make it look like a mountain, and write the various elevations on the layers.

2. Explain the exercise on the facing page, being sure to give special instructions if hatching rather than coloring must be used.

Answers to the Exercise

1. [Check their maps for proper completion. Make sure that the "airspace" between the land and water masses is not filled in.]

2. [Check your students' maps for correct coloration or hatching.]

3a. Red   b. Gray   c. Green   d. Brown

Name _____

Date _____

USING COLOR TO SHOW ALTITUDE OR ELEVATION

COLORS AND THE ELEVATIONS THEY SHOW

ELEVATION	COLOR	HATCHING
10,000'	Red	(cross-hatch)
5,000' to 10,000'	Brown	(wavy)
1,000' to 5,000'	Yellow	(grid)
0' to 1,000'	Green	(brick)
Land below Sea Level	Gray	(pencil)
Water below Sea Level	Blue	(ball point)

3. Some places and their elevations are listed below. On the lines next to the places, tell what color they would be on a map.

a. Mount Whitney (California)   14,494' _____

b. Death Valley (California)   − 282' _____

c. Chicago* (Illinois)   672' _____

d. Denver* (Colorado)   5,470' _____

*Highest elevation

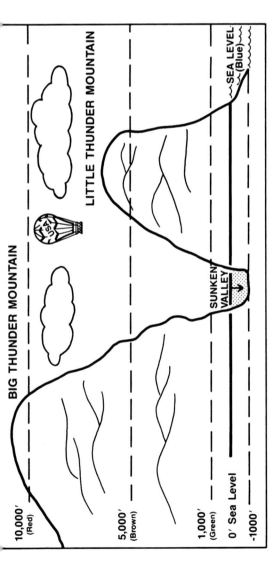

BIG THUNDER MOUNTAIN

LITTLE THUNDER MOUNTAIN

SUNKEN VALLEY

SEA LEVEL (Blue)

10,000' (Red)

5,000' (Brown)

1,000' (Green)

0' Sea Level

-1000'

1. Color the land and water in the map-diagram above as shown in the color key. Notice that *Sunken Valley*, which is below sea level, has already been darkened. Note: If you do not have crayons, use the substitutes for color shown in the key.

10,000' _____

5,000' _____

1,000' _____

0' SEA LEVEL _____

-1,000' _____

2. In the space above, draw your own land and sea profile. Include land at all levels, land below sea level, and some ocean water. Color all the land and water. Use the color key at the top of the page. As in Part 1 above, substitute for color if you do not have crayons.

More Reading and Interpreting Maps:
Determining Elevation on Flat Maps Through Color

Background

1. It is relatively easy to visualize elevation when it is shown in cross-section, as was done in the preceding activity. However, visualizing elevation on flat maps is much more difficult. This is because one is looking down at a two-dimensional map, yet elevation by its nature is three-dimensional.

Some students are able to quickly perceive the relationships between symbols for elevation and reality. Others require considerable explanation and illustration before true understanding comes about. In any case, all students should benefit from the following procedure for demonstrating elevation as symbolized by color.

Directions for making a three-dimensional model:

—Obtain four pieces of board with the following dimensions:

    1 pc. @ 1″ × 8″ × 12″ (green)
    1 pc. @ 1″ × 6″ × 10″ (yellow)
    1 pc. @ 1″ × 4″ × 8″ (brown)
    1 pc. @ 1″ × 2″ × 4″ (red)

—Paint the boards as indicated in the parentheses above.
—Glue or nail the pieces together to make a pyramid.
—Your finished model should look like the diagram that follows:

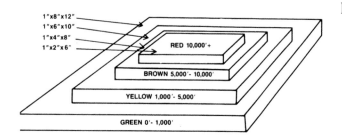

Note: As an alternative to using wood, jar lids of varying diameters can be painted and glued one on top of the other, as with boards. In some respects, this procedure

results in a better model, because the round layers appear to be more natural.

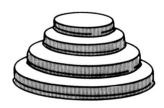

2. Show the model from a side view; then show it from an "aerial" view. By looking down on the model, one gets the same visual impression that a flat map would give.

3. After showing the model, make a drawing on the chalkboard. Color the drawing appropriately and write in the elevations.

Student Involvement

If colored crayons are not available, substitute hatching for color, as follows:

Answers to the Exercise

1. [Check for appropriate coloring or hatching.]
2. 5,000–10,000 feet
3. 1,000–5,000 feet
4. Sea level–1,000 feet

DETERMINING ELEVATION ON
FLAT MAPS THROUGH COLOR

1. The map is an uncompleted elevation or altitude map of Jugoland, a make-believe country.

The numbers on the map tell the elevation of the land. You can find what elevations the numbers represent by looking in the key of the map.

Color the land represented on the map according to the numbers in the key.

Color the water light blue.

2. What is the elevation of the land at the source, or beginning, of the Rocky River?

3. What is the elevation of the land at the source of the Park River?

4. What is the elevation of the land where the Park River joins the Rocky River?

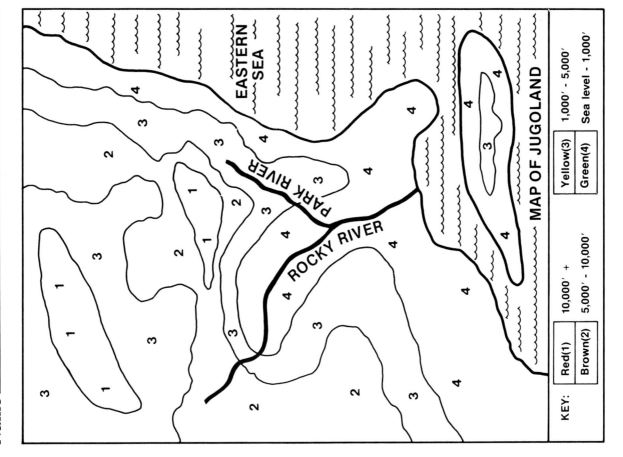

EASTERN SEA

PARK RIVER

ROCKY RIVER

MAP OF JUGOLAND

KEY:

Red(1)	10,000' +	
Brown(2)	5,000' - 10,000'	
Yellow(3)	1,000' - 5,000'	
Green(4)	Sea level - 1,000'	

More Reading and Interpreting Maps: Determining Elevation from Contour Lines

Background

1. What is a contour line? Simply stated, it is an imaginary line on land on which every point is the same height above sea level.

2. Consider the ocean coastline as the zero-foot contour line, as shown in the diagram below. The next contour line has *20'* printed on it. This means that everything on the line is 20 feet above sea level.

3. Every fifth line has its elevation printed on it, and the printing on that line is heavier than on the other four lines.

4. The distance between contour lines is called the *contour interval*. All maps that show contour lines will state the contour interval somewhere on the map.

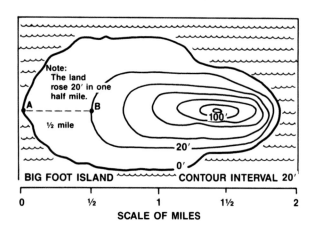

BIG FOOT ISLAND **CONTOUR INTERVAL 20'**

0   ½   1   1½   2
SCALE OF MILES

5. The scale of miles on the next diagram shows that the island is 2 miles long. The dotted line from point A on the coast to point B on the second contour line represents a distance of one-half mile. Thus, the land rises 20 feet in one-half mile.

6. The diagram in the next column is a side view of Big Foot Island. Notice that the left side of the island shows a gradual slope, whereas the right side shows a steep slope.

7. The gradual slope is portrayed on the map in the first column by contour lines that are widely separated. The steep slope is portrayed by lines that are much closer together.

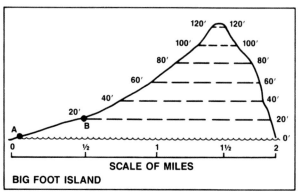

BIG FOOT ISLAND

0   ½   1   1½   2
SCALE OF MILES

Student Involvement

1. Explain contour lines and contour intervals. Sketch the two diagrams on the board.

2. Have your students complete the contour map on the facing page.

Answers to the Exercise

1. Lines should be numbered from 1,000' as follows: 1,020', 1,040', 1,060', 1,080', 1,100'

2. A to B

3. 2 miles

4*a.* 1,020 *b.* 1,040 *c.* 1,080 *d.* Between 1,100 and 1,119 *e.* 1,040 *f.* 1,020 *g.* Between 1,000 and 1,019

5. Four

Name _____ Date _____

DETERMINING ELEVATION FROM CONTOUR LINES

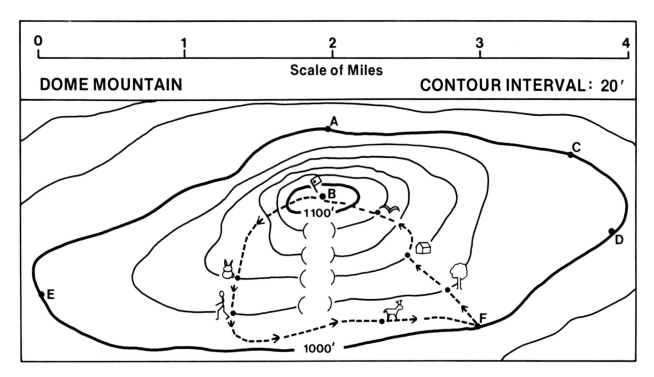

DOME MOUNTAIN   Scale of Miles   CONTOUR INTERVAL: 20'

1. Most contour maps have elevations printed on every fifth line, as in the map above. However, to understand contour maps better, print the elevation of each contour line in the parentheses on the lines.

2. When contour lines are close together, the slope is steep. With this in mind, can you tell which is the steepest climb to the top of the mountain?

_____ A to B   _____ D to B

_____ C to B   _____ E to B

3. Approximately how many miles is the climb to the top of the mountain from D?

_____ 1 mile   _____ 2½ miles

_____ 2 miles   _____ 3 miles

4. Notice the dotted line starting from F. The line shows the path that Beth and Sue took to the top of the mountain and down again. At what elevation in feet did they meet each of the following things? Note: The dot next to the thing shows the actual location of the thing.

Thing		*Elevation*
a. Oak tree		_____
b. Cabin		_____
c. Eagle		_____
d. Flag		_____
e. Rabbit		_____
f. Hiker		_____
g. Deer		_____

5. About how many miles did Beth and Sue walk?

_____ 2   _____ 4

_____ 3   _____ 5

More Reading and Interpreting Maps:
Finding Man-made Things on Topographical Maps

Background

A topographical map is one that, through the use of standardized symbols, shows all the man-made (cultural) and natural (physical) features of a given area. Topographical maps are useful for several reasons:

1. The scale of the maps is such that a relatively small area is shown in great detail. This allows the map to show features such as houses that were in existence at the time the map was made. Caution: Features may be shown on the map that no longer exist, such as a house destroyed by fire.

2. The elevations of places shown on the map are readily determined by contour lines. Also, the elevations of prominent places are stated on the map.

3. Man-made features such as buildings, pipelines, and bridges are printed in black so that they can be easily located and identified.

4. Natural land and water features are shown in color: blue for water, brown for land shapes, green for vegetation, red for special emphasis on certain man-made features.

5. Lines of latitude and longitude are indicated in the margins of the map.

6. The magnetic declination of the mapped area is printed on the map.

7. North is always at the top of topographical maps. Caution: Students should realize that not all maps show north at the top. For example, polar projections show north at the center of the map.

The map on the facing page is part of a larger topographical map. The lack of color limits its usefulness because features such as orchards, forests, and water are not shown. Nevertheless, a black and white topographical map still offers a great amount of data to the perceptive observer.

Student Involvement

1. If you have a topographical map in its entirety, show it to the students. If not, point out that an original map would have various colors.

2. Describe or illustrate what the symbols look like in actuality before students start to work independently; for example, "A trail is a walking path through woods, fields, and mountains." Notice that in the map key more than one symbol may be shown on a line; for instance, the line for buildings shows that they are designated either as "dwellings" (all black) or as "place of employment" (dots within an outline of the structure).

Answers to the Exercise

1. Checked: church, cemetery, houses
2. Three
3. No
4. Forty
5. Single track
6. Three
7. Power transmission line
8. Barns
9. Two

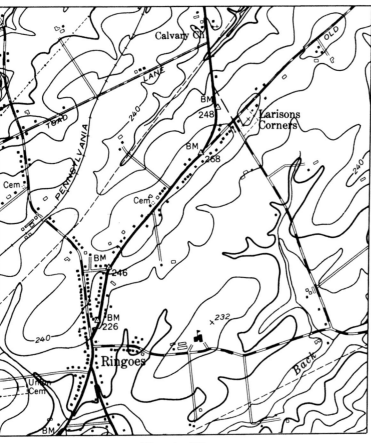

Key to Map

Hard surface, heavy duty road, four or more lanes	▬▬▬
Hard surface, heavy duty road, two or three lanes	━━━
Hard surface, medium duty road, four or more lanes	▬□▬
Hard surface, medium duty road, two or three lanes	═══
Improved light duty road	═══
Unimproved dirt road—Trail	========= -----
Dual highway, dividing strip 25 feet or less	═══
Dual highway, dividing strip exceeding 25 feet	═══
Road under construction	=======
Railroad: single track—multiple track	┼┼┼┼ / ┼┼┼┼
Buildings (dwelling, place of employment, etc.)	▪■▢
School—Church—Cemeteries	♠ ⊞ Cem
Buildings (barn, warehouse, etc.)	▫▭▨▨
Power transmission line	·—·—·—
Telephone line, pipeline, etc. (labeled as to type)	━ ━ ━
Wells other than water (labeled as to type)	○Oil ○Gas
Tanks; oil, water, etc. (labeled as to type)	•●⊘Water
Located or landmark object—Windmill	○ ☓
Open pit, mine, or quarry—Prospect	⚒ x
Shaft—Tunnel entrance	▪ Y

Name _____

Date _____

FINDING MAN-MADE THINGS ON TOPOGRAPHICAL MAPS

Note: Be sure to refer to the map key for help in understanding the symbols.

1. Check the things that can be found close to or at Larisons Corners.

_____ railroad   _____ mine

_____ cemetery   _____ church

_____ barns   _____ houses

2. How many cemeteries are shown on the map?

_____ 1 _____ 2 _____ 3 _____ 4

3. Is the road in front of the school designed to carry four lanes of traffic?

_____ Yes   _____ No

4. Suppose that there was an average of five people in each house on Toad Lane. How many people live on the road? _____

5. What kind of railroad line is shown in the northwest part of the map?

_____single track _____multiple track

6. How many churches are shown on the map?_____

7. Find the line in the northwest part of the map that looks like this: •- - - -•- - What does the line show?

_____

8. Suppose that you were in a classroom on the west side of the school. What kind of buildings would you see closest to the school?

_____

9. How many roads does the Pennsylvania Railroad cross? _____

More Reading and Interpreting Maps:
Locating Unnamed Places on Topographical Maps

Background

One purpose for which topographical maps are used is to help people walk "cross-country" to a known but unlabeled destination such as a crossroad.

Those who use topographical maps have developed a unique and simple way to locate unnamed destinations. They use place names printed on the map as starting points for locating other places. Once a starting place name has been established, two other map-reading skills—finding direction and finding distance—come into play. However, distances are measured in inches with rulers.

The following is an example of how the technique works:

Suppose that several people are to meet at a certain place. Let's assume that the place is Point A on the map below. How can everyone know the location of the place? Steps to follow:

1. Find the printed word that is nearest to the place. In this example, the word is TAN.

2. Find the letter of the word that is nearest to the place. In this example, it is the letter N in TAN.

3. Measure with a ruler the distance from the bottom of the N in TAN to A. The distance is almost 1⅛ inches. (Round distances to the nearest ⅛- or ¼-inch.)

4. Determine the direction that Point A

is from the N. In this example, the direction is southeast.

5. The full description of point A may be written in the following manner: Point A is at the Transmission Line–Road Crossing, 1⅛ inches southeast of the N in TAN.

(Abbreviations may be used: e.g., SE for southeast, Tran L for Transmission Line, etc.)

Student Involvement

Explain the need for locating unnamed places on topographical maps. Illustrate the procedure for locating unnamed places by completing with the students the first example on the facing page.

Answers to the Exercise

1. Road T
2. Pond
3. Bend in trail
4. Road Y
5. Road end
6. Building
7. ¼ inch SW of the E in EAST
8. 2 inches NE of the e in Wertsville
9. ¾ inch W of the k in Brook
10. 1½ inches S of the e in Wertsville

[Note: Accept ¼-inch differences in the measurements for Items 7–10.]

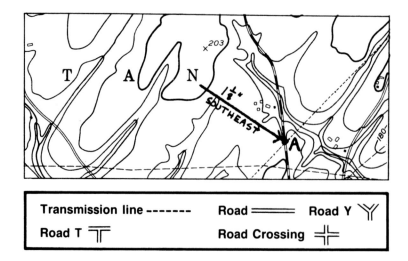

Transmission line -------   Road ═════   Road Y

Road T   Road Crossing

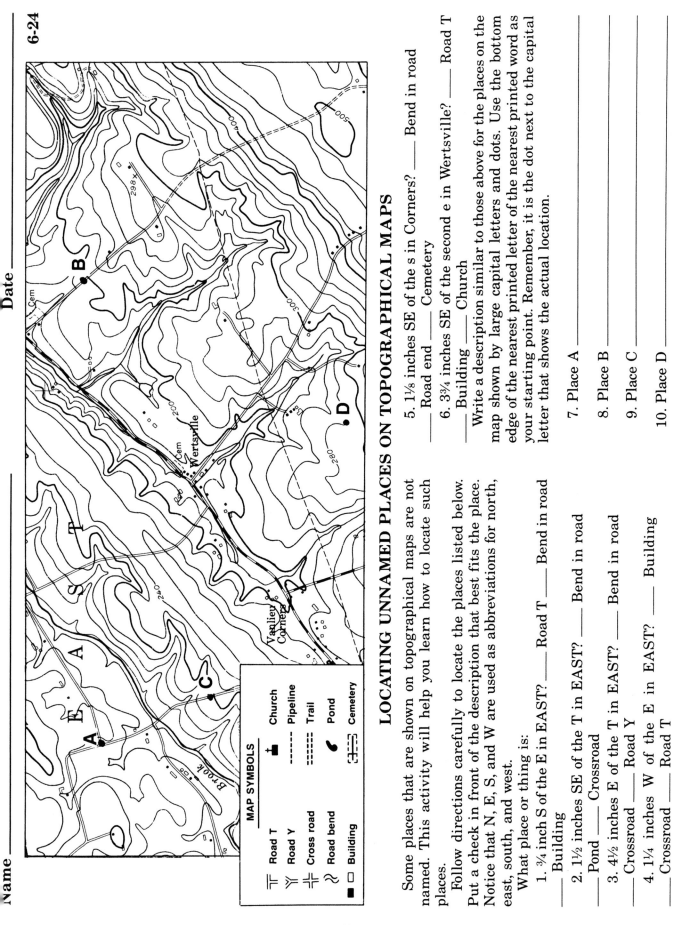

MAP SYMBOLS

丅 Road T	⬛ Church		
丫 Road Y	----- Pipeline		
十 Cross road	∷∷ Trail		
≈ Road bend	✎ Pond		
■ □ Building	▥▤ Cemetery		

LOCATING UNNAMED PLACES ON TOPOGRAPHICAL MAPS

Some places that are shown on topographical maps are not named. This activity will help you learn how to locate such places.

Follow directions carefully to locate the places listed below. Put a check in front of the description that best fits the place. Notice that N, E, S, and W are used as abbreviations for north, east, south, and west.

What place or thing is:

1. ¾ inch S of the E in EAST? ____ Road T ____ Bend in road ____ Building

2. 1½ inches SE of the T in EAST? ____ Bend in road ____ Pond ____ Crossroad

3. 4½ inches E of the T in EAST? ____ Bend in road ____ Crossroad ____ Road Y

4. 1¼ inches W of the E in EAST? ____ Building ____ Crossroad ____ Road T

5. 1⅛ inches SE of the s in Corners? ____ Bend in road ____ Road end ____ Cemetery

6. 3¾ inches SE of the second e in Wertsville? ____ Road T ____ Building ____ Church

Write a description similar to those above for the places on the map shown by large capital letters and dots. Use the bottom edge of the nearest printed letter of the nearest printed word as your starting point. Remember, it is the dot next to the capital letter that shows the actual location.

7. Place A _____

8. Place B _____

9. Place C _____

10. Place D _____

More Reading and Interpreting Maps:
Taking a Walk with a Topographical Map

Background

The map on the facing page is a portion of a larger map called a *quadrangle*. A quadrangle is one of many that are required to map an entire state. For example, it takes 165 quadrangles to map New Jersey. Large states such as Texas require many more quadrangles. The figure to the right shows only one of New Jersey's quadrangles.

It would be useful to have topographical maps of the area where one teaches. Here is how the maps are obtained:

1. Write to the Map Information Office, Geological Survey, Washington, D.C., 20242.

2. Ask for the "Index to Topographic Maps" for your state.

3. The index you receive will help you easily find the name of the topographical map in which you are interested.

4. Complete the order blank and send it to the address above.

Student Involvement

1. Explain that topographical maps are useful for helping hikers plan their hikes. Scrutiny of a map can reveal what will be encountered before the excursion begins. Terrain, water features, roads, trails, distances, and direction are easily read from the map symbols.

2. Discuss the map on the facing page. Point out the symbols in the map key, the

NEW JERSEY

QUADRANGLE LOCATION

main road running in a general northwest direction, the Neshanic River (blue on the original map, but shown black because of reproduction limitations), the contour lines, and the hill summit elevations (shown by an X followed by a number).

3. Encourage your students to visualize the symbols on the map. Can they "see" the houses and barns, the land rising or falling to their left and right, a small village of perhaps one hundred people, a church, a crossroad, and the river? If their concepts of country roads, houses, and so on are limited, describe them and show pictures.

4. After the exercise is completed, your students may want to devise their own "walks."

Answers to the Exercise

These answers are given in the order in which they appear in the story:

1st Paragraph: East, road 239 feet + crossing, northeast, church, east

2nd Paragraph: 140 feet, downhill

3rd Paragraph: Northwest, house

4th Paragraph: Steep, 4

TAKING A WALK WITH A TOPOGRAPHICAL MAP

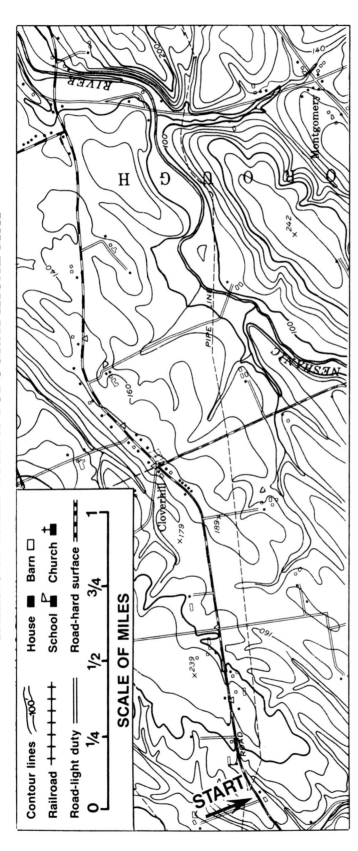

SCALE OF MILES

Contour lines 〰100〰 House ■ Barn □
Railroad +++++++ School ⌂ Church ✚
Road-light duty ═══ Road-hard surface ▪▪▪▪

0   ¼   ½   ¾   1

As you read the story below, study the map. Underline the words or figures in parentheses that best complete the sentences. Start the walk where it says START on the map.

At the start of our walk we are walking (east, west). One-eighth of a mile down the road, we look to our left and we see a (road, railroad). We walk about one-quarter of a mile further and to the north we see a hill. The elevation of the hill is (239 feet, 179 feet). We continue and soon we come to a (Y crossing, T crossing, + crossing). When we reach the first bend in the road we begin to walk (northwest, southeast, northeast). As we walk through a small town called Cloverhill, we see a (church, school). We continue walking until the road bends again. Now we are walking (east, west).

At Point A on the map, we wonder what our elevation is. We follow the contour line with our finger and see that we are (130 feet, 140 feet) above sea level. We started the walk at 200 feet above sea level, so we have been walking (uphill, downhill, level).

On we go. The first road we pass goes to the (northeast, northwest). We walk on and soon we reach a crossroad. What shall we do? We decide to not walk any further. It is time for lunch! We eat on the southwest side of the crossroad by a (barn, house).

After lunch we walk south on the road. Just after we cross the river (shown in heavy black on the map), we look to the east. The land is quite (flat, steep). It is pleasant walking along the river, but we are glad when we get to the crossroad in Montgomery. From start to finish it is a walk of (4, 7, 9) miles.

More Reading and Interpreting Maps

The next eight exercises are concerned with reading and making pattern maps.

Background

1. Pattern maps are given that name because they are designed to show patterns of distribution of things in the natural and cultural worlds. In fact, some geographers refer to pattern maps as distribution maps. Some examples of things from the natural world that can be shown on pattern maps are:

—Rainfall   —Volcanoes   —Deserts
—Minerals   —Wild animals —Fisheries
—Forests   —Glaciers   —Weather

Some examples of things from the man-made world are:

—Railroads —Airports —Nuclear plants
—Population —Historical sites

2. A pattern map is usually designed to show a particular set of things. The main idea of the map should be immediately apparent. For example, at a glance one should be able to determine on a United States precipitation map that the eastern half of the country receives more precipitation than the western half.

3. Pattern maps should first be read for the "facts" they show. But it should be understood that pattern maps do not always give exact and precise information. For example, on a precipitation map a sharp line may show where zero to 10 inches of yearly precipitation ends and 10 to 20 inches of precipitation begins. Actually, there is no sharp delineation. Rather, the two precipitation regions merge and overlap.

4. Inferences may be made from the facts shown on pattern maps. And two or more pattern maps used together can show relationships not otherwise easily found. At every opportunity learners should be encouraged to discover relationships among map facts and to make inferences. What is the relationship between the sparse rainfall shown on one map and the scarcity of farm products shown on another map? What may be inferred from a map that shows forest areas and another map that shows no railroads or highways leading in and out of the areas? These and similar questions can lead to fruitful discussions.

5. The two most important steps in reading pattern maps are first, to read the map title, and second, to study the map key.

6. In making pattern maps there are four basic steps: (1) Decide on a title that conveys the main topic of the map, (2) gather the data to be shown on the map, (3) devise a key for the map, and (4) arrange the data on the map.

Student Involvement

1. Show a variety of pattern maps, and illustrate each of the pattern map elements mentioned above.

2. Have your students complete each of the pattern map activities that follows. It may be most effective to discuss each map and the suggested answers immediately after each activity is completed. Inference-type questions should be thoroughly discussed, especially the rationale behind each inference.

Answers to the Exercises

Reading and Interpreting Pattern Maps I

1. ND, 7; KA, 6; TX, 4; OK, 3; MT, 3; WA, 3; MN, 3; MO, 2; CA, 2; NE, 2

2. Circled: a, d, e, f

Reading and Interpreting Pattern Maps II

Circled: a, c, d, g, h

Reading and Interpreting Pattern Maps III

1. Pacific Northwest, Western, Midwest, Southwest, Northeast, Southeast

2. Omaha, Nebraska

3. Virginia, 27,506,000

4. Arizona, 24

5. 381,500. It is difficult to get to; much of the year the weather is too severe for tourists

Reading and Interpreting Pattern Maps IV

1. a 2. a 3. c 4. c 5. c 6. d
7. a 8. a 9. b 10. c

Reading and Interpreting Pattern Maps V

1. b 2. d 3. c 4. c 5. c 6. b
7. b 8. a

Reading and Interpreting Pattern Maps VI

1. b

2. c

3. a, c, e, g

4. Coastal Range, Cascade Range, Sierra Nevada Mountains, Rocky Mountains

5. California and Nevada

6. Utah, Idaho, and Montana

7. Washington

Reading and Interpreting Maps VII

1. c 2. b 3. c 4. c, d 5. c 6. b
7. a, b, c, d 8. c 9. b 10. b 11. d

Making and Interpreting Pattern Maps VIII

1. [See chart.]

2. California, Wyoming

3. California, Oregon

4. Colorado, Wyoming

5. Arizona, Idaho

6. AZ, 167; CA, 179; CO, 178; ID, 178; MT, 157; NE, 172; NM, 166; OR, 173; UT, 166; WA, 166; WY, 177

Name _____   Date _____

READING AND INTERPRETING PATTERN MAPS I

1. The table below lists the major wheat-producing states and the number of bushels each state produced in a recent year (rounded to the nearest 50 million).

On the map show these figures with symbols. The symbols you should use are in the key of the map. Each symbol stands for 50 million bushels. So if a state produced 150 million bushels, you would draw three symbols in the state.

State (and abbreviations)	Millions of Bushels
North Dakota (ND)	350
Kansas (KS)	300
Texas (TX)	200
Oklahoma (OK)	150
Montana (MT)	150
Washington (WA)	150
Minnesota (MN)	150
Missouri (MO)	100
California (CA)	100
Nebraska (NE)	100

2. Draw a circle around the letters of the statements that are true. All statements concern facts shown in the table and on the map.

a. The list does not show the exact amount of wheat produced in each state.

b. Only one major wheat-producing state borders the Pacific Ocean.

c. The largest state in the list produces the most wheat.

d. Kansas produced as much wheat as Missouri, California, and Nebraska combined.

e. The greatest wheat-producing states are in the central part of the country.

f. If South Dakota (SD) were one of the first ten wheat-producing states, there would be an unbroken line of "wheat" states from Texas north to North Dakota (ND).

Name _____   Date _____

READING AND INTERPRETING PATTERN MAPS II

WHERE THE WATER FALLS

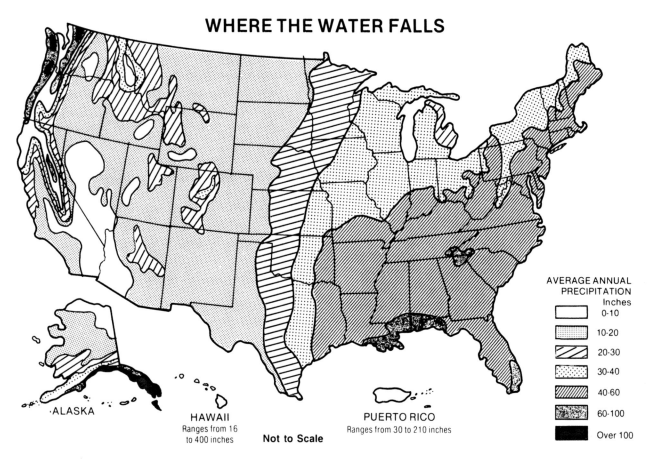

AVERAGE ANNUAL
PRECIPITATION
Inches
0-10
10-20
20-30
30-40
40-60
60-100
Over 100

ALASKA

HAWAII
Ranges from 16
to 400 inches   **Not to Scale**

PUERTO RICO
Ranges from 30 to 210 inches

Note: In the key to the map the word *precipitation* is used. Precipitation includes all forms of moisture falling on the earth: rain, snow, sleet, and hail.

A *general statement* is one that is mostly true, although there may be some exceptions. Following are some general statements about the precipitation map above. Circle the letter before each statement that is true.

a. Most of the southeast United States receives from 40 to 60 inches of precipitation a year.
b. Most of the land around the Great Lakes receives from 20 to 30 inches of precipitation a year.

c. The eastern half of the United States has more precipitation than the western half.
d. The northwest coast of the United States receives more precipitation than the southwest coast.
e. The farther north one goes in Alaska, the greater the precipitation.
f. Central Alaska has an average precipitation of 30 to 40 inches a year.
g. In some parts of Hawaii, as much as 33 feet of precipitation falls in a year. (Think: How many feet are there in 400 inches?)
h. In the West, the most rain falls in the mountain regions. (Think: Where are the mountains in the West?)

Name _____   Date _____

READING AND INTERPRETING PATTERN MAPS III

The map on the next page was developed by the National Park Service. It shows how many visits were made to our national parks in a recent year.

1. Notice that the map is divided into six areas shown by heavy dashed lines. The names of the areas are printed in heavy capital letters.

What are the six areas?

_____ _____

_____ _____

_____ _____

2. The cities shown on the map and marked with stars are where the main offices for each region are located. What city and state is the main office for the Midwest?

_____

3. Which state had the most visits, and how many visits were there? Hint: The state is east of the Mississippi River.

_____

4. Which state in the western half of the country has the most "areas," or parks, and

how many? _____

5. How many visits were made to national

parks in Alaska? _____

Can you think of a reason why there were so few visits in Alaska as compared to other

states? _____

_____

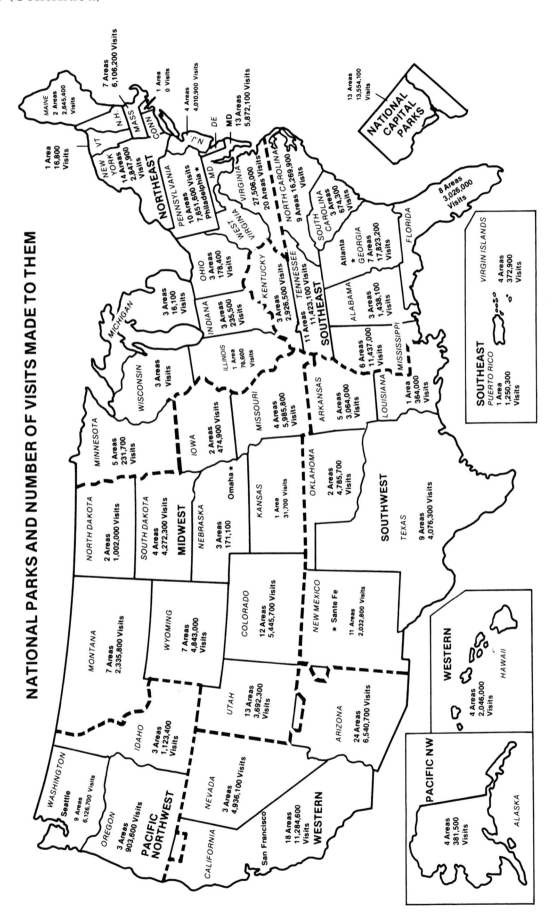

NATIONAL PARKS AND NUMBER OF VISITS MADE TO THEM

NORTHEAST

MAINE
2 Areas
2,645,400 Visits

7 Areas
6,106,200 Visits

N.H.

1 Area
0 Visits

MASS.

CONN.

VT

1 Area
16,800 Visits

NEW YORK
14 Areas
2,847,900 Visits

PENNSYLVANIA
10 Areas
7,651,600 Visits
Philadelphia *

N.J.

DE

4 Areas
4,010,900 Visits

MD
13 Areas
5,872,100 Visits

MD

WEST VIRGINIA

VIRGINIA
27,506,000
20 Areas Visits

NORTH CAROLINA
9 Areas 16,269,900 Visits

SOUTH CAROLINA
3 Areas
674,300 Visits

GEORGIA
7 Areas
17,823,200 Visits
Atlanta *

FLORIDA
8 Areas
3,026,000 Visits

NATIONAL CAPITAL PARKS
13 Areas
13,554,100 Visits

SOUTHEAST

KENTUCKY
3 Areas
2,926,500 Visits

TENNESSEE
11 Areas 11,423,100 Visits

ALABAMA
3 Areas
1,438,100 Visits

MISSISSIPPI
6 Areas
11,437,000 Visits

LOUISIANA
1 Area
364,000 Visits

OHIO
3 Areas
178,400 Visits

INDIANA
3 Areas
235,500

MICHIGAN
3 Areas
16,100 Visits

WISCONSIN
3 Areas
Visits

ILLINOIS
1 Area
76,600 Visits

MINNESOTA
5 Areas
231,700 Visits

IOWA
2 Areas
474,900 Visits

MISSOURI
4 Areas
5,985,800 Visits

ARKANSAS
5 Areas
3,064,000 Visits

MIDWEST

NORTH DAKOTA
2 Areas
1,002,000 Visits

SOUTH DAKOTA
4 Areas
4,272,300 Visits

NEBRASKA
3 Areas
171,100

Omaha *

KANSAS
1 Area
31,700 Visits

OKLAHOMA
2 Areas
4,785,700 Visits

SOUTHWEST

TEXAS
9 Areas
4,076,300 Visits

MONTANA
7 Areas
2,335,800 Visits

WYOMING
7 Areas
4,843,000 Visits

COLORADO
12 Areas
5,445,700 Visits

NEW MEXICO
11 Areas
2,032,800 Visits
* Sante Fe

IDAHO
3 Areas
1,123,400 Visits

UTAH
13 Areas
3,692,300 Visits

ARIZONA
24 Areas
6,540,700 Visits

WASHINGTON
Seattle
9 Areas
6,126,700 Visits

OREGON
3 Areas
903,600 Visits

PACIFIC NORTHWEST

NEVADA
3 Areas
4,936,100 Visits

CALIFORNIA
San Francisco
18 Areas
11,284,600 Visits

WESTERN

WESTERN

HAWAII
4 Areas
2,046,000 Visits

PACIFIC NW

ALASKA
4 Areas
381,500 Visits

SOUTHEAST
PUERTO RICO
1 Area
1,250,300 Visits

VIRGIN ISLANDS
4 Areas
372,900 Visits

Name _____   Date _____

READING AND INTERPRETING PATTERN MAPS IV

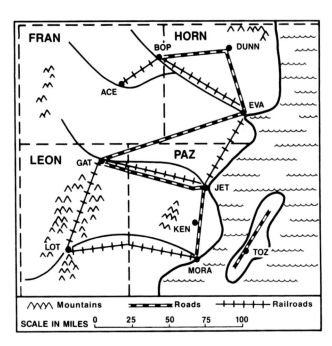

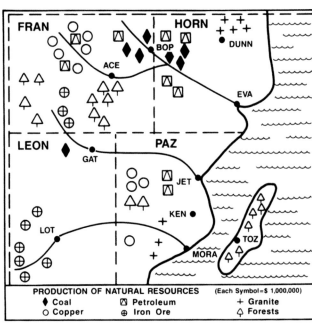

Circle the letter before the best answer to each question.

1. What is the best reason why it would be hard to build a railroad from Ace to Gat?

   a. The forests are too thick.

   b. It is too far from the coast.

   c. There are too many mountains.

   d. There are too many rivers to cross.

2. Which of these railroads would be likely to carry the most iron ore?

   a. Lot to Mora b. Gat to Jet c. Bop to Eva

3. Which of these port cities would most likely export the most coal?

   a. Mora b. Jet c. Eva

4. Which would most likely be carried on the railroad from Jet to Eva?

   a. lumber b. copper c. passengers d. oil

5. What railroad has a road on its south side and a river on its north side?

   a. Bop to Eva b. Lot to Mora c. Gat to Jet

6. Which resource has the greatest value for the state of Fran?

   a. petroleum b. forests c. coal d. copper

7. If it cost $.08 to carry one ton of ore one mile on a railroad, how much would it cost to ship 1,000 tons from Lot to Mora?

   a. $6,800 b. $8,200 c. $7,000 d. $8,000

8. Which state has the most valuable amount of resources?

   a. Fran b. Horn c. Leon d. Paz

9. Which product is most likely to be manufactured in Toz?

   a. gasoline   b. lumber   c. cans
d. automobiles

10. Which city is most likely to have a ski resort?

   a. Bop b. Ace c. Lot d. Jet

Name _____ Date _____

READING AND INTERPRETING PATTERN MAPS V

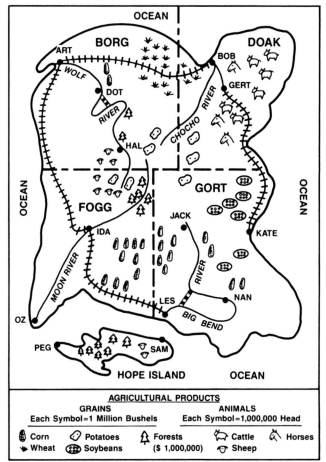

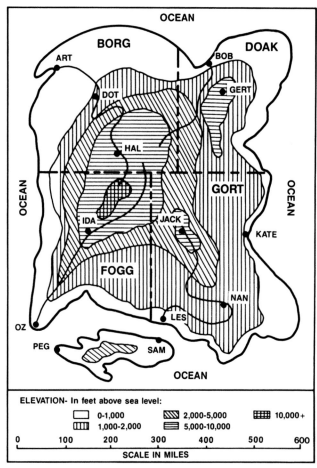

Circle the letter before the best answer to each question.

1. At what elevation is most of the corn grown?

a. 0–1,000 feet   c. 2,000–5,000 feet
b. 1,000–2,000 feet   d. 5,000–10,000 feet

2. What is the highest elevation at which potatoes are grown?

a. 0–1,000 feet   c. 5,000–10,000 feet
b. 1,000–5,000 feet   d. Over 10,000 feet

3. Which river is the only one that begins at the 10,000 feet and over level?

a. Big Bend River   c. Wolf River
b. Moon River   d. Chocho River

4. Which of the following is most likely to be the elevation of Jack?

a. 700 feet   c. 6,200 feet
b. 2,500 feet   d. 10,800 feet

5. How many bushels of wheat were produced in all four states?

a. 8 million   c. 15 million
b. 12 million   d. 18 million

6. Which state probably has the greatest number of cowboys?

a. Borg   c. Fogg
b. Doak   d. Gort

7. Suppose you could take a sightseeing tour on any of the rivers. Which one would have the most forest scenery?

a. Big Bend River   c. Wolf River
b. Moon River   d. Chocho River

8. Which river shortens its length by almost 300 miles because of a canal?

a. Big Bend River   c. Wolf River
b. Moon River   d. Chocho River

Name _____ Date _____

READING AND INTERPRETING PATTERN MAPS VI

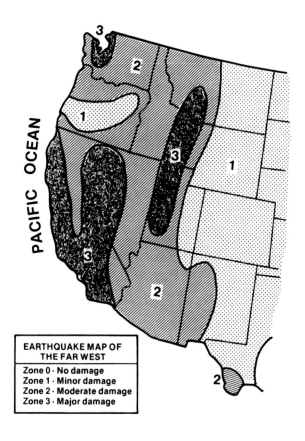

MOUNTAINS
OF THE FAR
WEST

The "Earthquake Map of the Far West" at the top of this column shows where in the West earthquakes are likely to occur. The key to the map tells how much damage might occur in certain zones as a result of an earthquake.

For the first three questions circle the letter or letters before the best answer to each question.

1. In which one of the following groups of states would an earthquake probably do the most damage?

   a. Wyoming and Colorado
   b. California and Nevada
   c. Washington and Oregon

2. In which one of the following groups of states would an earthquake do the least damage?

   a. Idaho and Utah
   b. Arizona and New Mexico
   c. Wyoming and Colorado

3. Which of these states are totally, or almost totally, in Zone 1 or Zone 2?

   a. Arizona b. Utah c. New Mexico
d. Idaho e. Colorado f. Washington
g. Oregon h. California i. Nevada

4. Earthquakes can occur anywhere, but they occur most frequently in mountain regions. What are the four mountain ranges shown on the "Mountains of the Far West" map?

_____ _____

_____ _____

5. What two states are in a Zone 3 area *and* the Sierra Nevada Mountains?

_____ _____

6. What three states are in a Zone 3 area *and* the Rocky Mountains? _____

_____ _____

7. What state is in a Zone 3 area *and* the Cascade Mountains? _____

Name _____   Date _____

READING AND INTERPRETING PATTERN MAPS VII

RAILROAD AND RIVER MAP

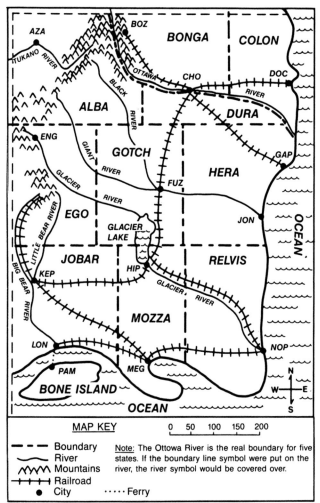

MAP KEY

0   50   100   150   200

– – – Boundary
〰〰 River
ʌʌʌ Mountains
+–+–+ Railroad
● City
····· Ferry

Note: The Ottowa River is the real boundary for five states. If the boundary line symbol were put on the river, the river symbol would be covered over.

Circle the letter or letters before the best answer to each question.

1. What two cities are not connected by rail to any other city?
  a. Doc and Jon   c. Aza and Eng
  b. Gap and Eng   d. Nop and Fuz

2. Which one of these cities probably has the most railroad activity?
  a. Boz   b. Cho   c. Fuz   d. Nop

3. What two cities are located where two rivers join?
  a. Fuz and Hip   c. Fuz and Kep
  b. Cho and Kep   d. Hip and Kep

4. On what *two* rivers would you be able to see mountains on both sides of the river?
  a. Great River   c. Tuckaho River
  b. Glacier River   d. Ottawa River

5. What *two* things are most likely to keep Aza from trading with other cities on the map?
  a. A mountain range separates Aza from other cities.
  b. Aza is too far north.
  c. Aza has no river or railroad connection to the other cities.

6. How do people get to Pam from Lon?
  a. bridge b. ferry c. tunnel d. railroad

7. Which of these states have the Ottawa River for all or part of their boundaries?
  a. Dura b. Alba c. Hera d. Colon

8. How many rivers would you fly over if you flew from Kep to Cho?
  a. 1 b. 2 c. 3 d. 4

9. What is the *shortest railroad trip* from Kep to Nop?
  a. Fuz to Hip to Nop
  b. Kep to Meg to Nop
  c. Cho to Hip to Nop
  d. Kep to Hip to Nop

10. What is the *shortest* way to go from Cho to Jon?
  a. By rail to Fuz, then by river boat
  b. By rail to Gap, then by ocean boat
  c. By river boat to the coast, then by ocean boat
  d. By rail to Doc, then by ocean boat

11. How many miles is the railroad from Lon to Meg to Nop?
  a. 100 miles   c. 300 miles
  b. 175 miles   d. 500 miles

Name _____   Date _____

READING AND INTERPRETING PATTERN MAPS VIII

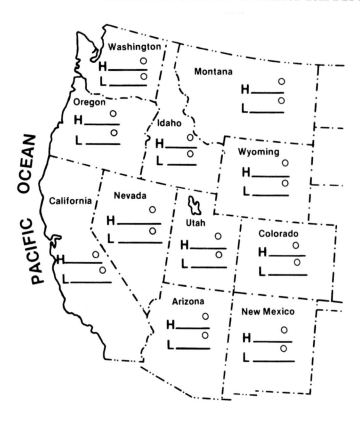

STATE	HIGH TEMP. (F)	LOW TEMP. (F)	DIFFERENCE BETWEEN HIGH AND LOW TEMPERATURES
Arizona	127°	−40°	_____
California	134°	−45°	_____
Colorado	118°	−60°	_____
Idaho	118°	−60°	_____
Montana	117°	−40°	_____
Nevada	122°	−50°	_____
New Mexico	116°	−50°	_____
Oregon	119°	−54°	_____
Utah	116°	−50°	166°
Washington	118°	−48°	_____
Wyoming	114°	−63°	_____

RECORD TEMPERATURES FOR ELEVEN WESTERN STATES

1. The table of figures on the right shows the lowest and highest temperatures recorded in the eleven far western states. The records have been kept for more than eighty years.

Write the temperatures for each state on the lines shown in each state on the map.

2. Which state had the highest recorded temperature? _____ Which state had the lowest recorded temperature?

_____

3. Which of the three states bordering the Pacific Ocean had the highest recorded temperature? _____

Which of the three states had the lowest recorded temperature?

_____

4. Which of the four states farthest east had the highest temperature?

_____

Which of the four states had the lowest recorded temperatures?

_____

5. Which of the states between the Pacific Coast states and the easternmost states had the highest recorded temperature?

_____

Which of the four states had the lowest recorded temperature?

_____

6. How many degrees' difference is there between the lowest and highest temperature in each state? To find the difference for any state, add the *below-zero* figure to the *above-zero* figure. Example for Utah: Add 50 and 116. The answer is 166 degrees of difference.

Write your answers in the blank spaces in the table. Utah's figures have already been entered.

WORLD'S CONTINENTS, OCEANS, AND IMPORTANT WORLD PASSAGES

7-1   Locating the Continents and Oceans
7-2   The Panama Canal
7-3   The Suez Canal
7-4   The Strait of Gibraltar

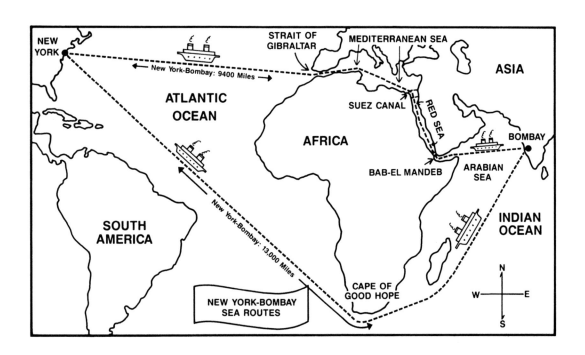

Important World Passages:
Locating the Continents and Oceans

Background

1. Item 2 of the exercise calls attention to the fact that Europe and Asia are physically one continent. But for historical, cultural, and political reasons, Europe and Asia are referred to separately.

The physical boundary between Asia and Europe is considered by some geographers to be the "line" created by the Ural Mountains (a north–south range) and the Caspian Sea (a north–south-oriented body of water) and that continues west to the Black Sea through the Caucasus Mountains.

2. Sometimes a map or globe will include an "Antarctic Ocean." However, it should be realized that the so-called Antarctic Ocean is really made up of the southern parts of the Atlantic, Pacific, and Indian Oceans. The Arctic Ocean is well-enclosed by the northern edges of North America, Europe, and Asia, as well as by many islands, notably Greenland, but, the "Antarctic Ocean" is not enclosed in any way.

In reality, there is only one great ocean (all of the oceans are connected), and the four "oceans" are merely divisions of it.

Student Involvement

1. Meaningful context, activity, and repetition are the keys to your students' development of a clear mental image of the world's major configurations—an image that can be evoked instantly, as the need arises. Thus, throughout this skill-development book there will be numerous activities concerned with world maps.

2. Your introduction of continents, oceans, and hemispheres to the children should begin with a simplified globe. Then your students should be helped to transfer what they see on the globe to the flat map of the exercises.

There are obvious distortions to any flat map that attempts to show a round world. Make your students aware of this by comparing the globe and the map. Some discrepancies to which you should call their attention are shape, size, distance, and proportion. Just as the students resort to the dictionary for the correct way to spell or syllabicate words, so should they refer to a globe for true depictions of the world. But be sure to not destroy their confidence in flat maps, which are useful tools if their strengths and weaknesses are understood.

Answers to the Exercise

1. Seven
2. Eurasia
3. Pacific, Atlantic, Arctic, Indian
4a. Northern b. Southern c. Southern d. Southern e. Northern
5a. Atlantic b. Atlantic c. Indian

Name _____   Date _____

LOCATING THE CONTINENTS AND OCEANS

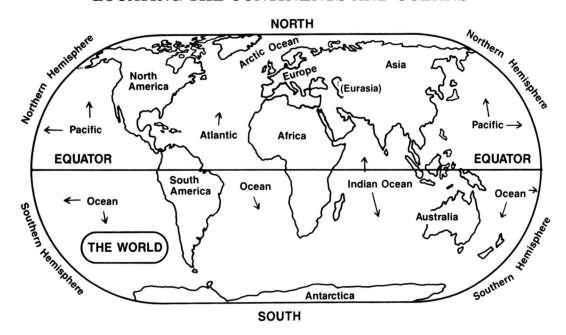

1. Continents are the great land masses of the earth. They are shown and named on the map above. How many continents are there?

_____

2. Sometimes Europe and Asia are called one continent because they are joined together. According to the map, what is the name of the one combined continent?

_____

3. Oceans are the great water bodies of the world. What are the names of the world's four oceans?

_____

_____

_____

4. Find the line on the map called *equator.* This lines divides the earth into two parts called *hemispheres.* A *sphere* is a ball, which is what the earth appears to be. *Hemi* means "one-half." So a hemisphere is one-half of a ball, or one-half of the earth.

The half of the earth that contains the North Pole is called the *Northern Hemisphere.* The half that contains the South Pole is called the *Southern Hemisphere.* The small globe map above shows these two hemispheres.

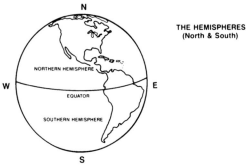

THE HEMISPHERES
(North & South)

Following are some incomplete sentences about hemispheres, continents, and oceans. Draw a circle around the word that correctly completes each sentence.

a. Most land is in the (southern, northern) hemisphere.

b. Most water is in the (southern, northern) hemisphere.

c. Australia is in the (northern, southern) hemisphere.

d. Most of South America and all of Antarctica are in the (northern, southern) hemisphere.

e. Europe, Asia, and North America are all in the (northern, southern) hemisphere.

5. What ocean would you cross to go from:

a. North America to Europe? _____

b. Africa to South America? _____

c. Australia to Africa? _____

Important World Passages:
The Panama Canal

Background and Interpretation

The Isthmus of Panama has been important to the development of the Americas since Vasco Núñez de Balboa first crossed it in 1513 and "discovered" the Pacific Ocean. The distance across the isthmus, about 50 miles, was tantalizingly short, but the path across was studded with mountains, forests, and swamps infested with snakes and disease-bearing mosquitoes. For three hundred years, ships wishing to sail from the east coast of North America to the west coast had to sail around the southern tip of South America. The trip could take from three to six months. This all changed when the Panama Canal, built by the United States, was completed in 1914.

Following is more factual information relative to the canal:

—Statistics: 50 miles in length; lifts ships 85 feet above sea level through a series of six locks, three on the Atlantic side and three on the Pacific side; each lock is 1000 feet long, 110 feet wide, and 40 feet deep.

—Under a treaty with the United States, Panama will take over the canal on December 31, 1999. Until that time, it will be operated jointly by the United States and Panama.

Student Involvement

Some aspects of the exercise map that should be brought to the attention of your students:

—The map is a modified Mercator projection that results in an exaggeration of the polar portions of the earth. However, this projection is useful for showing sea routes of travel.

—The oceans are shown as North Pacific and South Pacific, North Atlantic and South Atlantic, thus making it easier to locate places. However, there are but four oceans: Atlantic, Pacific, Indian, and Arctic.

—The sea route distances are told in "land," or statute, miles because students are more familiar with them. However, seafarers speak in terms of nautical miles. A land mile is 1.15 times the length of a nautical mile. Thus, the distance from Boston to San Francisco can be expressed as 13,043 nautical miles if the route around South America is taken. If the Panama Canal route is taken, the distance is 5,217 nautical miles.

—As a sea route, the Bering Strait is little used, but it is still important because it is a major entrance to the Arctic Ocean.

Answers to the Exercise

1. [Check for correct labeling.]

2a. 6,000 miles b. 15,000 miles c. 9,000 miles

3. Straits of Magellan

4. 13,500 miles

5, 6. [Check for correct labeling.]

Name _____   **Date** _____

THE PANAMA CANAL

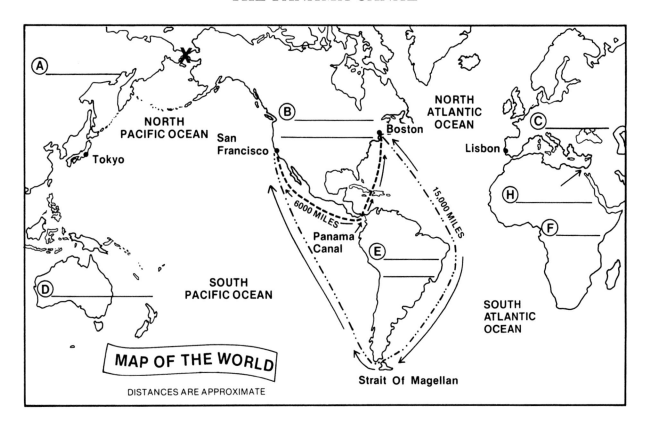

1. Label the following places on the map.

   (A) Asia   (D) Australia

   (B) North America (E) South America

   (C) Europe   (F) Africa

2a. How many miles is the water trip from Boston to San Francisco if the Panama Canal is used? _____

   b. How many miles is the water trip from Boston to San Francisco if the ship sails around the southern tip of South America and then north to San Francisco?

_____

   c. What is the difference in miles between the two water routes? _____

3. What narrow passage would a ship sail through on the longer route from Boston to San Francisco? _____

4. Draw a route of travel line from Lisbon, Portugal, to the Panama Canal. Write *4,700 miles* on the line. Then draw another line from the Panama Canal to Tokyo, Japan. Write *8,800 miles* on the line.

   What is the total distance in miles from Lisbon to Tokyo? _____

5. Label another famous water passage, the Suez Canal, at H on your map.

6. Asia and North America are separated by a water passage that is sometimes ice-blocked. Label the passage, the Bering Strait, at X on the map.

Important World Passages:
The Suez Canal

Background

The Suez Canal activity offers an opportunity not only to understand a crucial world location, but also to gain skill in map reading. Here are some background facts about the canal:

—A French company built the canal (1859–1867), but Great Britain gained control of it in 1875. Some 75 years later, in 1956, the Egyptians took over the canal and have been operating it ever since.

—The canal is about 100 miles long. Its average width is about 200 feet, and its average depth is about 36 feet.

—The Suez is a sea-level canal; there are no locks. The canal has been widened and deepened several times. One of the biggest maintenance problems is dredging sand from the sides and channel. Ships' speeds are carefully monitored because the waves the ships make, and even the motor vibrations from the ships, break off parts of the sand banks.

—The Suez carries about two times more tonnage yearly than the Panama Canal. Oil boats from Saudi Arabia and other Middle East countries are among the canal's greatest users.

—A little known-fact: A canal connecting the Mediterranean Sea and the Red Sea was completed about 1300 B.C. But wars and neglect contributed to its destruction, and the water passage was forgotten for more than three thousand years.

Student Involvement

1. Use the foregoing information to build some background of understanding about the historical and contemporary aspects of the Suez Canal. It is especially important that your students realize that the Strait of Gibraltar, the Suez Canal, and the Bab el Mandeb have the potential to control the trade and traffic of the Mediterranean Sea countries. Also of significance: The Russians have always been concerned about control of these Mediterranean Sea passages because they are the Russians' chief means of entering the oceans of the world, especially during the winter months when most of their other ports are frozen.

2. The most important skill to be developed in this activity is following a route of travel. The most important understanding is the great savings of time (and money) gained by use of the canal.

3. At the completion of the activity, it would be helpful to illustrate the mathematical computations on the chalkboard.

Answers to the Exercise

1. East

2a. Southeast   b. Northeast

3. Strait of Gibraltar

4a. Red Sea   b. Bab el Mandeb   c. Arabian Sea

5a. 13,000 miles   b. 9,400 miles c. 3,600 miles

6. 120 hours, or 5 days

Name _____   Date _____

THE SUEZ CANAL

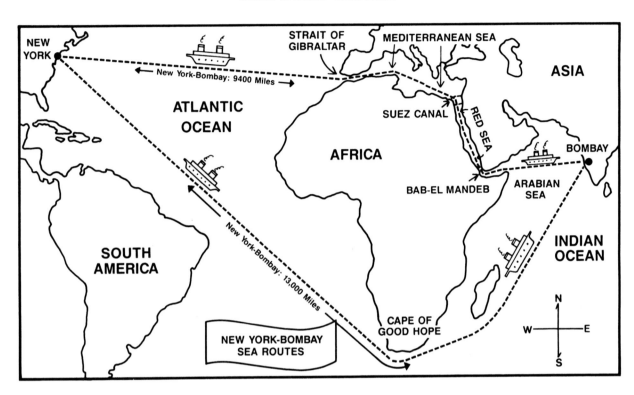

1. In what general direction does a boat travel when it sails from New York to Bombay, India, through the Suez Canal?

_____

2a. What direction is the Cape of Good

Hope from New York City? _____
   b. What direction is Bombay from the

Cape of Good Hope? _____
   c. What is the name of the narrow passage at the western end of the Mediterranean Sea?

_____

4a. What sea does a boat enter at the southern end of the Suez Canal?

_____

   b. What is the name of the narrow passage at the southern end of the Red Sea?

_____

c. What is the last body of water that must be crossed to reach India from the Red Sea?

_____

5a. According to the map, how many miles is the water passage from New York to Bombay, India, around the Cape of Good Hope?

_____

   b. How many miles is the water passage from New York to Bombay through the Suez Canal?

_____

   c. What is the saving in miles if the Suez Canal route is taken over the Cape of Good

Hope route? _____
   6. Challenge: If a boat traveling at an average speed of 30 miles per hour is going from New York to Bombay, how much time will it save if it takes the Suez route rather than the Cape of Good Hope route?

_____

Important World Passages:
The Strait of Gibraltar

Background

It is possible that no other water passageway has played a more important part in history than the Strait of Gibraltar. The passage, 8 to 27 miles wide, was a gateway to the Atlantic Ocean for Phoenician and Roman ships centuries before the modern era.

Today it is even more important as a major transportation route. The opening of the Suez Canal in 1869 at the eastern end of the Mediterranean increased the significance of Gibraltar because the Middle East, the Far East, and the West gained ready access to one another via an uninterrupted water route.

Militarily, the Strait of Gibraltar is of tremendous importance. The aphorism "Whoever controls Gibraltar controls the Mediterranean" is undoubtedly true. At this time, the controllers are the British. Gibraltar is a self-governing British colony in all matters except defense. For more than two hundred years the British have maintained a heavily fortified base on "the Rock," as it is called.

Student Involvement

1. Some additional instruction and demonstration on measuring distances, as called for in Item 2 of the student activity, may be desirable. Refer back to Activity 1-9 for suggestions on measuring distances on maps. Also, to demonstrate how to measure the route shown on the map, make a transparency of the map. Then, following the directions to students given on the opposite page, project the transparency and show how to measure the distances.

As a supplementary measuring exercise, ask: "What is the air distance from London to Athens?" To compute it, draw on the map a straight line between the two cities. Using the described technique of measurement, you will find that the distance is approximately 1,500 miles, some 1,900 miles less than the sea route.

2. As frequently as possible, have your students estimate distances while using the scale of miles as a reference. Then check the estimate with an actual measurement. In time, student estimates will become more and more accurate.

Answers to the Exercise

1. In order from London: English Channel, Bay of Biscay, Lisbon, Strait of Gibraltar, Spain, Morocco, Sicily, Aegean Sea

2. The approximate distance is 3,400 miles, as measured along the sea route shown on the map. Student measurements of plus or minus 300 miles are quite acceptable.

THE STRAIT OF GIBRALTAR

There are three important water entrances into the Mediterranean Sea. You have already learned about one of them—the Suez Canal. One of the other entrances is called The Dardanelles, and the third is called the Strait of Gibraltar. This exercise is concerned with the Strait of Gibraltar.

1. The dashed line on the map shows a route you might take in traveling from London, England, through the Strait of Gibraltar to Athens, Greece. The numbers on the map locate some of the places you would see on the trip. Match the number of the place with one of the descriptions below. Write the name of the place on the line next to each description.

Narrow water passage separating England from France _____

A large bay west of France _____

Portugal's capital city _____

Narrow water passage separating Europe and Africa _____

Country on the northern side of the Strait of Gibraltar _____

Country on the southern side of the Strait of Gibraltar _____

Island at the "toe" of Italy _____

Sea off the east coast of Greece _____

2. Compare the route of travel from London to Athens with the map's scale of miles. Make an estimate of the distance.

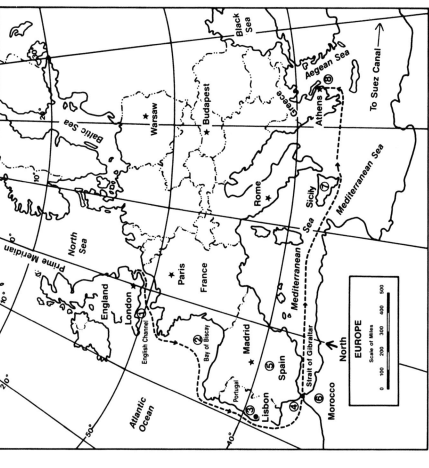

Take the long edge of a piece of paper and lay it along the route, starting at London. At each big curve in the line, make a mark on the paper. Start the next measurement from the last mark and continue. Twist and turn the paper as needed.

Next, lay the paper edge along the scale of miles. Make a mark for every 500 miles. Add up the units of 500. What is your total? _____

Compare your measurement total with your estimate total.

WATER AS A UNIVERSAL GEOGRAPHY SIGNIFICANT

8-1   Our Water Is Running Out
8-2   Raindrops Falling in a Watershed
8-3   Water Goes 'Round and 'Round
8-4   Thunder, Lightning, and Rain
8-5   Rain in the Mountains
8-6   The Battle of the Air Masses
8-7   Water for Cities from Rivers and Lakes
8-8   Water from Under the Ground
8-9   When Does the Rain Come Down?
8-10 Dams—Water Controllers
8-11 High Dams of the United States and Canada
8-12 Electric Power from Water
8-13 Polluted Water Kills Fish
8-14 Making Water Pure Again

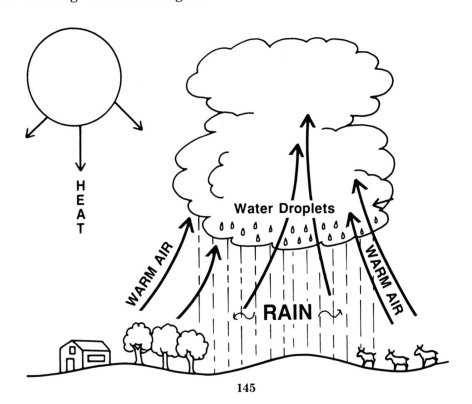

Water as a Universal Geography Significant: Our Water Is Running Out

Background

The activities in Sections 8 through 10 are developed within the context of such topics as water, air, and soil. At the same time that competency in geographic skills is developed, knowledge of universal elements of geography will be gained.

The following information about water will add extra interest to water studies.

—The amount of water available on earth today is just about what it has always been. But because the earth's population has greatly increased, the same amount of water must be used by more people.

—Water covers about three-quarters of the earth's surface.

—Lakes, streams, and ponds occupy about 2 percent of the area of the United States.

—The average rainfall in the United States is about 30 inches per year. Some places receive less than 5 inches of rain yearly, while other places get as much as 120 inches yearly.

—Most of the water we use comes from surface sources. However, there is about six times as much water below the surface as on the surface.

—Pure water is virtually colorless. However, water may appear to be blue, green, or brown. Reflection of the sun's rays, reflection of the sky, and the presence of soil particles all affect the appearance of water.

Student Involvement

The table "Water Use in Your Home" is relatively simple to interpret. However, the graph may need explanation.

The title of the graph indicates that our usage is increasing. "Available Water Runoff" is a reminder that our upper limit of usage is 1,200 billion gallons daily. The amounts shown for the years 2000 and 2020 are predictions based on past rate of growth.

This is a line graph. The amounts are read at the point where the diagonal line (amount) crosses the vertical line (year). Interpolation is necessary, but precise figures are not available.

Answers to the Exercise

1a. 865 b. 383 c. 482 d. According to the trend shown on the graph, we probably will not have enough water. Reasoning: 482 billion gallons more will be used in 2020 than in 1980. That is a forty-year period. If this same gain is applied to the forty-year period beginning in 2020, total usage will exceed the 1,200 billion gallons available.

2. About one and a half times more

3. About three times more

4. About 10 gallons

5. 36 gallons

6. Cooking, cleaning, drinking, washing oneself, watering plants, watering lawns, washing car.

Name _____   Date _____

OUR WATER IS RUNNING OUT

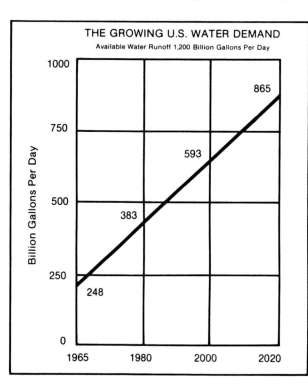

THE GROWING U.S. WATER DEMAND
Available Water Runoff 1,200 Billion Gallons Per Day

1a. About how many billions of gallons of water are expected to be used in 2020? _____

b. How many billions of gallons of water were used daily in 1980? _____

c. How many more billions of gallons of water will be used in 2020 than in 1980? (Subtract b from a) _____

d. At the rate we are using water, do you think there will be enough water in the year 2060? Explain your answer.

_____

_____

_____

_____

_____

WATER USE IN YOUR HOME

The average person uses 20 to 80 gallons of water each day in his or her home. Here is a list of some normal household uses of water and the amount of water required for each:

Washing dishes....................10 gallons
Flushing a toilet...................3 gallons
A shower bath ....20 to 30 gallons
A tub bath.................30 to 40 gallons
A washing machine load.....20 to 30 gallons

2. About how many times more water was used in 1980 than in 1965?

_____ About one and a half

_____ About two times more

_____ About three times more

3. About how many times more water will be used in 2020 than in 1965?

_____ About three times more

_____ About five times more

_____ About six times more

4. According to the table above, how many gallons of water could be saved by taking a shower instead of a bath? _____

5. Suppose each person in a family of four flushed the toilet three times a day. How many gallons of water would be used?

6. Think of five ways water is used in a home that are not mentioned in the table.

_____

_____

_____

_____

Water as a Universal Geography Significant:
Raindrops Falling in a Watershed

Background

It has been said that to understand water conservation, one must first understand watersheds. When it is realized that the United States has hundreds of thousands of watersheds, it is easy to recognize the truth of this statement.

This activity will not only provide another opportunity to develop skill in using diagrams, but also will develop significant geographic understandings.

Student Involvement

1. Read to the learners the story below. Be sure that they are looking at the diagram as they listen to the story.

2. When a number is met in the story, pause and have the learners write the italicized word or words on the corresponding numbered line in the diagram.

Journey of a Raindrop

Let's trace the journey of a drop of rain that fell on the roof of Tom Smith's house.

First, the drop drained into a wooden gutter and then into a copper leader. From the leader the drop flowed over an asphalt driveway that slants toward a ditch.

Once in the ditch, Tom's raindrop moved rapidly until it became caught in the flow of *Little Horse Brook* (1). This stream swept the raindrop along at a swift pace until it met a larger stream, *Big Horse Brook* (2). Finally, Big Horse Brook joined the *Mohican River* (3), which completed the job of carrying Tom's raindrop to the *ocean* (4).

The whole area from which all of the water eventually drained into the Mohican River is called a *watershed*. Because the Mohican River is the major river of the area, the watershed is called the *Mohican Watershed*.

As you can see, the Mohican Watershed is made up of a number of smaller watersheds. The drainage areas surrounding Little Horse Brook and Big Horse Brook are two other, but smaller, watersheds. The area around Eagle River, shown in the diagram, is still another watershed, and so on.

Answers to the Exercise

1. [Check for completed line and green color.]

2. [Check to see that *Source* is written at every S and *Mouth* at every M.]

3, 4. [Check for blue waters and black road.]

5. [Check for title.]

6. Three

7. 50 miles

8. A tree—the "trunk" is the Mohican River, and the "branches" are the tributaries.

RAINDROPS FALLING IN A WATERSHED

1. The Mohican Watershed is all the area shown within the dashed lines in the diagram. To better show the limits of this watershed, connect the dashes with a heavy solid line.

Now, in the diagram, color green the "slopes" on both sides of the line.

2. Some of the terms used to describe the parts of a river system are listed below.

a. *Source*—the place where a stream begins. Write *Source* at all the places in the diagram where an S is printed.

b. *Mouth*—the place where a stream empties the water it carries. Write *Mouth* wherever an M is printed on the diagram.

3. Color blue the oceans and rivers.

4. Color black the road and driveways that run from Tom's house to the ocean.

5. Write in the box in the lower right corner of the diagram the title of the diagram: *Mohican Watershed.*

6. How many beginning river systems are shown *outside* the Mohican Watershed?

7. About how many miles did the raindrop that fell on Tom Smith's house travel before it got to the ocean?

_____ 50 miles   _____ 200 miles
_____ 100 miles   _____ 250 miles

8. Study the entire diagram. What thing in nature does the Mohican Watershed look like?

Water as a Universal Geography Significant: Water Goes 'Round and 'Round

Background

Since the beginning of time, water has been in continuous movement from the earth to the atmosphere and back to the earth. During the movement, water is constantly changing from vapor to liquid (rain), and sometimes to solids in the form of sleet, snow, hail, or ice. The movement of water is known as the *hydrologic cycle,* or the water cycle.

Student Involvement

Trace the movement of water through the cycle by beginning at the numeral 1 in the diagram.

1. *Water is drawn from the oceans by evaporation.* It is the heat energy of the sun that causes the water to evaporate. The oceans furnish most of the water for evaporation. However, large quantities of water are drawn from humans, animals, plants, trees, lakes, rivers, and marshes. When automobile, tractor, and airplane engines burn fuel, they also give off moisture in the form of vapor.

2. *Advancing warm air masses and winds transport the water vapor across the ocean and land masses.*

3. *Clouds are formed.* When the advancing warm air meets colder air, the water begins to change back to its liquid form. "Young" clouds made up of millions of drops of water begin to take shape.

4. *Rain clouds are formed.* As the young clouds meet colder and colder air, the tiny drops become larger and larger.

5. *Precipitation occurs.* When the water drops become too large and heavy, they fall.

6. *Some of the precipitation runs off the surface.* If the precipitation falls on bare ground, hard-surfaced parking lots, city streets, and similar surfaces, it will flow quickly into ditches, streams, and rivers. Some of it will be stored in ponds and lakes. Most of the runoff water will find its way to the ocean in a few hours or days.

7. *Most precipitation soaks into the ground.* Water that soaks into the earth is called *groundwater.* Almost all of this water eventually finds its way back to the ocean. Some groundwater is used by plants and trees and then evaporates. Some groundwater is drawn into the atmosphere directly from the soil.

Water moves through the hydrologic cycle again and again. Water is never destroyed. Thus, the water that early humans scooped from pools for drinking may very well be the water that will be used in homes and industries today.

Answers to the Exercise

1, 2, 3. [Check for completion.]

4. Ocean, boat, airplane, crops, animals, tractor, lake

5. It will push the clouds over the land.

6. Snow, hail

7. The sun

8. The boat's smoke and the path of the sailboat are moving counter to the upper winds.

Name _____ Date _____

WATER GOES 'ROUND AND 'ROUND

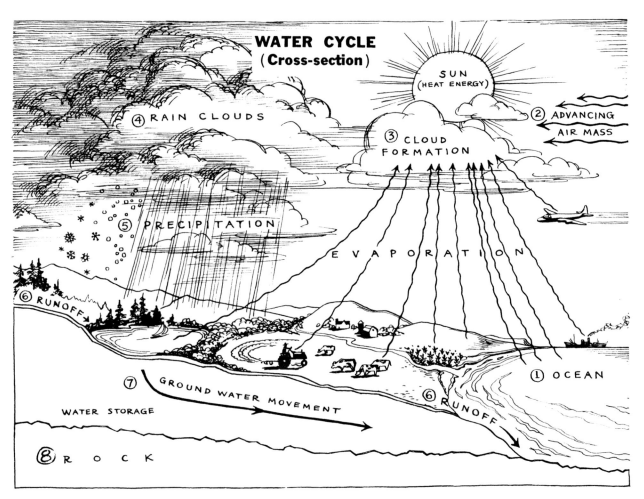

1. The water storage area (7) shown in the diagram usually consists of sand and gravel. Show this layer more clearly by drawing small circles and dots (⚬∘⚬∘∘⚬∘⚬) in it.

Show the rock layer (8) with light diagonal (///////) lines.

2. Color the ocean, the lake, and the river blue.

3. Color the sun yellow.

4. Name seven things in the diagram that are giving off water vapor.

_____ _____

_____ _____

_____

5. Find the "Advancing Air Mass" (2). How will this moving air affect the clouds that are

forming? _____

_____

6. Rain falling from the clouds is shown by slanting lines. What two other forms of precipitation are shown? _____

_____

7. It takes heat energy to evaporate water. What is the source of heat energy in the

water cycle? _____

8. Challenge: What evidence is there in the diagram to show that the winds in the upper atmosphere are blowing in one direction, but the winds near the surface are

blowing in another? _____

_____

Water as a Universal Geography Significant: Background for Teaching the Three Basic Causes of Rainfall

The next three exercises are concerned with the three major weather conditions that cause precipitation.

Background

1. Precipitation—how much, how often, and when—has always been a crucial factor in determining how we live. The United States and other nations are constantly searching for ways to make rain when it is needed.

—The basic thing to remember about precipitation is that it is formed when air moisture rises as a vapor, condenses around a nucleus, cools, and changes into rain or snow, which then falls of its own weight.

—Warm air can hold more water vapor than cold air.

—Air derives moisture from the earth and things on it, including vegetation and rivers.

—As the moisture in air condenses, minute droplets of water are formed. These droplets combine with other droplets. One drop of rain that falls may have been formed from millions of very tiny droplets.

2. Types of rainfall (in order of activity):

—*Convectional:* Heated air rises in a *convection* current. In rising, it cools until the *dew point* is reached. At the dew point, the water condenses, forms drops, and falls.

—*Orographic:* Surface winds meet a mountain range head-on or obliquely. The winds flow up the slope of the mountains. As the winds rise, the air cools. Condensation takes place and water drops form that fall as rain.

—*Cyclonic or frontal:* A mass of warm air meets a mass of cold air. The warm air rises over the cold air. As the warm air rises, it cools. As it cools, water vapor in it condenses, and precipitation occurs.

Student Involvement

1. Guide your students through the completion of the diagram of convectional rainfall (facing page).

2. The activities on orographic and cyclonic rainfall can be completed by your students on an independent basis, although some guidance to get them started would be helpful.

Answers to the Exercises

Thunder, Lightning, and Rain

[Check diagrams for correct labeling.]

Rain in the Mountains

1. 5, 1, 3, 4, 6, 2

2. Heavy rains on the west side increase tree growth

3. The top of the mountain receives more rain, thus increasing growth

4. Sleet

The Battle of the Air Masses

1, 3. [Check for accuracy of labeling, including *f*.]

2. Cold, cools, rain, drizzle, snow, sleet

4. Fourth sentence, second paragraph

Name _____ Date _____

THUNDER, LIGHTNING, AND RAIN

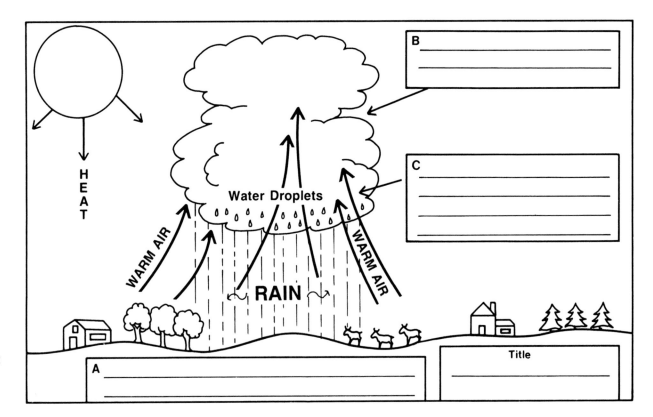

1. The diagram of convectional rainfall above is incomplete. Follow the directions below to complete the diagram.

—In the *a* box, write: Air close to the earth rises when heated by the sun.
—In the *b* box, write: Clouds form when the rising air becomes cooler.
—In the *c* box, write: Cooled water vapor changes into water droplets. As the drops become larger and heavier, they fall as rain.
—In the title box, write: Convectional Rainfall.

2. Convectional rainfall is often accompanied by thunder and lightning. Thun-derclouds are usually dark at the top. Darken the clouds near the top with a pen or pencil.

Show some lightning bolts (ϟ ϟ) in and near the cloud.

To give a better impression of rain, draw some large tear-shaped water drops (◊ ◊ ◊) among the vertical rain lines.

3. Airplane pilots avoid convection currents because the *updraft* (convection) can be very powerful. A plane can easily be damaged or even destroyed if caught in the suction of an updraft.

On the diagram, draw an airplane or two above the cloud.

RAIN IN THE MOUNTAINS

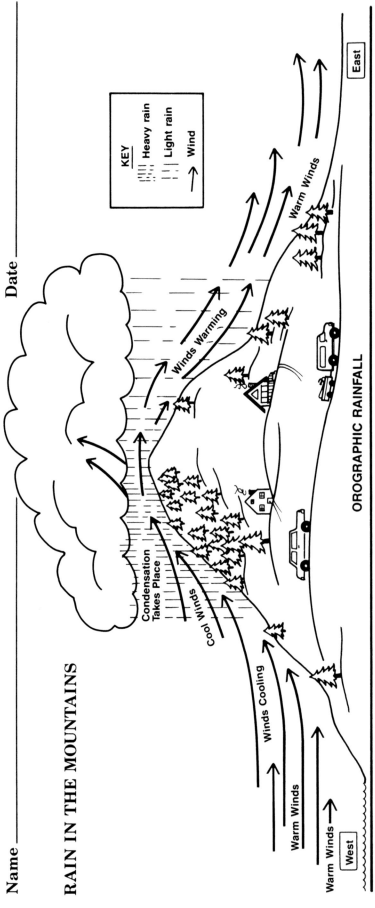

KEY

Heavy rain

Light rain

→ Wind

West

Warm Winds →

Warm Winds →

Winds Cooling

Cool Winds

Condensation Takes Place

Winds Warming

Warm Winds

East

OROGRAPHIC RAINFALL

OROGRAPHIC RAINFALL—Surface winds are forced to rise when they blow against a range of mountains. The winds cool as they rise against the mountain slopes. The moisture in the air condenses and changes into rain. If the rain freezes it becomes *sleet*. If the water vapor freezes and forms ice crystals, then we have *snow*. We call precipitation formed by winds rising against mountains *orographic* (from the Greek word *oros*, "mountain").

1. The "steps" in orographic rainfall are listed below in mixed order. Write a *1* before the first step, a *2* before the second step, and so on.

____ The winds become warm as they move down the mountain slopes.

____ Near the top of the mountains, the winds become cool and their moisture condenses.

____ After reaching the top of the mountains, some of the winds start going down the slopes.

____ At the foot of the mountains, the warm winds begin moving eastward along the earth's surface.

____ The winds begin to rise as they reach the mountains.

2. Why are trees more plentiful on the west side of the mountain than on the east side? _____

3. Why are trees on the west side of the mountain more plentiful at the top rather than at the bottom? _____

Name _____ Date _____

THE BATTLE OF THE AIR MASSES

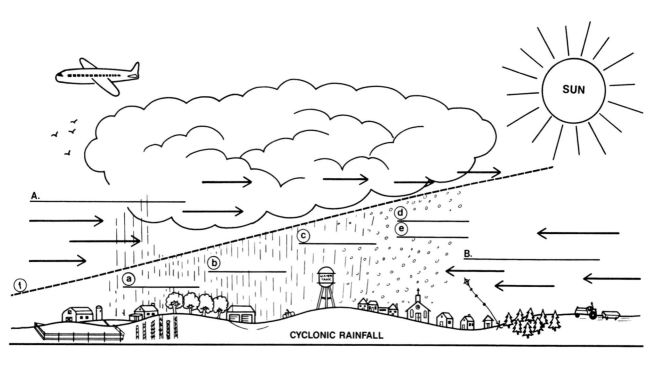

CYCLONIC RAINFALL

CYCLONIC OR FRONTAL RAINFALL—Think of a mass of warm air covering a large area, perhaps an entire state. Think also of a mass of cold air covering the area next to it. Think of each mass as a great army, each advancing toward the other. A clash is certain to occur.

And the clash does occur. Storm clouds gather. But the warm air, being lighter and less dense, begins to slide up and over the cold air. Then, when the warm air climbs high enough into the atmosphere, its water vapor begins to condense. Rain begins to fall through the cold air mass.

The warm air keeps moving along the top of the cold air, continuing to drop precipitation—sometimes heavy rain, sometimes drizzle, sometimes snow and sleet—at various places over the cold mass. This rainmaking process is known as cyclonic or frontal rainfall.

1. After reading the explanation of cyclonic rainfall, complete the diagram by following these directions.

On the line next to A, print *Warm Air.* On the line by B, print *Cold Air.*

Print these words next to the small letters in the diagram:

a—*Heavy Rain*   b—*Light Rain*   c—*Drizzle*
d—*Snow*   e—*Sleet*

2. Complete this sentence from what you have read in the explanation and from what you see in the diagram: As the warm air

mass climbs higher over the _____

air mass, the warm air mass _____.

From the warm air mass, precipitation falls

in the form of _____, _____,

_____, and _____.

3. A *front* is an imaginary line between the cold air and the warm air. There is usually much mixing of cold and warm air along a front. An airplane ride along a front would be very bumpy—and very dangerous—because of the *turbulence* (unrest) of the air.

The dashed line slanting upward from west to east on the diagram represents a front. At the three places on the line where there is an *f*, write *Front.*

4. Underline the sentence in the explanation that tells what happens to the water vapor in the warm air after the mass of warm air lies on top of the mass of cold air.

Water as a Universal Geography Significant:
Water for Cities from Rivers and Lakes

Background-Student Involvement

1. Explain that the picture-diagrams on the facing page show a generalized process for extracting and distributing water from rivers and lakes.

2. Read or explain the captions (below) for each step of the process. At the end of each step, inference questions related to the step are suggested. Suggested answers follow each question.

Picture-diagram 1: Some cities obtain their water from rivers. Trenton, New Jersey, draws water from the Delaware River. St. Louis, Missouri, draws water from the Mississippi River. *Question:* "What might interfere with a steady supply of water from the river?" (Periods of drought upstream, frozen water, diversion of water upstream for factories.)

Picture-diagram 2: Some cities obtain water from nearby lakes. Chicago, Illinois, uses Lake Michigan water. Burlington, Vermont has been drawing water from Lake Champlain for many years. *Question:* "Why do some cities ban the use of motorboats on lakes or reservoirs that are used for water?" (Motorboats discharge oil and gasoline, thus polluting the water.)

Picture-diagram 3: Water that is taken from lakes or rivers is first drawn through openings called *water intakes.* A screen over the intake blocks weeds, fish, and so forth from entering. From the intake, the water is piped to a treatment plant, where it is purified. *Question:* "Why is the intake at the bottom of the lake?" (Water at the bottom of a lake freezes last; in times of drought, water is more likely to be available at the bottom.)

Picture-diagram 4: The purified water may be pumped directly to users, or it may be pumped into a storage tank. *Question:* "Why must the storage tank be higher than all buildings in the community?" (Water will not rise higher than its source. Any outlet higher than the storage tank will not receive water.)

Picture-diagram 5: Water under pressure fills all the large *water mains* and all the smaller pipes in houses and other buildings. *Question:* "What might happen to the water pressure if all of the outlets in a house were turned on at once?" (The pressure, and hence the water flow, might decrease to the point of trickles.)

Answers to the Exercise

1. 4, 2, 3, 5, 1

2a. Watering, bathing, cooking, laundering

b. The arrows indicate direction

c. The suction created by the pumps draws in water, but also draws debris

Name _____   Date _____

WATER FOR CITIES FROM RIVERS AND LAKES

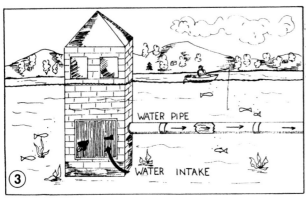

1. Write the number of the picture-diagram before the title below that best describes it.

_____ Water is pumped from the waterworks to the storage tank.

_____ Lakes furnish much of our drinking water.

_____ Water from a lake is piped to a waterworks.

_____ A household uses water in many ways.

_____ Rivers offer a constantly changing and fresh supply of water.

2. *Picture study:*

a. In what four ways is water being used by the family shown in Picture 5?

_____   _____

_____   _____

b. As shown in Picture 4, how do you know that water goes up one pipe and down another?

_____

c. Notice the items that are caught on the screen in Picture 3. Why would such items be attracted to the screen? _____

_____

_____

Water as a Universal Geography Significant: Water from Under the Ground

Background

1. Water from underground sources sometimes flows naturally from the earth. If the water flows without human assistance from a natural opening, it is called a *spring*.

Water issuing from an opening on the side of a mountain is most likely a gravity flow. The force of gravity makes the water within the mountain run downhill until it finds an opening and issues forth.

Water issuing from a natural hole in a valley floor is most likely a pressure flow. The weight of the water higher up in the hills presses the water out of the opening.

Some facts about springs:
—Some springs are mere trickles of water. They may not flow all year. Other springs may issue thousands of gallons of water daily.
—Most of the oases found in deserts are springs. The water may have traveled underground for hundreds of miles before finding an opening.

2. Nature doesn't always provide holes for water to reach the surface. So holes must be drilled or dug to where the water can be tapped. Sometimes a pipe can be driven into the ground to reach the water. Once the water is reached, a flow much like a fountain will begin. No mechanical or manual pumping is required; the flow is natural. Such wells are known as *artesian*.

Australia is one of the world's greatest users of artesian wells. Without them, much of Australia's interior would be practically useless for farming and ranching.

Student Involvement

The diagram should be carefully explained. The artesian well should be given special attention. An artesian well flows only when there is water in the layer that is higher than the surface opening. The pressure of the water at higher elevations than the opening pushes water out of the hole. Note that the small x in the diagram at the extreme left of the saturated layer is at a higher level than the opening of the artesian well.

Answers to the Exercise

1. Dug well, windmill, artesian well, drilled well

2. [Check for dots in the saturated area. If the layer is colored completely, it is incorrect, because this would give the impression of a pool of water, which it is not.]

3. Clay, rock

4. A pail is lowered into the water and then raised

5. Artesian well

6. The statement is true

Name _____ Date _____

WATER FROM UNDER THE GROUND

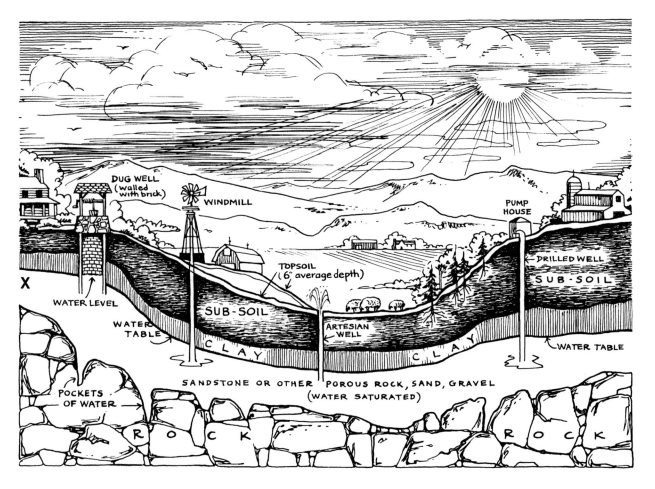

1. The diagram shows four ways to obtain water from under the ground. What are the four ways?

_____

_____

_____

_____

2. The blank layer on the diagram is the layer from which most well water comes. To understand how the water is stored there, think of the layer as a kind of sponge that is soaked with water—that is, saturated.

To represent the water, make many dots in the layer with a blue pen or crayon.

3. Complete this sentence: Above the saturated layer is a layer of _____.

Below this layer is _____.

4. According to the diagram, how is water obtained from the dug well?

_____

_____

5. In which one of the wells does water flow naturally (no pump or energy source of any kind is shown)? _____

6. Check this statement if it is true.

____ The water table is further below the surface in some places than others.

Water as a Universal Geography Significant:
When Does the Rain Come Down?

Background

Although it is helpful to know the average precipitation of an area, it may be even more helpful to know when the precipitation occurs. For example, if the rains occur during the growing season, there is reason to think that crops will thrive. But if the rain falls during the nongrowing season, the water may be of limited value for crop-growing purposes. For this reason, graphs or tables of monthly precipitation are very useful.

Student Involvement

1. Explain the importance of monthly precipitation data for farmers and others (for example, those who may be contemplating constructing a ski area that would be dependent on snow).

2. Refer to the table of statistics on the bottom of the facing page. Call attention to the following:
—Title: The averages were obtained from a thirty-year period, 1951–1980.
—Precipitation: Rain, snow, sleet, hail.
—Inches: Work toward an understanding of what "an inch of rain" really means—that is, 1 inch of rain over one acre (43,560 square feet) equals 27,154 gallons of water.
—Locate the four cities on a map.

—Ask some questions that require studying the table. For example: "How much precipitation can be expected in Philadelphia in September?"

3. Refer to the line graph. Call attention to the following:
—Title.
—Vertical axis and heading; horizontal axis and heading.
—Read Seattle's graph line with the students following along. Show how the line was derived from point to point with data from the table.

4. Have students complete the exercise. The steps in graphing a city's precipitation are these: (a) obtain the precipitation figure for each month from the table; (b) on the graph, show how a particular value is placed at the point where the horizontal and vertical axes intersect; (c) connect the "dot"; (d) proceed to the next city.

Answers to the Exercise

1. Seattle, 38½ inches; Albuquerque, 9 inches; Philadelphia, 42 inches; Miami, 58 inches

2. [No answer required.]

3. Miami

4. Summer, winter

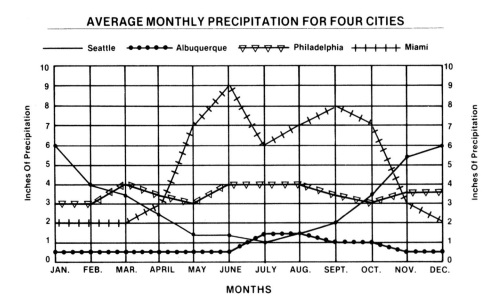

AVERAGE MONTHLY PRECIPITATION FOR FOUR CITIES

Name _____ Date _____

WHEN DOES THE RAIN COME DOWN?

AVERAGE MONTHLY PRECIPITATION FOR FOUR CITIES

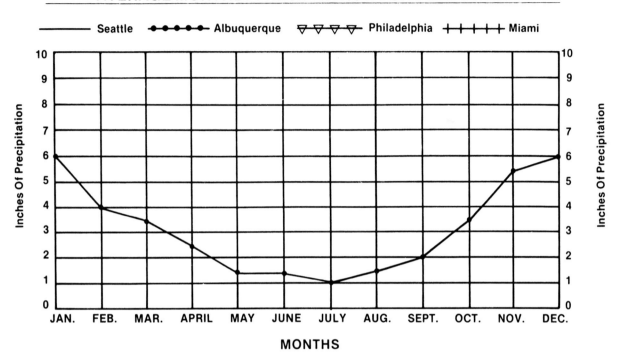

1. Figure out the average precipitation for each of the four cities listed in the table at the bottom of the page and write the answers in the "total" column.

2. Notice how Seattle's monthly precipitation is shown on the line graph. Do the same for the other three cities. Be sure to look at the key to the graph to see how each city should be shown.

3. In which city could you expect to sell the most umbrellas? _____

4. In what season of the year, summer or winter, does Miami have the greatest precipitation? _____

What is Seattle's greatest precipitation season? _____

	Jan.	Feb.	Mar.	Apr.	May	June	July	Aug.	Sept.	Oct.	Nov.	Dec.	Total
Seattle, WA	6	4	3½	2½	1½	1½	1	1½	2	3½	5½	6	
Albuquerque, NM	½	½	½	½	½	½	1½	1½	1	1	½	½	
Philadelphia, PA	3	3	4	3½	3	4	4	4	3½	3	3½	3½	
Miami, FL	2	2	2	3	7	9	6	7	8	7	3	2	

Water as a Universal Geography Significant:
Background for Teaching About Hydroelectric Dams

The next three exercises are concerned with dams.

Background

1. Dams are made for one or more of the following reasons:

a. To store water by blocking the flow of a river. Thus, a lake is created. The ready supply of water can be used for homes and businesses downstream or for irrigation.

b. To control flooding downstream. During times of heavy rains or melting snows, the lake behind the dam acts as a catch basin. The water can then be released gradually.

c. To supply water for the making of electricity. The water falling from the heights of the dam has tremendous weight. This weight, or force, can be used to turn blades, wheels, and gears in generators that produce electricity.

2. Silt will eventually fill a lake created by a dam unless a silt-removal program is in constant operation.

3. Dams can be damaged in many ways:

a. A dam's own massive weight may cause it to settle, causing cracks to develop.

b. The weight of the water pressing against a dam is enormous. The water pressure against a strip 1 foot wide and 200 feet high is 624 tons.

c. Earthquakes can cause a dam to crack.

d. Ice expanding and pressing against a dam may exert enough force to crack it.

e. Waves lapping against a dam may cause it to erode.

f. Weather elements cause erosion. For example, changes in temperature cause alternating expansion and contraction of the structure, which eventually weakens it.

Student Involvement

Present the foregoing information to build some background and readiness for studying dams and hydroelectric power.

Answers to the Exercises
Dams—Water Controllers

1. [Check pictures for correct labeling.]

2a. A road that acts as a bridge
b. A powerhouse and transmission lines

3. Swimming, boating, fishing, waterskiing

4. [Check for correct labeling.]

5a. Sun b. Waves c. Rain d. Ice

High Dams of the United States
and Canada

1a. Canada b. Mica c. 794 feet

2. 91 feet

3. [Check for diagonals in Mica and D. Johnson bars.]

4. Oroville

5. [Check for horizontals in the five United States bars.]

6. 272 feet

7. 684 feet

8. [Check for completion.]

Electric Power from Water

[Check for correct labeling of boxes.]

Name _____   Date _____

DAMS—WATER CONTROLLERS

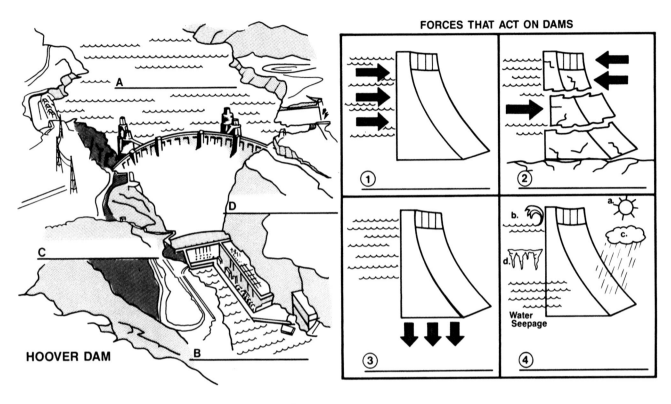

FORCES THAT ACT ON DAMS

HOOVER DAM

1. Label lines on the picture of Hoover Dam as follows:

        A: Lake Meade
        B: Colorado River
        C: Nevada
        D: Arizona

2. Study the picture carefully.

    a. What is there along the top rim of the dam that is helpful to transportation?

_____

    b. What is in the drawing that helps you to know that the water in the dam is used to make electricity?

_____

3. The answer to this question is not shown in the drawing, but you can answer it if you think carefully: What are four possible recreational uses of the lake and its water?

_____

_____

_____

4. Hoover Dam looks, and is, very strong. But there are forces that can weaken the structure. Those forces are shown in the drawings at the top of the page.

    On the blank lines in the drawings, label the forces as follows. At 1: *Water Pressure;* 2: *Earth Movement;* 3: *Weight;* 4: *Weather.*

5. Five things that make up weather and that can cause damage to dams are shown in Diagram 4. Try to identify the five things. One has been done to help you get started.

    a: _____ ;

    b: _____ ;

    c: _____ ;

    d: _____ ;

    e: Water seepage _____

Name _____ **Date** _____

HIGH DAMS OF THE UNITED STATES AND CANADA

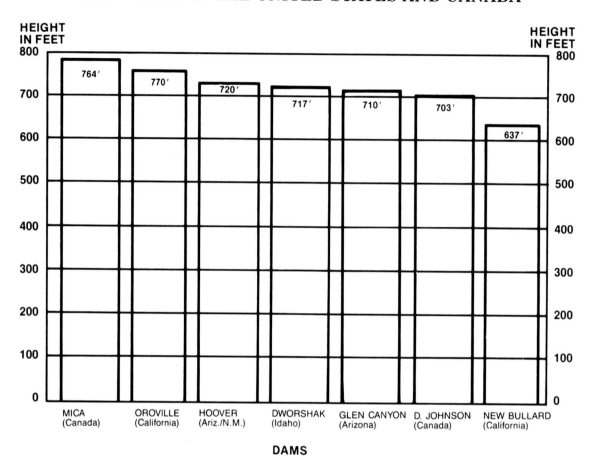

1a. Which country has the highest dam?

_____

b. What is the name of the dam?_____

_____

c. How high is it in feet?_____

2. How many feet of difference is there between Canada's first highest and second

highest dams? _____

3. Show Canada's dams by drawing diagonal (//////) lines in the bars that represent them.

4. What is the name of the United States' highest dam? _____

5. Show the United States dams by drawing horizontal (≡) lines in the bars that represent them.

6. The world's highest dam, the Rogun, is 1,066 feet high. It is in Russia. How much higher is it than Canada's Mica Dam?

_____

7. The world's tallest building, the Sears Tower, is 1,454 feet high. It is in Chicago, Illinois. How much higher is the building than the highest dam in the United States?

_____

8. Add to the information that your graph shows. Carefully print at the bottom of the bars the names of the rivers where the dams are located. Mica: *Columbia R.;* Oroville: *Feather R.;* Hoover: *Colorado R.;* Dworshak: *N. Fork Clearwater R.;* Glen Canyon: *Colorado R.;* D. Johnson: *Manicouagan R.;* New Bullard: *North Yuba R.*

Name _____   Date _____

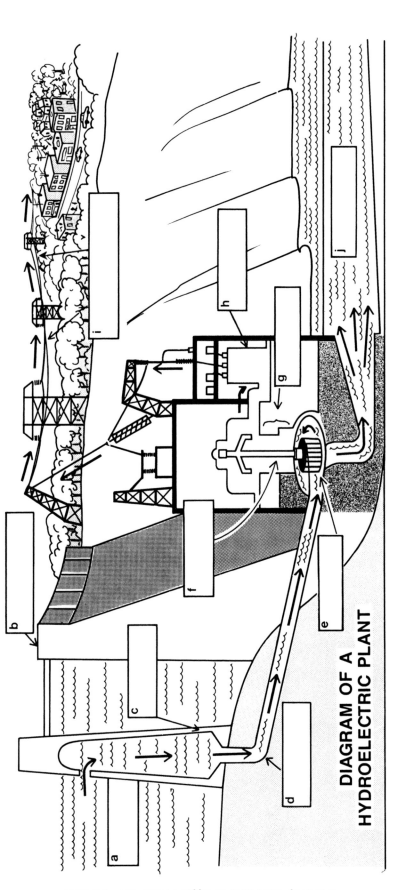

DIAGRAM OF A HYDROELECTRIC PLANT

ELECTRIC POWER FROM WATER

How does water help make electricity? The steps in the process are listed below. Follow the directions to complete the diagram.

1. Water is stored behind a *dam* in a *reservoir*, or lake.
Write *reservoir* in Box a. Write *dam* in Box b.

2. The water from the reservoir enters an *intake tower* and drops to a *pipe* in the powerhouse.
Write *intake tower* in Box c. Write *pipe* in Box d.

3. The force of the falling water in the pipe turns the blades of a *turbine*.
Write *turbine* in Box e.

4. A *shaft* is attached to the turbine. The shaft turns with the turbine.

Write *shaft* in Box f.

5. The shaft turns the machinery in the *generator*. It is in the generator that the electricity is created.
Write *generator* in Box g.

6. A *transformer* controls the electricity produced by the generator.
Write *transformer* in Box h.

7. From the transformer, the electricity flows to the *transmission lines*, and then through the transmission lines to homes and businesses.
Write *transmission lines* in Box i.

8. After the water has turned the turbine, the water flows out of the powerhouse into the *river*.
Write *river* in Box j.

Water as a Universal Geography Significant:
Polluted Water Kills Fish

Background

Each year, many millions of fish are killed needlessly by water pollution. Newspaper stories accompanied by photographs of dead or dying fish are commonplace. Some revealing figures on pollution-caused fish kills in a recent year:

—Estimated number of fish killed: 41 million.

—Largest single kill reported: 26 million.

The two greatest killers of fish are industry and agriculture. For the year reported, insecticides alone accounted for the deaths of 6 million fish, while waste food products killed some 27 million.

It should be realized that many more fish are killed than are reported. Many "small" kills caused by water pollution go undetected and unreported. Also, it is not only fish that are killed by poisoned waters. Newspaper photographs attest to the slow deaths of oil- and tar-covered ducks and geese.

Student Involvement

1. Present and discuss the foregoing information on fish kills. Be alert for reported news stories on the problem. Stories that occur on the local level have the greatest impact.

2. Refer to the pictures. Every picture has a main idea, sometimes more than one, and supporting detail. Have the students think of a main idea for each picture. Suggestions: Picture A—"No fishing today"; Picture B—"Frequent pipe inspections might have prevented this accident"; Picture C—"Must we kill fish to have paper?"; Picture D—"Oil on water means death to fish."

3. The completion of the activity will require the learners to observe closely for supporting details.

Answers to the Exercise

1. Pesticides leaking from drums.

Picture B: 2,000 fish were killed when a pipeline broke and leaked fuel oil into a stream.

Picture C: Government agents found 1,000 fish dead in a local stream. They said that wastes from a paper factory caused the damage.

Picture D: A derailed tank car that has been on its side for three days is still leaking diesel fuel. So far, 29,000 fish have been killed.

3. The air is being polluted by smoke.

4. Wooden posts could support the dock, or styrofoam floats could have been used.

Name _____ **Date** _____

POLLUTED WATER KILLS FISH

Pesticides leaked from drums that were used to support a dock, causing the death of 3,000 pounds of fish.

_____

_____

_____

_____

_____

_____

_____

_____

_____

1. When a fish kill is caused by polluted waters, newspaper reports often explain how it happened. Read the report under Picture A. What was the cause of the fish kill?

_____

2. On the lines below each picture, write your own brief report from what you see in the picture. In your report, imagine the cause of the fish kill. In Picture B, 2,000 fish were killed; Picture C, 1,000 fish; Picture D, 29,000 fish.

3. In Picture C, what else besides water is being polluted? _____

4. In Picture A, what could have been used to support the dock that would not have polluted the water? _____

Water as a Universal Geography Significant:
Making Water Pure Again

Background

An important consideration in the teaching of geography is the conservation of natural resources. Water is unquestionably a natural element that is being seriously abused.

Fortunately, unlike most other resources, water may be used again and again if it is given proper treatment. Unfortunately, untreated and polluted water can destroy other resources, such as plant and animal life, that cannot be revitalized and recycled.

The following is information about the recycling of water, which is the topic of the exercise on the facing page.

1. In the United States alone there are over 1,000 communities that dump their sewage into rivers without treating it in any way. Of those communities that have sewage disposal plants, only two in every three follow all the steps that are necessary to return water to its original purity. In most cases only solids are removed from the sewage. Germs that cause disease and organic matter that robs oxygen from streams are not treated.

2. Other water treatment problems:

—How to get towns, cities, and states, as well as countries, to work together on waste disposal problems.

—What laws to make to regulate waste disposal.

—How to treat wastes resulting from the use of atomic energy.

—What to do about household wastes, including detergents, that are difficult to treat by ordinary methods.

Student Involvement

1. Bring to your students' attention the whole problem of polluted water and how to cleanse it.

2. Survey with the learners the seven basic steps depicted in the sequence of diagrams. Depending on the ability of the class, you may need to read the captions with them.

The diagram shows a common method of treating wastes. It is known as the *activated sludge* or *aeration* (air) method. In this approach, sewage is treated in three major ways:

—Solid wastes are removed by separation.

—Air and helpful bacteria work together to destroy harmful bacteria and other tiny organisms.

—Chlorine gas is added to the water in the final stages of the purification process.

Answers to the Exercise

1. Bottles, rags, logs, sticks

2. Step 3

3. Steps 5 and 7

4. Step 5

5. Chlorine gas

6. The fish might die from lack of oxygen. Some plants might die, but others might thrive because of increased nutrients added to the water.

Name _____ Date _____

MAKING WATER PURE AGAIN

HOW COMMUNITY WASTEWATER IS PURIFIED

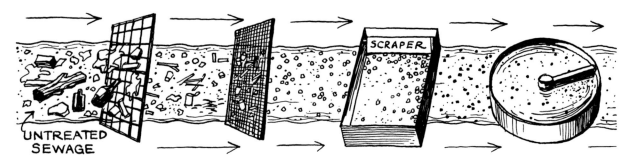

1. **COARSE SCREENING**
   - Large logs, bottles, rags, etc., are blocked.

2. **FINE SCREENING**
   - Small objects such as cans, paper cups, sticks, etc., are caught in the small openings.

   Screens are cleaned of objects by manual or mechanical rakes.

3. **GRIT TANK**
   - Dirt, gravel, sand settle to the bottom.
   - From time to time grit is scraped off the bottom and is trucked away.

4. **SEDIMENTATION TANK**
   - Fine soil particles, and other bits of matter settle to the bottom as sludge.
   - A revolving scraper pushes the sludge to an outlet where it is removed.

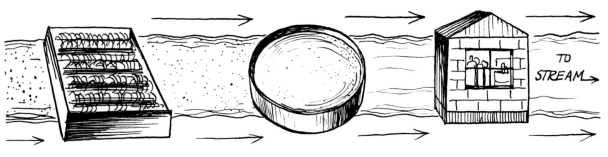

5. **AERATION TANK**
   - Air and sludge, which are loaded with helpful bacteria, are mixed with the sewage. After several hours most of the harmful bacteria and small organisms have been made harmless.

6. **FINAL SEDIMENTATION TANK**
   - At this point in the purification process about 90% of the harmful bacteria have been destroyed, but the water is not clear. It contains fine bits of matter. This sediment, or sludge, is allowed to settle.

7. **CHLORINATION PROCESS**
   - Chlorine gas is added to the water making it about 99% pure. The "pure" water is allowed to flow into a running stream. There is now very little danger of polluting the stream with sewage.

The diagram shows and explains the steps that can be taken to help polluted water become pure. Study the diagram and then answer the following questions.

1. What are some of the objects removed from the water in Step 1?_____

_____

2. In which step are sand, gravel, and dirt removed?_____

3. Which two steps are not concerned with removing objects from the sewage?

_____

4. In which step are harmful bacteria (germs) made harmless?_____

5. What is added to the water in the final step that makes the water almost 100 percent pure? _____

6. What might happen to the fish and plants in the stream if the water were not purified before entering the stream?

_____

_____

AIR AS A UNIVERSAL
GEOGRAPHY SIGNIFICANT

9-1   Air Pollutants and the Atmosphere
9-2   How Does Air Become Polluted?

Air as a Universal Geography Significant:
Air Pollutants and the Atmosphere

Background

Air quality is becoming increasingly important as a factor of our environment. For example, *acid rain*—rain polluted by acids collected from the air—is causing the death of untold millions of trees around the world each year.

Student Involvement

1. Direct the reading of the information in the box that is next to the diagram. A key concept to emphasize is that air has weight, and that weight is made up of particles and vapors.

To illustrate that air has weight, give the following demonstration:

a. Obtain a yardstick, or a dowel about 3 feet long. Find the middle of the stick and tie a string tightly around the stick at that point. This is the balance point of the stick.

b. Tie an uninflated balloon at each end of the stick. Demonstrate that the stick remains balanced when suspended by the string.

c. Detach one of the balloons and blow it up. Reattach the inflated balloon to the stick. What happens? The end of the stick with the inflated balloon goes down. Why? Because the air in the inflated balloon has weight.

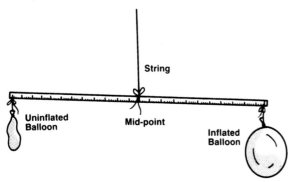

2. To illustrate the weight of air at increasing altitudes, draw a diagram on the board as illustrated in the next column. Notice that at sea level air weighs about 15

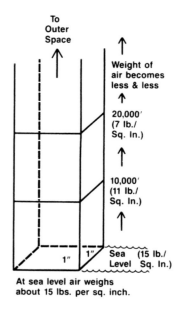

At sea level air weighs about 15 lbs. per sq. inch.

pounds per square inch, at 10,000 feet about 11 pounds per square inch, and at 20,000 feet about 7 pounds per square inch.

Point out that because of their weight and the pull of gravity, particulates are much more prevalent at the bottom of the illustration (the surface of the earth) than at the top (the upper atmospheres).

3. Discuss the diagram of the earth's atmosphere, giving special emphasis to

a. the cross-sectional aspects of the diagram;

b. the fact that the thicknesses of the layers are not drawn to scale.

Answers to the Exercise

1. Troposphere

2. Exosphere

3. Troposphere, exosphere

4. 3, 40°

5. The particles have weight, and gravity pulls them toward the earth.

6. 5½ miles, 6½ miles

7. 2,000°

8. Troposphere

Name _____ Date _____

AIR POLLUTANTS AND THE ATMOSPHERE

Air extends above the earth in layers that gradually blend into one another. Each layer has certain characteristics, as shown by the diagram.

All "normal" air contains solid particles such as pollen from plants, microbes, dust, and even salt from the sea. Air also contains invisible gases such as nitrogen and oxygen. All of these things give air weight. At sea level, a column of air extending from sea level to the top of the atmosphere with a base of one square inch would weigh about 15 pounds.

Because air pollutants have weight, they tend to settle toward the earth. There is usually greater air pollution near the surface of the earth than far above the earth. Since most human activities occur within 50 feet of the earth, it is important that this portion of the earth's atmosphere be kept clear of harmful particles and gases.

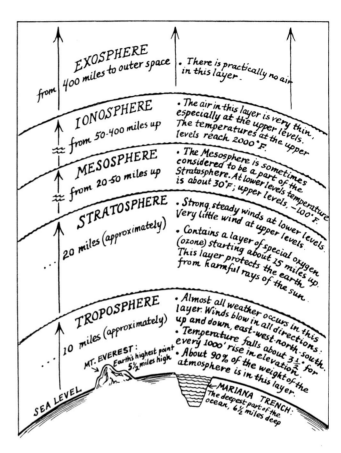

The answers to the questions below can be found in either the diagram of the earth's atmosphere or the story next to it.

1. Which layer of the atmosphere is closest to the surface of the earth?

_____

2. Which layer of the atmosphere is farthest from the earth?

_____

3. Which layer contains the most air?

_____

The least air? _____

4. Complete these two sentences: For every 1,000-foot rise in elevation, there is a decrease in temperature of about ____ degrees. If it is 70° F at the surface of the earth, it is about ____ F at 10,000 feet overhead.

5. Why are more air particles found near the surface of the earth than high above the earth? _____

_____

6. How high is the highest point on earth? _____ How deep is the deepest point on earth? _____

7. Rocket ships that reach the ionosphere must have some kind of insulation to protect them from the sun's heat. How hot does it get in the ionosphere? _____

8. In which layer, the exosphere or the troposphere, could you expect the most severe weather?

_____

Air as a Universal Geography Significant:
How Does Air Become Polluted?

Background/Student Involvement

1. To impress your students with the seriousness of air pollution, read to them the story that follows. At the point in the story where temperature inversion is explained, it would be helpful to have a transparency of the diagram (below) to show them.

2. At the conclusion of the story, discuss the implications of excessive air pollution. Mention that temperature inversions have happened all over the world many, many times. No one really knows how many people have died from such weather phenomenons, but certainly there would be thousands. This is one reason why the United States Department of Environmental Protection strictly enforces rules regulating air pollution.

DONORA, PENNSYLVANIA

In October 1948, a dense fog settled on Donora, Pennsylvania, a town of about 14,000 people. A layer of warm air hung over the town. The warm air prevented the colder air from moving. This kind of weather condition is called a *temperature inversion*.

Smoke from a steel mill, from chemical plants, and from other nearby factories and exhaust gases from automobiles and trucks could not escape into the upper atmosphere. Sulphur dioxide, other gases, and particulates continued to build up in the trapped air.

The result: About half of the people in Donora became sick. Twenty people died. Scientists and doctors who investigated the sicknesses and the deaths decided that heavily polluted air was the cause of the illnesses and deaths in Donora.

For years afterward, people who had become sick in the Donora incident continued to get sick more easily and die earlier than other people.

3. Explain that the exercise drawings show some of the things that contributed to the air pollution in Donora.

TEMPERATURE INVERSION
Under certain weather conditions a blanket of warm air may form over an area. When this happens the air near the surface is trapped because it cannot penetrate the warmer air above.

Answers to the Exercise

1. Picture 4

2. Picture 6

3. Picture 3

4. Exhaust from the truck and tractor

5. Fields and orchards, painting, insect spraying

6. Cars, trucks, airplanes

7. Volcanoes, sandstorms, wild forest fires

Name _____ Date _____

HOW DOES AIR GET POLLUTED?

1. TRANSPORTATION — Automobiles, airplanes, trucks, etc., pour more than 100 million tons of deadly carbon monoxide, other gases, and particulates into the air each year. Motor vehicles are our number 1 polluter.

2. POWER PLANTS AND FACTORIES — Industrial plants that burn coal and oil yearly exhaust some 75 million tons of pollutants including poisonous sulphur and nitrogen gases, carbon monoxide, vapors, and particles.

3. MISTS — When farmers spray their fields and orchards, or when a building is spray-painted, or when a marsh is sprayed to kill mosquitoes, liquid particles may escape into the atmosphere.

4. NON-INDUSTRIAL BURNING — When leaves are burning, the town or home incinerator is roaring, or even when ice skaters are warming themselves, smoke is entering the atmosphere. Smoke contains poisonous gases and particles.

5. VAPORS — Large quantities of gasoline evaporates from storage tanks, from gas station filling-operations, etc. Another source of vapors is unburned, or partially burned, gasoline from motor vehicles.

6. DUST — Dust can come from many sources other than soil. Chemical dusts are especialy dangerous to breathe. Some sources of dust are: quarries, chemical plants, saw mills, flour mills, cement plants, and cattle herds. Bare fields yield large quantities of dust.

1. Which picture shows situations that the average person could eliminate?

_____

2. Which picture shows a situation where a water spray could cut down air pollution?

_____

3. Which picture shows pollution resulting from an agricultural activity? _____

4. Picture 6 shows air pollution caused by dust. What other things in the picture contribute to pollution? _____

5. What three kinds of spraying situations are mentioned in the caption for Picture 3?

_____   _____

6. What three kinds of vehicles are shown as polluters in Picture 1? _____

_____   _____

7. Think of one situation where nature is an air polluter. _____

NATURAL CONDITIONS
AND PHENOMENA
THAT MODIFY THE EARTH

10-1 Forces that Act on Rocks
10-2 A Slice of Soil
10-3 The Making of a Volcano
10-4 The Moving Earth
10-5 The Beginning of an Earthquake
10-6 Glaciers—Masses of Moving Ice
10-7 All About Icebergs
10-8 The Work of Glaciers
10-9 The Ice Age

Natural Conditions and Phenomena That Modify the Earth: Forces That Act on Rocks

Background and Preparation

1. Section 10 is concerned with soil as a universal element of geography. The subject matter is used as a vehicle to develop skills in interpreting symbolic representation of ideas and realities via words, pictures, graphs, tables, and diagrams.

2. Some background information on soil:
—Six to eight inches is the average depth of topsoil over the face of the earth, although some places may have as much as two feet while others may have scarcely an inch. The figure for the average depth should be startling. Why? Because the earth has been in existence millions of years, and six inches of topsoil is all that has been produced. If our topsoil is depleted, how will it be replaced?
—It has been estimated that in the Mississippi River watershed alone—the land between the Rockies and the Appalachians and all the rivers and streams within—136 million tons of sediment are carried to the Gulf of Mexico each year.
—The chief natural forces of erosion are:

• the *heat of the sun*, which breaks down rocks through alternate heating (expansion) and cooling (contraction);

• *wind*, which "sandblasts" rocks and then transports the loose particles;

• *rain*, which loosens soil and then transports it;

• *frost and ice*, which freeze water in rock cracks, causing bits and pieces to split off;

• *rivers and streams*, which wear away banks and channels and carry away loose soil;

• *glaciers*, which scrape land and transport the pieces;

• the *sea*, which wears away coasts through wave action;

• *chemicals*, which combine to break down soil.

It should be kept in mind that none of the above acts alone; they work together. For example, wind may blast grains of rock loose, but water will eventually transport the pieces.

Student Involvement

After the information above is conveyed to the learners, the exercise on the facing page will serve as a follow-up.

Answers to the Exercise

1. From left to right the numbers in the picture are: (top row), 3, 2, 6; (bottom row), 5, 4, 1.

2. Water expands when frozen. The pressure forces the two sides of the crack apart.

3. The wind carries sand. The force of the moving sand dislocates small particles of the rocks.

4. They break the soil into smaller particles, which aids cultivation.

5. The alternating heat and cold puts stress on the rocks, causing them to split.

Name _____   **Date** _____

FORCES THAT ACT ON ROCKS

HOW ROCKS ARE BROKEN DOWN

1. Moving water, such as waves breaking on a shore, wears away rocks into fine bits.

2. Water in a rock crack expands when it freezes. The expansion force is so great it can split the rock.

3. Oxygen, carbon dioxide, and moisture are all present in air. When they combine with chemicals in rocks, the rocks break down and decay.

4. The pelting, grinding action of wind-driven dust or sand can reduce great rocks to small grains.

5. Earthworms take soil into their systems. After they have taken food from the soil, they discard the soil, but in much smaller grains than when they took it in.

6. Changes in temperature will help turn rocks into soil. During the day, rocks expand as they are warmed by the sun. After the sun goes down, rocks cool and contract (shrink). The expansion and contraction puts stress on the rocks and may cause them to split.

1. Powdered rock is the most common part of soil. The information in the box at the right tells how rocks are turned into powder.

Match the numbered descriptions in the box with the pictures above. Write the numbers of the descriptions in the circles in the pictures.

2. How is it possible for a small amount of ice to crack a rock?

_____

_____

3. What part does the wind play in wearing away rocks?

_____

_____

4. Why would earthworms be good to have in gardens?

_____

_____

5. Many deserts are cold at night and warm during the day. How does this affect rocks in a desert?_____

_____

_____

Natural Conditions and Phenomena That Modify the Earth:
A Slice of Soil

Background

1. The earth's surface is covered with layers of soil. Soil profiles are easily noticeable in embankments along roads or in excavations for buildings.

2. The upper layer, Horizon O in the accompanying exercise, is rich in organic materials. The layer is dark because of the decay that is occurring. Horizon O is not topsoil. When it is mixed with soil from Horizon A, it is considered to be part of the topsoil.

3. Horizon A becomes enriched by the materials from Horizon O that are moved downward through water percolation. Horizon A, which is sometimes called the "leaching zone," dissolves (leaches) minerals and nutrients from the Horizon O materials.

4. Horizon B, subsoil, accumulates much of the dissolved materials from Horizon A. Eventually—over a period of many, many years—Horizon B could become capable of sustaining plants.

5. Horizon C, through weathering processes, mostly chemical action, is in the process of breaking down rock into smaller particles.

Student Involvement

1. The soil diagram your students will be studying represents the "average" cross section of soil. Be sure they understand that no two samples of soil will be alike, although there may be general similarities. Even soil samples taken a few feet apart may be different. Soils from around the world differ greatly.

2. Explain the diagram and emphasize the following:

—A *horizon* is a layer of soil. It is not the horizon that we see in the distance where the sky and the earth seem to meet.

—The thickness of soil horizons can vary greatly from place to place.

—In the diagram, these symbols (⬭) represent the larger stones and rocks, while these (⁖⁘) represent smaller stones and gravel bits.

—The plants shown in the diagram are about 6 to 8 inches high. As they grow, the root system will become denser and the roots will penetrate more deeply into the horizons.

—If trees were shown on the surface, we could expect the roots to be heavier and deeper.

Answers to the Exercise

1. Four

2*a*. 2 inches   *b*. Young plants

3*a*. 10 inches   *b*. 12 inches

4. 30 inches

5. A

6. It has larger rocks, no roots, fewer small particles, and the layer is thicker than the others

7. Horizons A and B

8. The soil in Horizons A and B would be mixed from plowing. The layers would not be discernible.

Name _____ **Date** _____

A SLICE OF SOIL

ORGANIC MATERIAL: Many dead and decaying plants and animals...loose and crumbly...lots of air spaces...black or dark brown

TOP SOIL: Contains various minerals *leached* (dissolved) from the decaying plants above... loose and crumbly...dark brown to yellow

SUBSOIL: Thicker and heavier than the materials in Horizons 0 and A...very poor soil for growing plants

ROCK AND ROCK PARTICLE: Useless for growing plants...color varies according to the kind of rock

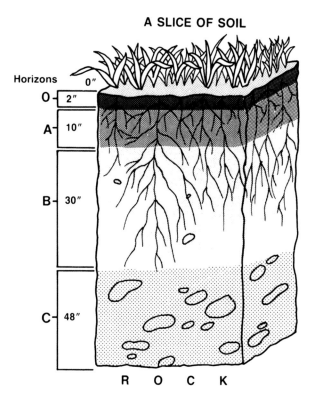

A SLICE OF SOIL

If you cut a slice of soil out of a field that has never been farmed, it would look something like the diagram. Of course, the slices would look different from field to field.

Study the diagram to get the answers to the questions that follow.

1. How many layers, or horizons, of soil are shown?_____

2a. About how thick is the O horizon?

_____

 b. What is growing out of the O horizon?

_____

3a. About how thick is the A horizon?

_____

 b. How far below the surface is the bottom of the A horizon?_____

4. How thick is the B horizon?_____

5. Which horizon, A or B, has the densest root system?_____

6. What are three or four ways that the C horizon is different from the other horizons?

_____

_____

_____

_____

7. According to the information to the left of the diagram, what two horizons are the best for growing plants?

_____

8. Thought question: Why would a soil slice from a plowed field be entirely different from the slice shown in the diagram?

_____

_____

_____

Natural Conditions and Phenomena That Modify the Earth:
The Making of a Volcano

Background

Volcanoes are one of nature's great forces for altering the face of the earth. The materials they spew have created mountains and have filled in valleys and other depressions. Lava from volcanoes has leveled forests and turned the courses of rivers. Islands have been destroyed by volcanoes, and cities have been obliterated.

Following are some more facts about volcanoes:

—Many islands are of volcanic origin, including the Hawaiian Islands. Here is how they are formed: Underwater eruptions gradually build up layers of lava. Eventually, the pile of dried lava emerges from beneath the water and an island is begun. Continued eruptions enlarge the island. Gradually, seeds take hold in the fertile lava, and vegetation grows.

—The world has volcano "belts" where volcanic action is most likely to occur. One belt is the mountain range that runs along the west coast of North America and South America from Alaska through Chile. Another belt is located on the east coast of Asia from Siberia to New Zealand. Volcanoes are especially active in the islands of Southeast Asia.

—In 1883, a volcanic eruption on the island of Krakatau in Indonesia resulted in the deaths of 36,000 people from lava, debris, and a tidal wave caused by the explosion.

—About 65 percent of all volcanic eruptions occur in the northern hemisphere.

—The contiguous United States has two active volcanoes: Lassen Peak, California, and Mount St. Helens, Washington. However, Hawaii and Alaska have several volcanoes. There are thirty-two active vents in the Aleutian Islands. Mauna Loa in Hawaii is the largest volcanic mountain in the world, with a crater of 3.7 square miles.

—Even Antarctica has five active volcanoes, the last two of which were discovered in 1982.

—When volcanic ash falls on land, it eventually becomes part of the soil. It is a natural fertilizer that has significantly enriched soil in many parts of the world.

Student Involvement

The story "The Making of a Volcano" will cause the learners to interact with the diagram and thus lead to better comprehension. However, it may be necessary to explain the cross-sectional aspects of the diagram before the story is read.

Answers to the Exercise

1. [Check for correct labeling.]

2. The vents branching off the conduit offer means of escape for magma and gases.

3. Heat within the earth

4. Pressure "pushes" the magma to a natural opening, or else creates an opening.

5. They could be buried by magma, or set afire by the heat.

Name _____   Date _____

THE MAKING OF A VOLCANO

Beneath the outer surface of the earth it is very hot. It is so hot that rock is melted into a thick molasses-like liquid called *magma* (1). As the magma becomes heated, it expands. Gases and steam form. The pressure against the rock surrounding the magma is tremendous. If a weak spot in the earth's crust is found, the gases burst out of the opening. Rocks, ashes, sparks, and fire shoot into the air like giant fireworks. The magma flows out of the opening.

The "pipe" that the materials use to escape to the earth's surface is called a *conduit* (2). The hole at the earth's surface is a *crater* (3).

The magma that flows into the open air takes a new name—*lava* (4). As the lava flows, it cools and hardens into layers. Over a long period of time, perhaps hundreds or thousands of years, the layers may take the shape of a *cone* (5). The cone may reach thousands of feet into the air.

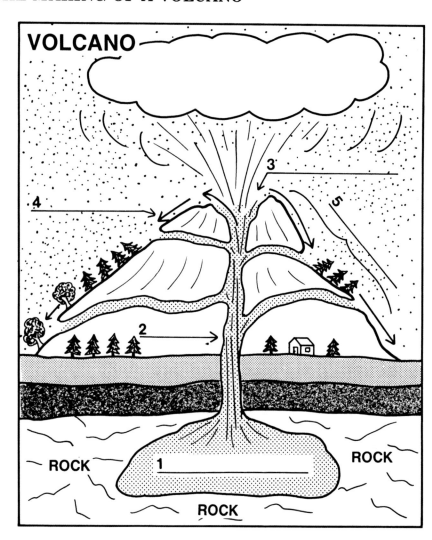

VOLCANO

ROCK   ROCK   ROCK

1. In the story in the box above, words that are special for understanding volcanoes are printed in italics. Each word is followed by a number in parentheses. Write on the lines in the diagram the words that identify the parts of the volcano.

2. According to the diagram, magma and gases escape through the volcano crater. What other means of escape is also used?

_____

_____

3. What causes magma to be formed?

_____

_____

4. What causes the magma to flow out of a weak spot in the earth's surface?

_____

_____

5. Thought question: What are two ways that trees on the sides of the volcano could be

destroyed?_____

_____

6. An erupting volcano is spectacular. Bright reds and yellows fly from the crater and dance and flash in the atmosphere. Color the air parts of your diagram as described above, and make the magma a brownish-orange color to show heat.

Natural Conditions and Phenomena That Modify the Earth:
The Moving Earth

Background

Earthquakes are a major force in shaping the earth. There is at least one earthquake every minute of the day, every day of the year.

Student Involvement

1. Drawings such as those on the opposite page are the artist's conceptions of real things. Every attempt is made to portray reality as simply and accurately as possible. However, it is virtually impossible to show by symbols exactly what the real object looks like.

Young learners are quite literal in their interpretation of symbols. They may not realize that artists cannot show, for example, a cross section of the earth in all its detail. If that were possible, much more space would be needed, and something else on the page would have to be omitted. It is up to the reader to recognize that there are limitations in every drawing, and to imagine what the artist cannot draw.

The drawings on the opposite page are a case in point. When using those drawings, and all others of a similar nature, instructors should be sure that their learners really understand what they are looking at. Consistent attention to the problem of accurate interpretation will bring about awareness in students and will increase their skills in observation and analysis.

2. To assist your students to interpret the diagrams, point out the following things:

—Diagram 1: The surface of the earth is not really smooth. Mountains, valleys, cliffs, and so on make the earth's surface quite rough. Also, the parts of the earth are not sharply separated by a dividing line.

—Diagrams 2, 3 and 4: The layers of the earth are greatly simplified in the diagram. They are not nearly as uniform in composition as depicted.

—Diagrams 5a, 5b, 5c: The sideslip is often accompanied by other actions. For example, one of the plates may "dip" at one end, as well as sideslip.

Ask the students if they notice any other elements of the diagrams that should be interpreted liberally. Perhaps they can make their own drawings showing the facts of the diagrams somewhat differently.

3. Have the students first read the story silently; then discuss it. Then have the learners respond to the questions at the bottom of the page.

Answers to the Exercise

1. Twelve (some scientists have estimated as many as twenty and as few as ten).

2. The plates move in various ways; this causes disruption on the surface of the earth.

3. Mantle

4. 50–70 miles; 1,800 miles; 2,200 miles

5. Movement apart

6. Diagram 4

7. It would probably have been torn apart.

Name _____ Date _____

THE MOVING EARTH

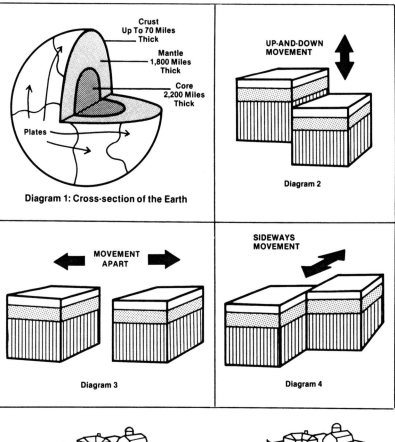

Diagram 1: Cross-section of the Earth

Diagram 2

Diagram 3

Diagram 4

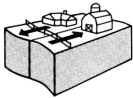

Diagram 5a: Before Earthquake

Diagram 5b: During Earthquake

Diagram 5c: After Earthquake

Earthquakes

What makes the earth "quake," or move? Many earth scientists believe that there are a dozen or so *plates* that cover the surface of the earth. If you can imagine a cracked egg, you will have an idea of what the earth looks like with its plates.

The plates, which are 50 to 70 miles thick, move slowly on the *mantle* of the earth. Diagram 1 shows a cross section of the earth, some of the plates, and the mantle on which the plates "float."

Sometimes one plate will drop lower than the plate next to it (Diagram 2). Sometimes the plates move away from each other (Diagram 3). Sometimes the plates slide against each other (Diagram 4).

When the plates move, the things on the surface of the earth move with them. When that happens, the result may be what you see in Diagrams 5a, 5b, and 5c.

1. According to the story "Earthquakes," about how many plates cover the earth?

_____

2. How do the plates cause earthquakes?

_____

_____

3. On what part of the earth do the plates "float?"_____

4. How thick is the earth's crust?_____

_____

the mantle?_____

the core?_____

5. Which of the movements shown in the diagram might result in a trench, or depression, in the earth?

_____ Up-and-down   _____ Sideways

_____ Movement apart

6. Which diagram—2, 3, or 4—shows what is happening in Diagrams 5a, 5b, and

5c? _____

7. What do you think would happen to the barn in Diagrams 5a, 5b, and 5c if it stood on the line between the two plates?

_____

_____

Natural Conditions and Phenomena That Modify the Earth: The Beginning of an Earthquake

Background

This activity concerns earthquakes that occur on the land surfaces of the earth. But it should be realized that thousands of earthquakes take place beneath the world's oceans.

Most ocean-floor earthquakes go unnoticed by the general public, but they are detected by the delicate instruments that record the earth's tremors. There are no observable results such as fallen buildings and rerouted rivers. However, if an opening in the earth's crust allows magma to escape, an undersea volcano may result. Or the magma may reach the surface, solidify, and become the basis for an island.

The most devastating effect of an underwater earthquake can be the *tsunami,* the Japanese word for *tidal wave.* Here is what happens: An earthquake causes the crust beneath the ocean floor to heave. The seismic waves produced by this upheaval create water waves on the ocean surface. The waves move with incredible speed—up to 400 miles per hour.

As the waves approach a shore, the *bottom* of the wave slows down because of friction with the ocean floor. The *top* of the wave hurtles on. Other waves crowd behind it and the water piles up, as much as 25 feet high.

When the *tsunami* slams against the shore, everything in its path gives way or crumbles: boardwalks, buildings, and streets. Huge ships are driven inland. People caught by a full-blown *tsunami* have little chance of surviving.

Student Involvement

It may be necessary to explain the diagram because it portrays two planes—one vertical, one horizontal. The vertical plane is a cross section of the earth. It should be noted that the focus of the earthquake in the diagram is arbitrarily set at 20 miles below the surface of the earth. Here are some other elements of the diagram to point out:

—The crust is shown as 40 miles thick, which is the distance from the focus to the surface, plus the distance down to the top of the mantle.

—The waves emanating from the focus move in every direction, not only in the set of concentric circles radiating from the focus.

—The horizontal plane starts at the surface of the earth. One should imagine oneself at the epicenter looking toward the horizon.

Answers to the Exercise

1. [Check for correct labeling of the diagram.]

2. Here are some of the elements of damage that could be reported in the learners' paragraphs: Overturned vehicles, buildings, water tower, fallen telephone poles, tangled wires, newly created waterfall.

Name _____ Date _____

THE BEGINNING OF AN EARTHQUAKE

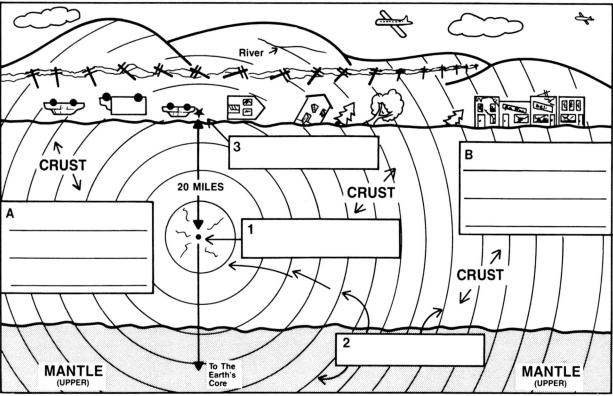

More About Earthquakes

An earthquake is born when huge masses of rock move below the surface of the earth. The point or place where the rocks begin to shift is called the *focus*. From the focus, seismic waves travel outward. Earthquake waves travel in much the same way that sound travels from a bell when it is rung. The sound travels in every direction—up, down, and sideways. Earthquake waves also travel in every direction from the focus.

The place where the seismic waves reach the surface of the earth is called the *epicenter* of the earthquake. Wave after wave follows the first wave, moving further and further out from the epicenter.

The waves shake the earth. Houses fall, streets heave, and water, gas, and oil lines break.

a. In Box 1, write *Focus,* which is where the earthquake begins.

b. In Box 2, write *Seismic Waves,* which is the energy created by the moving earth.

c. In Box 3, write *Epicenter,* which is the place where the seismic waves first reach the earth's surface.

d. In Box A, write *Waves travel in all directions*.

e. In Box B, write *Seismic waves weaken with distance*.

2. Think of yourself as a newspaper reporter at the site of an earthquake. You are reporting the damage as shown in the diagram. Describe in three or four sentences the kinds of destruction you observe.

_____

_____

_____

_____

1. Read the story "More about Earthquakes" before starting the exercise below. Then complete the diagram as follows:

Natural Conditions and Phenomena That Modify the Earth: Glaciers—Masses of Moving Ice

Background

Glaciers have been, and still are, primary shapers of the face of the earth. Although most of the glacial action has taken place in the Northern Hemisphere, great glacial action is still taking place in Antarctica, in the Southern Hemisphere.

Student Involvement

1. At the same time you are helping your students understand the glacier diagram, show them a simple three-dimensional model of a glacier. Here are some suggestions for making the model:

a. Obtain a piece of stiff cardboard, plywood, or styrofoam about 8″ × 12″.

b. Build a "valley" by creating two parallel mountain ranges. Block one end of the valley with another mountain range.

The mountains can be molded from clay, from a paste made of salt, water, and flour, or from wallboard spackle spread over crumpled paper. After the material hardens, paint it brown.

c. To represent "ice," fill one end of the valley with a soft, moldable material.

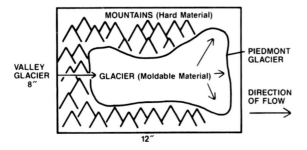

2. To demonstrate the movements of a glacier, do this:

a. Tilt the board slightly toward the open end of the valley.

b. Press the "ice" with the heel of your hand. Your hand pressure simulates the pressure brought about by the weight of the glacier ice.

Ask: "What else besides pressure or weight helps a glacier move?" (Gravity.)

3. Point out some of the limitations of the demonstration:

a. In a real glacier, the entire mass of the glacier moves.

b. The top of a glacier moves more swiftly than the base. Likewise, the sides move more slowly than the center. Frictional contact between the glacier and the valley floor and slopes causes the slowdown.

Answers to the Exercise

1. [Check the labeling of the diagram.]

2, 3. Weight and pressure

4. Approximately 38 miles (37.87)

5. Both rivers and glaciers flow through valleys.

6. As the ice at the beginning of a glacier flows out, new ice takes its place. (Ice at the terminal end of a glacier can be hundreds or thousands of years old.)

Name _____ Date _____

GLACIERS: MASSES OF MOVING ICE

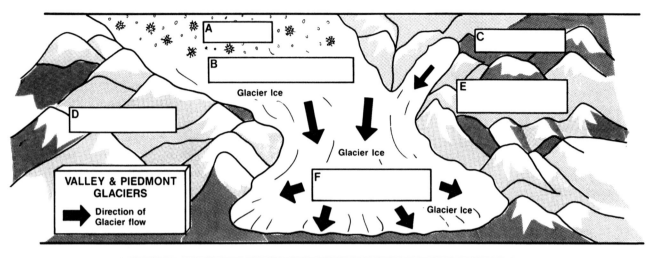

Imagine a lot of snow falling but not melting. Then imagine more snow falling on top of the first snow. This process goes on for thousands of years. The weight of each new snow presses on the old snow. The pressure turns the older snow into ice. More and more pressure from the top causes the packed ice to move slowly over the land. This great mass of moving ice is called a *glacier.*

There are many different kinds of glaciers, but the most common are *valley glaciers.* This kind of glacier begins high in the mountains. As the snow piles up and changes into ice, the glacier begins to move down the mountain valley. The downward slope of the valley helps the glacier move. The glacier may move only a few feet each year, or it may move hundreds of feet.

If the valley opens onto flat or level land, the glacier spreads out. This kind of glacier is a *piedmont glacier.* "Piedmont" means "at the foot of the mountains." Because of the spreading action, a piedmont glacier's ice may not be as deep as the ice in a valley glacier. The glacier will continue to move and spread in several directions.

1. After you read the story, complete the labeling of the parts of the diagram as follows:
Box A: *Snow*
Box B: *Valley Glacier*
Boxes C and D: *Mountains*
Box E: *Valley Glacier*
Box F: *Piedmont Glacier*
2. What are the forces that turn fallen snow into ice?_____
3. What are the forces that cause the great ice pack, or glacier, or move?
_____
4. Suppose a glacier moved 20 feet each

year. How many miles would this be in 10,000 years? (There are 5280 feet in a mile.)
_____
5. Valley glaciers are sometimes called "rivers of ice." Why is this a good way to describe valley glaciers?_____
6. Ice at the beginning of a glacier is said to be "young ice," while ice at the end of the glacier is said to be "old ice." Think of a reason why this is a true statement.
_____

Natural Conditions and Phenomena That Modify the Earth: All About Icebergs

Background

This activity is concerned with icebergs that emanate from valley glaciers. However, other types of glaciers, notably continental glaciers, which cover huge portions of the earth's surface, are accountable for large numbers of icebergs.

Continental glaciers are ice sheets or ice caps. The ice, which may be thousands of feet thick, spreads out on all sides. When the ice meets the sea, large chunks break off into icebergs. The most notable ice caps are in Antarctica and Greenland.

Student Involvement

After your students have completed the exercise on the facing page, further study of the story and diagram can be promoted by asking the following questions, which require critical thinking.

1. "Where on the glacier is it most likely that the next iceberg will split from the ice mass?" (The split will probably occur at the crevasse closest to the water because a crevasse will widen as the glacier moves down the slope.)

2. "Notice the ice 'shelf' on the iceberg second from the shore. The shelf is underwater. How does this present a danger to navigation?" (Such shelves cannot be seen by ships; consequently, many ships have been wrecked on icebergs. The sinking of the *Titanic* is probably the most famous of all the iceberg-caused shipwrecks.)

3. "Why are icebergs, which are very numerous each year, seldom seen off the coasts of northeast United States?" (Icebergs melt as the winds and currents carry them south into warmer waters, especially the Gulf Stream. Also, the United States Coast Guard dynamites icebergs that are in, or close to, shipping lanes.)

4. "How do icebergs reduce the salinity, or salt content, of the oceans?" (Most icebergs originate from snow, which is made up of fresh water. When the melted fresh water is added to the salt water, it dilutes the salinity of the ocean water.)

Answers to the Exercise

1, 2. [Check students' diagrams for correct markings.]

3. The rock was picked up by the glacier. It became embedded in an iceberg. The iceberg melted in the ocean and released the rock.

4. Some icebergs scrape the ocean floor, making grooves and other depressions.

5. A crevasse is a large crack in the surface of a glacier.

Name _____ Date _____

ALL ABOUT ICEBERGS

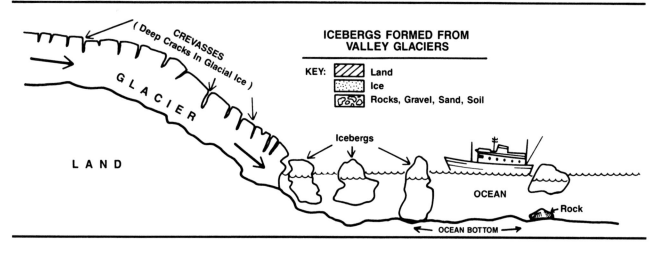

ICEBERGS FROM VALLEY GLACIERS

Some valley glaciers stop moving only when they meet the shores of an ocean. As the ice meets the salt water and warmth of the ocean, large pieces break off the front of the glacier. Waves, winds, and ocean currents move the *icebergs,* as the huge chunks of ice are called, out to sea.

Here are some interesting facts about icebergs:

—The frozen water in valley glacier icebergs is fresh. People in some ocean shore cities, such as Los Angeles, California, have thought about ways to get water from icebergs. One idea is to tow them to port and then melt the ice. The water could then be used for drinking, or to irrigate crops.

—Icebergs may carry large amounts of rocks, gravel, sand, and soil. Such materials are picked up by the glaciers as they scrape their way down the valleys. When icebergs melt, the materials they are carrying sink to the ocean floor.

—Some icebergs are so large that as they float out to sea, they scrape the ocean floor and cut long grooves in it.

—Icebergs come in all sizes. Some icebergs are as large as city skyscrapers. From a distance, they may look like mountain peaks.

—There is more to icebergs than the eye can see. Only about 13 percent of an iceberg is visible; the largest part is below the water level.

1. After reading "Icebergs from Valley Glaciers," complete the diagram as follows. Fill in the "land" portion of the diagram with the symbol for land shown in the key to the diagram. Then do the same for the "glacier" portion of the diagram.

2. Show with horizontal lines (≡) the parts of the icebergs that are below sea level.

3. Notice the huge rock on the ocean floor, below the iceberg farthest from the shore. From what you have read in the story, explain how the rock got there.

_____

_____

_____

4. Explain how icebergs carve the ocean floor._____

_____

_____

5. What is a crevasse?_____

_____

_____

Natural Conditions and Phenomena That Modify the Earth: The Work of Glaciers

Background

The traces that glaciers leave behind are readily visible. The long ridge in an otherwise level plain may be a terminal moraine; the turtle-backed hill, a drumlin; the lonely boulder, an erratic. It is hoped that this exercise will kindle in your students a curiosity that will motivate them to explore such natural phenomena further.

Student Involvement

The exercise on the facing page is designed not only to focus the attention of the learner on glacial terms, but also to provide practice in visualizing what is described in printed words.

It is sometimes difficult for young learners to visualize printed symbols, but it is even more difficult for them to "see" oral descriptions. This is because printed words may be read and studied over and over, but the spoken word, once uttered, is gone.

To provide an opportunity for students to experience visualizing the spoken word, the following activity is suggested.

1. Each student should have a blank piece of paper on which to draw.

2. Tell the students to listen carefully to the description that follows. They may take brief notes. After the description is completed, they are to draw their version of what was described. Brief annotations should be included in the drawing.

"I am going to describe what is called the *snow line.*

"Think of a range of mountains. The sides of the mountains are steep, and the peaks are high and sharp. The snow at the tops of the peaks is there all year.

"If one looks at the mountains from a distance, one can easily see where the white snow meets the darker rock and soil. The line between the snow and the land is uneven. This is the *snow line*—the line above which there is perpetual snow."

3. Examine your students' efforts. Perhaps one or two of the best drawings can be put on the chalkboard. The diagram at the bottom of the page is an idea of what the drawings might look like.

4. Think of other things to describe. Some suggestions for glaciers are medial moraines, cirques, hanging valleys, kettles, and kames.

Answers to the Exercise

1. First column: Lateral moraines, ice cave, erratic, striations. Second column: ice shelf, drumlin, terminal moraine, ice floe.

2. Rocks, stone, gravel, soil

3. Erratics are carried (in suspension, or rolled) by the glaciers.

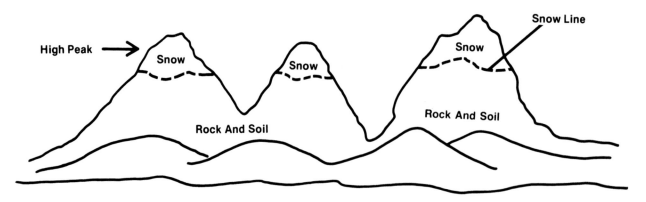

Name _____ Date _____

THE WORK OF GLACIERS

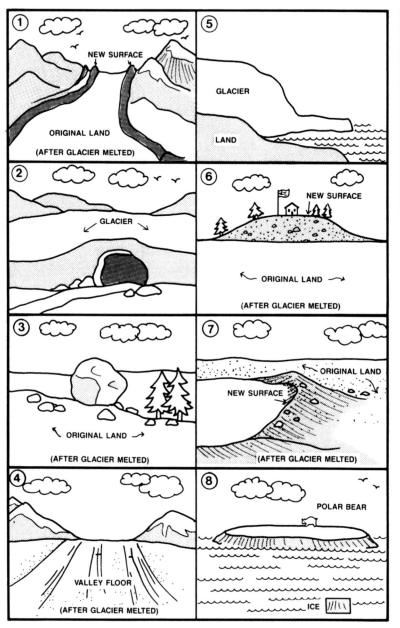

GLACIER VOCABULARY

Drumlin—An oval-shaped hill made up of glacial deposits. From the side, a drumlin has the appearance of a hard-boiled egg cut lengthwise and then laid on its flat surface.

Erratic—A large boulder that was picked up by a glacier and deposited far from its original surroundings.

Ice cave—An opening in the front, or face, of a glacier that is formed when glacial ice melts.

Ice floe—A large sheet of free-floating ice, usually flat on its top side.

Ice shelf—A large sheet, or shelf, of ice that extends into an ocean. The shelf is attached to a glacier, or to land.

Lateral moraine—A mounded glacial deposit at the bottom of the side of a valley. The deposit lies parallel to the sides of the valley.

Striations—Grooves in rocks made by passing glaciers.

Terminal moraine—A glacial hill or ridge deposit along the line that marks the end (terminal) of a glacier's forward movement.

The list above contains the special names given to some of the kinds of glacial deposits. Some other special glacial terms are also included in the list.

As glaciers move over the land, they scrape it. The scraping action loosens rocks and soil. These materials then become part of the glaciers and move with them.

When the glaciers melt, the materials that they have picked up are deposited. The deposits, called *drift,* may be in the form of huge rocks or gravel. Sometimes deposits take the form of ridges or mounds.

1. Each of the drawings above shows one of the terms listed in the "Glacier Vocabulary" in the opposite column. Match the terms with the pictures by writing the terms in the blank space in the pictures.

2. What are some of the materials that make up glacial drift?_____

3. How do glaciers help erratics, or large boulders, get moved to new locations?

_____

Natural Conditions and Phenomena That Modify the Earth: The Ice Age

Background

Ice was a major force in shaping the physical environment of the earth as it is today. Great ice sheets crept south from the northern latitudes into North America, Europe, and Asia on at least four separate occasions over a period of a million or more years. The effects of these ice invasions were profound:

—Some animal species were wiped out by the cold and the reduced availability of food. Other animals adjusted to their new environments through migration or physical adaptations.

—Valleys were gouged and mountains rounded by the moving ice. The debris that was displaced was deposited elsewhere.

—The formation of ice lowered the level of the oceans. Alternately, the melting of the ice increased the oceans' levels.

The map on the opposite page and the information above are concerned with ice in the Northern Hemisphere. However, Antarctica, in the Southern Hemisphere, is even today mostly ice-covered. One startling fact may serve to accentuate the immensity of the ice covering Antarctica: If it were spread over the United States, the ice would be more than 1½ miles thick.

Student Involvement

1. Point out that the map on the facing page is a pattern map; it is designed to portray information on a particular subject.

2. In order to complete the exercise, it will be necessary to use a map from another source that names the states and cities. This should be a helpful learning experience for the students because comparisons between maps will have to be made.

3. The table in the exercise lists only eleven of the fifty states. For a complete tabulation, it might prove useful to list all of the states.

The students should be made aware of the value of reorganizing information from one source (the map) into another format (the table).

Answers to the Exercise

1. Completely covered: Maine, Massachusetts, Michigan, Minnesota. Partly covered: Montana, New Jersey, Pennsylvania, North Dakota. No ice: Arkansas, South Carolina, Virginia.

2. Alaska, Washington, Oregon, California

3. Chicago, Boston

4. Greenland

5. Ice Age glaciers also covered water, as shown on the map by the shaded areas. Examples: The Great Lakes and the Atlantic and Pacific coastal areas.

Name _____   Date _____

KEY

Existing Glaciers

Areas covered by ice during the Ice Age

THE ICE AGE

The map shows how much of North America was once covered with ice. All of Canada and about 25 percent of the United States carried glaciers. The ice was so thick that even high mountains were covered.

A great drop in the world's temperatures caused the ice to form. When temperatures climbed, the ice melted and the land became green again. Then, for reasons that are not completely understood, temperatures dropped again. Snow fell for hundreds of years. The land was once more smothered in ice. The "freeze-melt" sequence occurred several times.

No one is sure, but it is thought that the "Ice Age," as the period was called, lasted at least 1 million years. The Ice Age ended about 10,000 years ago.

1. According to the map, which of the states listed below were once completely covered with ice, which were partly covered, and which were not covered at all? Place checks in the proper columns of the table.

State	Completely Covered	Partly Covered	No Ice
Arkansas			
Maine			
Massachusetts			
Michigan			
Minnesota			
Montana			
New Jersey			
North Dakota			
Pennsylvania			
South Carolina			
Virginia			

2. Which four states have glaciers today?

_____

_____

_____

3. Which two cities are located on land that was once ice-covered?

____ Chicago, IL   ____ San Francisco, CA

____ Memphis, TN   ____ Boston, MA

4. What great island in northern North America is still almost completely covered with ice?_____

5. Did the glaciers cover only land? Explain your answer._____

_____

STATISTICAL INFORMATION ON WORLD POPULATION AND PRODUCTION

11-1   The Sizes and Populations of the Continents

11-2   Wheat and Flour for the World's Bread

11-3   The World's Rice Bowls

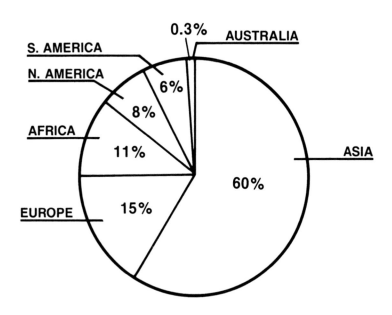

Statistical Information on World Population and Production: The Sizes and Populations of the Continents

Background

How people use the land on which they live is of crucial importance. The population cannot exist without the land, so it behooves all to understand the land and to take care of it. Some significant land and population facts:

—In 1650, there were about 5 million people on earth; today, the population is approaching 5 billion.

—75 percent of the earth is covered with water. It seems likely that given the finite amount of land and the earth's exploding population, we will have to turn more and more to the sea as a source of food.

—Only a small percentage of the land is suitable for producing food crops. Most land is too dry or too mountainous for agriculture, or its growing season is too short.

—China with 25 percent of the earth's people, has only 5 percent of the world's land. The United States, slightly smaller than China, has only 5 percent of the world's people. The Soviet Union, with 17 percent of the world's land, has only 6 percent of the earth's people. Implication: Land and people are not equally distributed and balanced.

Student Involvement

Demonstrate how the segments of the graphs were determined. Here is an example:

a. Asia occupies 30 percent of the world's area.

b. Multiply .30 by 360. The result is 108 degrees.

c. Thus, 108 degrees of the total 360 degrees in the circle is allotted to Asia.

d. With a protractor, measure 108 degrees on the circumference of the circle.

e. Draw lines from the center of the circle to the end points of the 108 degree arc.

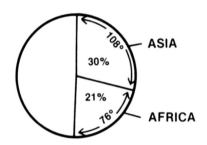

f. Proceed in the same manner with the next segment, Africa, which should be allotted 21 percent of the circle, or 76 degrees.

The area and population percentages shown in the circle graph are as follows:

Continent	Area %	Degrees	Population %	Degrees
Asia	30	108	60	216
Africa	21	76	11	40
North America	16	58	8	29
South America	12	43	6	22
Antarctica	9	32	–	–
Europe	7	25	15	54
Australia	5	18	0.3	1

Answers to the Exercise

1, 2. [Check for correct labeling.]

3. Asia

4. Antarctica

5. Asia

6. Africa, Antarctica

7. 4 percent

8. 2,907,000,000; 726,750,000

Name _____ Date _____

THE SIZES AND POPULATIONS OF THE CONTINENTS

AREAS OF CONTINENTS

POPULATION OF CONTINENTS

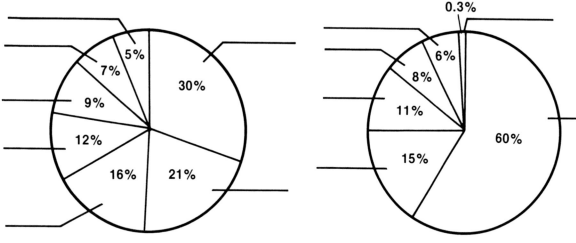

**World Population
4,845,000,000**

1. In the *Areas of Continents* circle graph, print the names of the continents listed below on the proper lines in the graph.
—At the 30 percent segment: *Asia*
—At the 21 percent segment: *Africa*
—At the 16 percent segment: *North America*
—At the 12 percent segment: *South America*
—At the 9 percent segment: *Antarctica*
—At the 7 percent segment: *Europe*
—At the 5 percent segment: *Australia*

2. In the *Population of Continents* circle graph, print the names of the continents listed below on the proper lines outside the graph.
—At the 60 percent segment: *Asia*
—At the 11 percent segment: *Africa*
—At the 15 percent segment: *Europe*
—At the 8 percent segment: *North America*
—At the 6 percent segment: *South America*
—At the 0.3 percent segment: *Australia*
Note: Antarctica has no population.

3. Which continent has both the largest

area and the largest population?_____

4. Which continent has no population?

_____

5. Which continent contains more than one-half of the people of the world?

_____

6. What two continents combined have

about the same area as Asia?_____

_____

7. How much more of the world's area does North America have than South America in

percentages?_____

8. Challenge Question: The estimated population of the world is 4,845,000,000. Using this fact, what is the approximate population

of Asia? _____

of Europe? _____

Hint: Continent Population equals Population Percent times the World Population. Don't forget the decimal point when you write the percent!

Statistical Information on World Population and Production: Wheat and Flour for the World's Bread

Background

There are some countries in the world, one of which is the United States, that are fortunately located for the production of grain, especially wheat. Their growing seasons are lengthy, rainfall is sufficient, soil is fertile, temperatures are mild, and terrain is level. The crops of these countries are so abundant that they not only feed their own populations, but also feed populations of less fortunate areas of the world.

This activity will help your students know who are the world's great food producing nations. It will also increase their geography data interpretation skills.

Student Involvement

1. If the single-bar bar graph is new to your students, it would be helpful if you explain its arrangement. Important aspects to emphasize are:

a. Each bar represents 100 percent of something (a commodity, group of countries, etc.). The sections of the bar show the portions of the total amount belonging to the various "contributors" to the bar. For example, in the graph titled "Who Buys American Wheat and Flour?" the bar for 1978 shows that Europeans bought approximately one-quarter of the wheat and flour exported by the United States, while Asians bought one-half of the wheat and flour exported.

b. The vertical axis labeled "Million Metric Tons" shows another statistic. It shows for example, that in 1978 Europeans bought about 8 million metric tons of wheat and flour from the United States.

c. The sections of a single bar could be shown by separate bars, as in a typical bar graph. Here is how the single 1978 bar of "Who Buys American Wheat and Flour" could be shown:

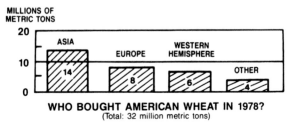

WHO BOUGHT AMERICAN WHEAT IN 1978?
(Total: 32 million metric tons)

2. Single-bar bar graphs are often shown in a horizontal rather than a vertical position.

Answers to the Exercise

1a. 1981   b. 1978   c. 1981   d. 1978

2. Asia

3. Europe

4. Africa (South America would be part of the Western Hemisphere, shown on the graph)

5. 1981

6. 1979

7. United States

8. 1981, 1983

9. 15

10. 200

Name _____ Date _____

WHEAT AND FLOUR FOR THE
WORLD'S BREAD

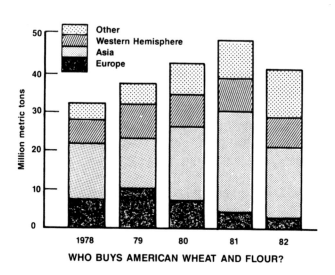

WHO BUYS AMERICAN WHEAT AND FLOUR?

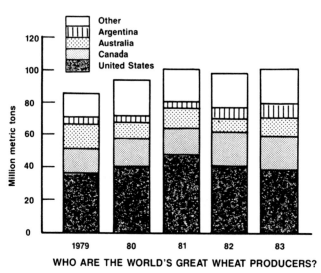

WHO ARE THE WORLD'S GREAT WHEAT PRODUCERS?

The following questions refer to the graph at the top of this column.

1. In what year did the United States
   a. produce the most wheat and flour?

_____

   b. sell the least wheat and flour?_____
   c. sell almost 50 million metric tons of

wheat and flour?_____
   d. sell about 32 million metric tons of

wheat and flour?_____
2. The people of what continent buy the most wheat and flour from the United States?

_____

3. Starting with 1979, what continent bought less and less flour each year from the

United States?_____
4. "Other" in the key to the graph refers to all the places in the world that buy wheat from the United States but that are not listed in the key. Which would most likely be one of the "other" places, Africa or South

America?_____

The following questions refer to the graph at the top of this column.

5. In what year was the most wheat and flour

produced?_____
6. In what year was the least wheat and flour

produced?_____
7. Of all the producers, which one produced the most wheat and flour each year?

_____

8. In what two years was the amount of wheat and flour produced about the same?

_____   _____

9. About how many more metric tons of wheat and flour were produced in 1983 than

in 1979?_____
10. About how many total millions of metric tons of wheat and flour did the United States produce in the years shown on the graph?

_____100 million   _____300 million

_____200 million   _____400 million

Statistical Information on World Population and Production: The World's Rice Bowls

Background

Wheat, rice, and corn are the three grain crops that are most important in feeding the world's ever-increasing population. Whether these crops are abundant or lean is largely dependent upon geography and climate.

Student Involvement

1. Before proceeding with the "bar graph building" activity on the facing page, it would be meaningful to point out on a map the rice-producing countries listed in the table. Arrive at the generalization that Asian countries dominate the production of rice.

2. It may be helpful to complete with the students Items 1 to 3 of the exercise. Then they should be able to complete Items 4 to 6 independently.

3. Item 6 calls for questions to be composed by the students. Have some of the questions read by the students and answered by others in the class. To help the class understand the kinds of questions they should ask, read to them the two sample questions that follow:

—"What percent of the world's rice did China grow?" (Thirty-eight percent.)

—"How much more rice did China grow than India?" (Twenty-one percent.)

4. At the completion of the activity, have your students construct their own single-bar bar graphs using the statistics on corn listed below. Graph paper should be used for this activity because lines are already drawn and conveniently spaced. A title, key, and horizontal numbering should be included. The rice graph may serve as a model.

THE WORLD'S LEADING CORN PRODUCERS*

Country	Percent
United States	47
China	14
Brazil	5
Rest of the World	34

*in a recent year

Answers to the Exercise

The facing page activity does not call for answers to questions; however, the learners' completed bar graphs should be checked for neatness and accuracy. A completed graph is shown at the bottom of this page.

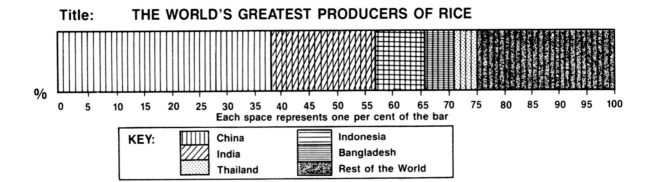

Title: **THE WORLD'S GREATEST PRODUCERS OF RICE**

%

0 5 10 15 20 25 30 35 40 45 50 55 60 65 70 75 80 85 90 95 100

Each space represents one per cent of the bar

KEY: China / India / Thailand / Indonesia / Bangladesh / Rest of the World

Name _____ Date _____

THE WORLD'S RICE BOWLS

COUNTRY	PERCENT OF THE WORLD'S CROP
China	38
India	17
Indonesia	8
Bangladesh	5
Thailand	4
Rest of the world	28

The information in the table above can be shown in another way—with a single-bar bar graph. It is often better to show information on such a graph because comparisons may be more easily made.

Complete the graph at the bottom of the page by following the instructions.

1. The figures in the table tell a particular country's share of the world's total rice production. What percent of the world's total rice was grown in China? The table tells you that it was 38 percent.

2. Realize that the bar at the bottom of the page stands for 100 percent of all the rice produced in the world. From the left side of the bar, count off thirty-eight spaces (38 percent) on the bar. Draw a heavy line at the end of the last space.

3. Fill in China's portion of the bar with the symbol shown in the key to the graph.

4. What percent of the bar "belongs" to India? The answer is 17 percent.

Count off seventeen spaces from the end of China's portion and draw a line at the end of the last space. Fill in India's portion with symbols from the key to the graph.

5. Complete the graph with information from the table for Indonesia, Bangladesh, Thailand, and Rest of the World.

6. Think of a title for the graph and write it on the title line above the graph.

7. Make up three questions and answers that can be answered from the graph or table.

Question:_____

_____

Answer:_____

Question:_____

_____

Answer:_____

Question:_____

_____

Answer:_____

Title: _____

% 0 5 10 15 20 25 30 35 40 45 50 55 60 65 70 75 80 85 90 95 100

Each space represents one per cent of the bar

KEY: China India Thailand Indonesia Bangladesh Rest of the World

APPENDIX

GEOGRAPHY ENRICHMENT ACTIVITIES

Three-Dimensional Elevation Model

A three-dimensional map made of modeling clay can do much to make altitude more understandable.

1. For a base, obtain a piece of plywood or stiff cardboard about 9″ × 10″.

2. Color the base blue. This represents sea level.

3. Make a key for the map.
    a. Decide on a scale. Each 2,000 feet can be shown by 1 inch of height.
    b. Make a color key for the map. A simple key could be:

> Blue—Sea level (the sea)
> Green—Sea level to 2,000′
> Yellow—2,000′ to 4,000′
> Brown—4,000′ to 6,000′
> Red—6,000′ or more

4. With clay, mold a coastline and inland elevations. Make at least one elevation 4 inches high (8,000 feet).

5. Color the map to conform to the key. That is, up to 2,000 feet (1 inch), color green; 2,000 feet to 4,000 feet (4 inches) color yellow; and so on.

6. At each 2,000 feet of elevation place a small paper sign that tells the elevation at that point. A toothpick can be used to hold the sign.

7. At the 6,000-foot mark attach a thread to the toothpick. Extend the thread to the sea on a horizontal level. Then tie the thread to a stick stuck in the "sea." From this your students will see that elevation is measured as the height of a place above sea level.

8. Various additions can be made to the basic model: snow lines, trees, lakes, islands, and so on.

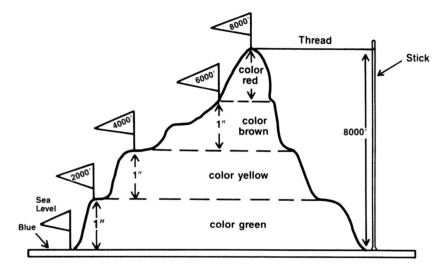

Finding Compass Directions with a Bar Magnet

A commercial compass can be used to establish the north, south, east, and west walls of a classroom. However, you can produce the same results with a bar magnet and at the same time make the experience all the more meaningful.

1. Obtain a milk carton, preferably the half-gallon size, and cut windows in its sides.

2. With a string, suspend a bar magnet from the top of the carton. If possible, paint the north end of the magnet red or blue.

3. Allow the magnet to swing until it comes to rest. Keep the carton well away from electric lines. In fact, it would be best to turn the electricity off in the room. (Electric current flowing through a wire produces a magnetic field.)

4. Mark the sides of the carton north, south, east, and west as indicated by the set of the magnet. Realize that the magnet is pointing toward magnetic north, not true north.

5. Label the walls of the room accordingly.

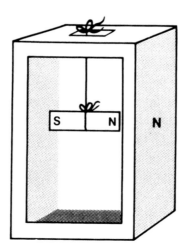

Map Jigsaw Puzzles

This activity can do much to help your students learn the conformations and place names of continents, countries, and states.

1. Obtain a number of maps from old textbooks and other sources.

2. Carefully cut the maps out of the books and trim them. Mount the maps on stiff cardboard. Gum cement and diluted white glue are good adhesives.

3. Cut the maps into a number of segments, as in a jigsaw puzzle.

4. Store the pieces in a manila envelope and label the envelope (for example, "Map of North America, 15 pcs.").

5. The map puzzles can become a part of your students' independent work activities, or they can be used as activities in a geography learning center.

Demonstrating Contour Lines

On a map, a contour line is a line on which every point is the same height from the sea as every other point on the line.

Contour lines are parallel to the level of the sea.

1. Obtain an open bowl, preferably glass. Pour about 1 inch of water in the bowl.

2. Place a rock in the bowl. Using a waterproof crayon or marker, draw a line around the rock at the level of the water. The water represents "sea level." Notice that the line follows all the rock's indents and bumps.

3. Pour another inch of water into the bowl. Draw another line around the rock, as in paragraph 2 above. Continue adding contour lines to the rock at height intervals of 1 inch.

4. Take the rock out of the water. With the crayon or marker, assign and write elevations on the rock's contour lines: Sea level, 1,000', 2,000', 3,000', and so on.

5. Remove all but one inch of the water from the bowl. Put the rock back in the water so that the first line drawn on the rock is at sea level. Keep the rock and water on exhibit and refer to it frequently.

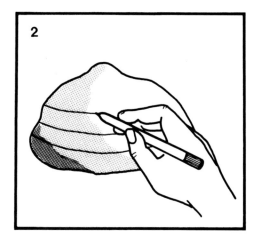

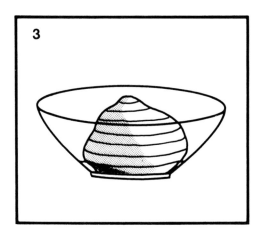

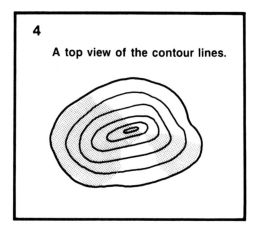

A top view of the contour lines.

Three-Dimensional Pattern Maps

1. Select a country, state, or region that the class is studying.

2. Determine with the children what is to be shown on the maps. One map may show a distribution of agricultural products, another a distribution of people, another a distribution of oil wells, or mines, or forests, or state parks, and so on.

3. Have the learners research in world almanacs, encyclopedias, textbooks, yearbooks, and other sources for statistical information about the product that will be mapped. For younger learners, it may be necessary to provide information of a simple and uncomplicated nature.

4. Choose three-dimensional symbols to represent the realities that will be shown on the map. For example, the southern part of one state may have produced 1 million bales of cotton in a recent year. Ten cotton balls, each representing 100,000 bales, may be glued to the southern part of the map.

Perhaps the northern part of the state produced 500,000 bushels of corn. Twenty corn kernels, each representing 25,000 bushels of corn, could be glued to the northern part of the map.

5. Each map should have a title and a key that explains the symbols and the quantities they represent.

Reading Road Maps

State road maps can usually be obtained from your state department of transportation. If possible, each student should have his or her own map. Once the maps are available, there are a number of interesting activities that can be carried out.

1. List all the names on the map that are of Indian origin, French origin, Spanish origin, and so forth. This experience will help your students realize that the ethnic and racial origins of our country are diverse.

Example for California (Spanish): San Diego, Los Angeles, Sacramento, Sierra.

2. As gleaned from the map, list the rivers and/or lakes of your state. Organize the information, perhaps alphabetically.

River	Towns and Cities Located on It
Passaic	Paterson, Kearny, Newark

3. Set up a series of "Which is the shorter route?" questions. Example: "Which is the shorter route, in miles, from Largo to Pilot Point via State Highway 17 through Kingston, or via County Road 322 through Pittstown?"

4. Set up a series of "What routes do I take?" questions. Example: "What

county, state, and federal roads does one take to go from Andover to Hamburg?" (County 517, State 181, State 94.)

5. Set up a series of "What towns do I pass through?" questions. Example: "What towns does one pass through, in order, when going from Florham Park to Chester on State 24?"

6. Place a compass (for measuring circles and arcs) on the scale of miles of the map. Let's say that the span between the compass point and the point of the pencil is 10 miles. Thus, 10 miles is the radius of a circle, and the diameter is 20 miles.

Select a city on the map and use it as the center of the circle drawn on the map. The task is to name all the cities and towns within a radius of 10 miles from the city.

Give the task a meaningful context. Example: "You are looking for work. However, on your bicycle you can't go any more than 10 miles from your home. Where could you work?"

Silhouette Map Flash Cards

From large maps, trace on cardboard the outlines of states and countries. Carefully cut out the shapes. On the back of the map write the name of the place shown.

For a few minutes each day drill the class on the names of the places. In some drills the maps should be shown in various positions, such as upside down. This technique helps the learners realize that maps can be read from a north-to-south orientation as well as a south-to-north orientation. Point out that on polar projections places are frequently shown in alternate ways.

Clocks That Show "Times" Across the Country

1. Make four "clocks" from large cardboard plates. Print on the faces of the clocks large numerals from 1 to 12. Cut out "hands" for the clocks and attach them with brass fasteners to the centers of the plates.

2. Attach the following signs to the clocks: New York, 75° W; St. Louis, 90° W; Denver, 105° W; Fresno, CA, 120° W.

3. Set the New York clock at 5:00 P.M., St. Louis at 4:00 P.M., Denver at 3:00 P.M., and Fresno, CA at 2:00 P.M.

4. Display the clocks with a backup map that shows the locations of the cities and their longitudes.

5. Play a game with the students: Set the St. Louis clock at 7:00 A.M., then have them show the correct times on the other clocks. Use a variety of settings.

6. If real clocks can be obtained, set them as explained, then display them. The advantage of this alternate procedure is that the clocks advance in time as the day wears on.

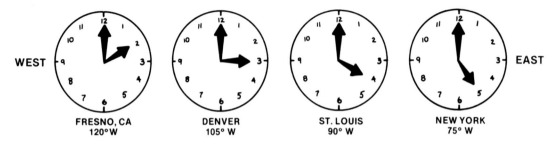

WEST			EAST
FRESNO, CA 120° W	DENVER 105° W	ST. LOUIS 90° W	NEW YORK 75° W

Making Rain

As air rises, it cools. After the air has cooled to a certain temperature (the dew point), it changes from a gas or vapor to water droplets. Because the water droplets have accumulated weight, when they get heavy enough they fall to the earth as precipitation. This process is called the hydrologic cycle.

This phenomenon can be easily demonstrated:

1. Boil water in a pan until steam rises. (The steam represents water evaporating from the earth.)

2. Over the rising steam, hold a cookie pan that contains several ice cubes. The pan, which has been cooled by the ice cubes, represents the cool upper atmosphere. (Be sure to use several paper towels as "insulators" between your fingers and the pan.) An alternate way to cool the pan is to cool it in a refrigerator. Remove the pan just before the demonstration.

3. Observe that the steam condenses into water droplets when it strikes the pan.

4. Observe that the water droplets fall to the floor. Literally, it is "raining."

5. This three-step process—moist air rising, air cooling, condensation of the moist air—is repeated over and over in the real world.

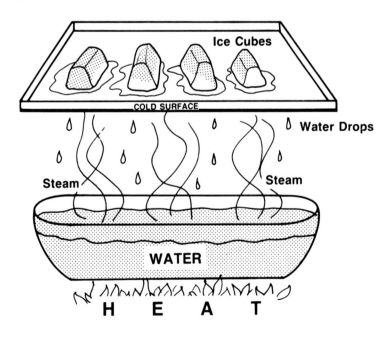

Water Waste

1. Set a water faucet so that there is a slight drip. Catch the drops in a measuring jar for an hour. Multiply the volume of the drip for one hour by the number of hours in a day (24); in a week (168); in a year (8,736). Convert to gallons.

Suppose that 10 million faucets in the United States dripped at the same rate. How many gallons would be wasted nationally in a year?

2. Students in the class may make surveys of their own homes to determine how many faucets are leaking and how much is leaking from each faucet. A class total may be determined.

Model Conservation Farm

1. *Information Background*

Help your students understand the following practices in conservation of soil and water.

a. *Contouring*—Plowing and planting crops across a slope rather than down a slope. Results: Water run-off is slowed down, allowing for greater soil saturation and decreased sediment carry.

b. *Windbreaking*—Planting trees in rows to break the forces of winds. Result: Pickup of soil particles from bare fields is considerably decreased.

c. *Terracing*—Shaping land slopes into "steps." Result: Similar to contouring; also permits marginal farming land on steep slopes to become usable.

d. *Strip cropping*—Planting fields with alternating strips of crops; for example, corn, soybeans, corn, soybeans, and so on. Result: Conserves water and soil nutrients.

e. *Willow planting*—Planting willow trees on the outside curves of streams and rivers. Result: Decreases amount of soil cut from banks as the water flows downstream. Thus, channels are not filled with sediment, and sediment is not deposited at the mouths of the streams.

f. *Lying fallow*—Setting aside fields to allow them to "rest and recuperate" by not being worked. Result: The land recovers some of its nutrients and general fertility in natural ways. Often, the land may be used for pasture and naturally fertilized by the animals.

2. *Activity*

a. Obtain styrofoam insulating boards and cut them to 6″ × 9″ × ¾″. Least expensive source: Lumberyards.

b. Obtain spruce twigs for "trees"; corn, wheat, rye kernels for "plants"; bits of hay for "pasture"; cardboard for "terraces"; glue; scissors.

c. Students sketch a conservation farm plan that shows contours, terraces, strip crops, fallow fields, windbreaks, and a stream with a sharp curve. Arrows show the direction of the prevailing winds and the direction of stream flow. They may show the location of a house, windmill, and so on.

d. After obtaining teacher approval of their sketches, students construct a three-dimensional styrofoam-based model of their sketch.

e. Some suggestions:
   —A heavy blue line can show the stream.
   —Brown or green lines may show the curves of the contours and strips.
   —Liquid glue can be lightly spread to follow the crayoned lines. Various seeds representing crops are then planted in the glue. Bits of hay and straw can be glued on the fallow field.
   —Spruce or other twigs can be planted along stream curves and windbreak rows. Stick the twigs in holes punched into the styrofoam.
   —A house made of cardboard may be placed on the farm. Windbreaks can be planted around the house to give protection.

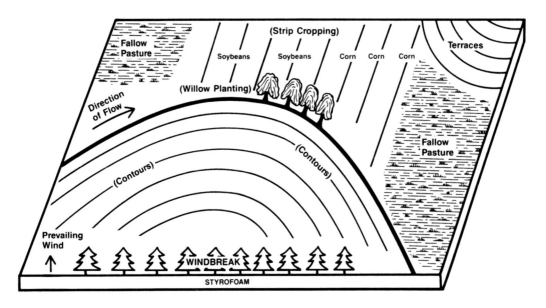

Making Soil

An effective way to demonstrate the composition of soil is to make some soil. However, your learners should realize that the soil they are going to make in a few minutes would not be made so quickly in nature.

1. Ask: "What are the things that make up soil?" (Powdered rock, bits of rock, decayed vegetable matter, decayed animal matter, fecal matter, and various minerals such as iron, potassium, nitrogen, phosphate, and lime.)

2. Obtain some soft rocks, especially limestone or sandstone. However, old bricks or even concrete will do. Have your students rub the rocks together. This simulates the action that occurs when physical changes and the forces of wind and rain combine to reduce rocks to powder. The powder and bits of rock obtained from the rubbings should be gathered and placed in a pot.

3. Mix some decayed vegetable matter such as peat moss with the rock.

4. Some dried insects and dried fish food should be entered into the mix. These things represent the remains of dead animals, such as deer and squirrels, that contribute to the organic composition of the soil.

**1. Rocks rubbed
   together**

**2. Add organic and
   inorganic materials
   to rock powder**

**3. Plant seeds,
   place in sunlight,
   add water**

5. Small quantities of a commercial fertilizer that contains potassium, phosphate, and nitrogen can be entered into the mix. These ingredients represent the minerals found in soil.

6. Dried cow manure, available in commercial preparations such as Bovung, represents the droppings of animals such as cows and horses. Fecal matter is rich in organic matter.

7. Add some limestone, another mineral.

8. Fill a suitable container with the mixture. Plant some quick-growing seeds such as lima beans, water them, and observe the results—a thriving plant.

Sediment in Water

1. Pour soil into a jar so that it is about one-third filled. Pour water into the jar. Shake well. Observe and then make a sketch of the layers of sediment. Where are the finest grains?

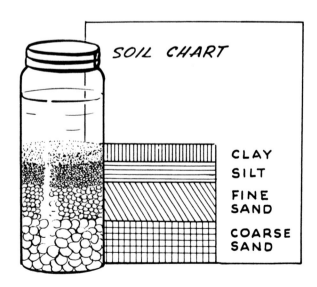

2. Place funnels in the openings of two jars. Fill one funnel with a mixture of soil, grass, leaves, pine needles, and so forth. Fill the second funnel with the same amount of soil, but no vegetation. Pour the same amount of water into each funnel. Compare the amount of time it takes for the water to drip through each funnel. Which jar contains the most sediment? How are the results related to sediment erosion of covered and uncovered fields?

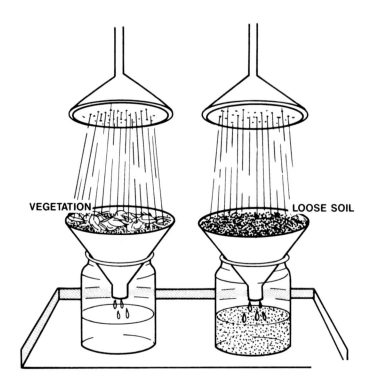

3. Before a rain, obtain a jar of water from a stream. Obtain a second jar of water from the same stream after a heavy rain. Observe and compare the sediment in the two jars. What conclusions may be drawn about soil erosion in the area drained by the stream?

Contours

Make two boxes about 2 feet long, 1 foot wide, and 6 inches deep. Cut a hole in the end of each box. Put equal amounts of soil in the boxes. Contour the soil in one box. In the second box, make straight rows running the length of the box. Elevate the ends of the boxes. Sprinkle the same amount of water in each box. Which box drains more rapidly? Why?

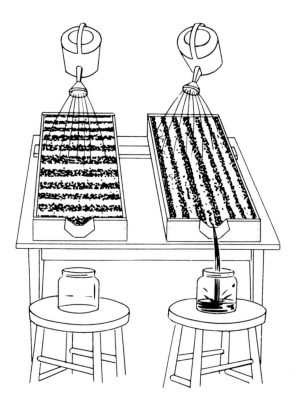

Reducing Rocks by Changes in Temperature

In nature, rocks are broken down in a variety of ways, including freezing and thawing, and expanding and contracting. In both of the following demonstrations, change in temperature is the cause of the rock action.

1. *Freezing and Thawing*
a. Obtain a piece of sandstone or other soft rock.
b. Soak the rock in water overnight.
c. Remove the rock from the water and set it in a tray. Place the tray in the freezer part of a refrigerator.
d. After 24 hours, remove the rock from the freezer. Allow the rock to thaw.
e. Observe on the bottom of the tray the fine grains that have separated from the rock.
The process illustrated by this demonstration goes on for thousands of years in nature. Whole mountains have been reduced by this process.

2. *Expansion and Contraction*
a. Heat in a pan a rock about the size of an orange. The heat will cause the rock to expand.
b. Plunge the rock into a pan of cold water. The sudden change in temperature should cause the rock to split or parts of the rock to flake off.

Mountain Ranges and Peaks

1. Obtain a number of rocks ranging from about 4 inches to 7 inches in height.

2. Arrange the rocks in a row in a long box about 6″ × 6″ × 18″. A plastic planter box used for windows and ledges would be quite suitable.

3. Pour plaster of Paris in the box to a height of about 3 inches. Allow it to harden, as in a mold.

4. "Break out" the mold. Now you have a mountain range.

5. Paint the mountains brown. On the highest peaks paint a snow line.

6. Devise an altitude scale. Let 1 inch = 1,000 feet.

7. Students may draw a profile of the range. Name each peak and write its altitude (measured from the level of the plaster of Paris) next to each peak's name.

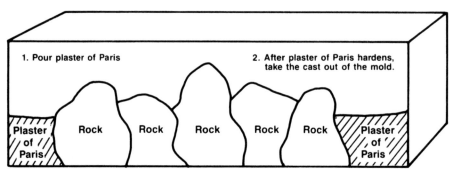

NOTE: Keep the rocks in the center of the mold. Do not allow the rocks to touch any of the sides of the box during pouring and hardening. The result should be an island mountain range. The top of the hard plaster is "sea level."

Erosion

Take a walk around the school grounds and the immediate neighborhood. Look for signs of erosion, such as soil that has washed on the top of asphalt in the playground or parking lot, soil that has collected in depressions along the curbs, rills or small gullies that have appeared at construction sites, small piles of sand or silt that have collected at the bases of fences as a result of wind erosion, small stones or gravel that have washed onto the road after a heavy rain, and end-of-driveway drainpipes that have become so clogged with sediment that water no longer flows through them.

Ask: "Where will all the sediment eventually go?" (Into the streams, eventually to the sea or some other inappropriate depository.)

Evidence of Air Pollution

Lightly coat plastic lids or cardboard squares with vaseline. Place the collectors in several locations around the classroom or school, including outside the building. Make a map showing the locations. After a day or so, collect the lids. Examine the lids for evidence of pollution. Try to identify some of the collected materials. Compare the lids with respect to locations and amounts of pollution.

Community Air Pollution

Take pictures of air pollution situations in the community: open burning in dumps, factory chimneys, home incinerators, dust from quarries, car exhausts, dust blowing across fields, and so on. Caption the pictures and display them.

Air Pollution and Plant Growth

Take two plants of the same kind, size, and age. Place one plant in a situation where polluted air will easily reach it, such as next to a smoky chimney. Place the second plant in a situation where air pollution is at a minimum. Keep all other conditions, such as amount of sunlight and water, the same for each plant. Observe and record the differences in growth, color, and general health of the plants over a six-week period. What conclusions can be drawn? How would large fields of crops be affected by polluted air?

Wind, Dust, and Air Pollution

The winds are significant contributors to air pollution. But polluted air is not the only effect of the wind. Winds blowing over unprotected soil bring about yearly losses in the United States and the world of millions of tons of topsoil.

Using a fan, demonstrate the power of the winds to erode soil, as follows:

1. Take a fan to a part of the school grounds where the soil is bare. Bring power to the fan with an appropriate length of extension cord.

2. Place clean pieces of white paper at varying distances from the fan: 10 feet, 15 feet, and so on.

3. Turn on the fan. Observe the clouds of dust that rise into the air.

4. Turn off the fan. Observe the dust that has settled on the pieces of paper.

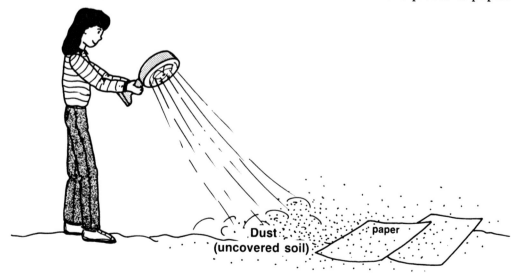

5. Perform the same demonstration at a location well covered with grass. Observe how the dust in the air and the dust collections on the papers have been considerably reduced as a result of the protective covering of grass.

Picture Collections

Enlist your students' aid in collecting pictures that show natural features. Some of the possibilities are islands, peninsulas, rivers, lakes, mountain ranges, mountain peaks, glaciers, mesas, plains, waterfalls, volcanoes, bays, and straits.

Each picture should be mounted (laminations add to the life of the pictures). Captions should be written that tell something about each picture, including the location of the scene. If possible, draw the picture as a map, or have the students make a map from the picture as one of their tasks. Classify the picture for filing and ready retrieval.

Especially helpful: Devise five to ten factual and inferential questions about each picture. Then place the pictures in a geography learning center where your students can independently study and respond to the pictures and the questions.

Travel Posters

Travel posters may be classified as follows: those that show a variety of the attractions of a country or city and those that single out a particular highlight. An example of the former would be a Mexican poster that shows Mayan ruins, a quaint rural village, the beaches and hotels of Acapulco, and snow-covered Mount Popocatapetl. The latter type of poster might show a bagpipe band marching in Edinburgh, thereby featuring only one of Scotland's attractions.

Your students can combine research and organizational skills with the gaining of geographical knowledge by making posters.

1. Obtain some travel posters to display and discuss.

2. Suggest that each student, or team of two students, make a poster about a country or city.

3. Read about the place to be illustrated in references such as textbooks, *National Geographic,* and encyclopedias.

4. Make a list of the attractions of the place.

5. Decide whether the poster is to focus on a single feature or multiple features.

6. Design the poster on a sheet of paper.

7. Transfer the design of the poster to a larger surface, preferably cardboard. Line drawings are fine for a poster, especially when color is added. However, drawings that are made, cut out, and then pasted on poster board have special appeal. Also, collage posters are generally simpler than drawn posters.

8. Don't forget captions for the posters.

9. Arrange a display in the classroom or the hallway.

Sand Table Models of Basic Environments

1. Decide what environment will be shown on the table.

2. For reference, find pictures that show various aspects of the environment.

3. Gather simple materials that can represent real things.

4. Example: a herder's camp in North Africa.

a. Arrange sand in the table so that dunes and flat places are part of the landscape. Scatter some gravel and small stones around the table.

b. Create an oasis with blue construction paper laid on the floor of the sand table. Surround the pool with simulated trees made of toothpicks topped by frond-like leaves.

c. Place brush in scattered spots of the landscape.

d. Construct several tents from paper or cloth.

e. Make cutout figures of people, goats, and camels.

Diorama Models

Dioramas require simple and inexpensive materials, help your students to see things in three dimensions, offer opportunities for the development of research and organizational skills, and provide enjoyable learning through hands-on activities. It is the kind of activity in which teams of two children can work together in a productive manner.

1. A topic is chosen, for example, a fishing harbor scene.

2. A shoebox that will house the diorama is obtained.

3. A typical fishing village background is drawn. The paper on which it is drawn should fit neatly on the back wall of the shoebox.

4. In the foreground, which should resemble water, paper cutout fishing boats are placed.

5. In the middleground, pilings and docks are shown.

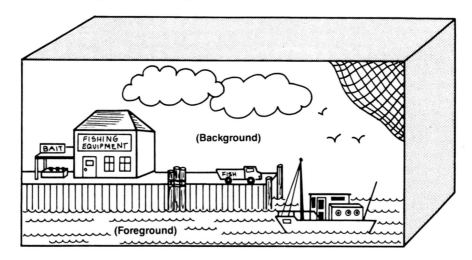

6. Symbols representative of fishing villages are made and placed: nets are hung, lobster traps made of popsicle sticks are placed in various spots, and perhaps a lighthouse is made and located.

Clay Models of Land Features and Land Usage

1. *Contours and Terraces*
Mold a pound or so of soft clay into an oval-shaped lump, with one end steep and the other end a more gentle slope. With a dull knife or spatula, carve or gouge out terraces on the steep slope.

Ask: "How do contours and terraces conserve water and soil?" (The water is slowed in its travel down the slope. Thus, less soil is carried by the water, and the water has time to saturate the ground.)

2. *Land Features*
Mold clay into steep-sided canyons, plateaus, cliffs, mountain ranges and peaks, rivers and valleys, waterfalls, and fiords. The children can shape their own models with small amounts of clay. The clay may be used over and over again as new land elements are introduced.

Weather Charts

Design a chart on which daily weather observations may be recorded. Notations on the chart may be made by the class, a group, or individuals. Adjust the sophistication of the chart and the kinds and depths of observations to fit your students. A sample chart is suggested below. It is condensed so that it may fit this column, but in a chart for young learners there should be ample space for writing things in. Note: All temperatures should be taken in the sun.

Weather Item

	M	T	W	T	F	
Sky* (S,C,V)	S	S	C	V	S	Weekly Average Temperature
Temperature* F°	12°	70°	68°	70°	65°	69° (9:00 AM)
	18°	77°	75°	75°	70°	75° (2:00 PM)
Precipitation** (R,S,O)	-	-	R	R	-	
Wind*** (N,M,S)	M	S	M	N	M	

Notes
 *Sky abbr.: S-Sunny, C-Cloudy, V-Varied
 **Precipitation abbr.: R-Rain, S-Snow, O-Other
 ***Wind abbr.: N-None, M-Mild, S-Strong
All temperatures should be taken in the shade.

Weather Graphs

Bar graphs and line graphs can be drawn on the chalkboard or on chart paper. Data can be gathered by the students or may be obtained from daily newspapers. To reduce the number of graphs that have to be made, design the graph for use over a month's time.

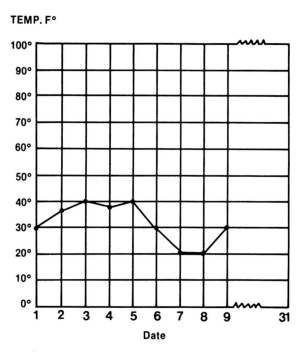

TEMPERATURE GRAPH

Postage Stamp Design

Students select countries or states for which they will design stamps. Through research they determine what outstanding geographical feature or features can be shown on their stamps. For example, Iceland might be symbolized by hot springs, Japan by Mount Fujiyama, Florida by an orange tree, Arizona by the Grand Canyon, and Kansas by waving grain.

After preliminary sketches have been made, the final drawing is made on a 5" × 8" index card. All of the usual items found on stamps should be included. Pinking shears can be used to make perforated edges.

Floating Icebergs

One of the dangers that icebergs present to ocean shipping is that only one-third of an iceberg is visible; the other two-thirds are submerged. This characteristic of icebergs can be easily shown by filling a clear glass or plastic bowl with water. Place two or three ice cubes in the water and note the portions that are above sea level and below. If irregular pieces of ice can be obtained, the demonstration is even more meaningful.

Geography Bulletin Board

You or your students can make bulletin boards on a great variety of geography topics.

Countries	Land features
Cities	Water features
States	Products
Basic environments	

Sequences (for example, the growth of a volcano or valley)
A helpful procedure to follow in making a bulletin board:

1. Decide on the topic. Subdivide the topic into its components.

2. Gather information on the topic (do research).

3. On paper, make a drawing of the board. Decide if the board will answer a question, show a sequence, or give a general overview. Perhaps some of the elements of the board may be shown in three dimensions.

4. Think of a title. Draw and cut out attractive letters.

The diagram below shows an interesting board on the uses of wood. (There are over 5,000 uses!) To help everyone feel that they are a part of making the board, each student may make a contribution, either a drawing or a real object.

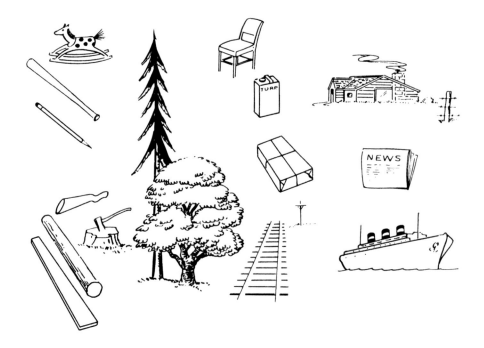